The Silence of Amor. Where the Forest Murmurs

The Works of
"FIONA MACLEOD"

UNIFORM EDITION

ARRANGED BY
MRS. WILLIAM SHARP

VOLUME VI

UNIFORM WITH THIS VOLUME
THE COLLECTED WORKS OF FIONA MACLEOD
(WILLIAM SHARP)

In Seven Volumes. Crown 8vo. Price 6s net. With Photogravure Frontispieces from Photographs and Drawings by D. Y. Cameron, A.R.S.A.

I. PHARAIS: THE MOUNTAIN LOVERS
II. THE SIN EATER; THE WASHER OF THE FORD AND OTHER LEGENDARY MORALITIES
III. THE DOMINION OF DREAMS: UNDER THE DARK STAR
IV. THE DIVINE ADVENTURE: IONA: STUDIES IN SPIRITUAL HISTORY
V. THE WINGED DESTINY: STUDIES IN THE SPIRITUAL HISTORY OF THE GAEL
VI. THE SILENCE OF AMOR · WHERE THE FOREST MURMURS
VII. POEMS AND DRAMAS

ALSO UNIFORM WITH THE ABOVE
SELECTED WRITINGS OF WILLIAM SHARP
In Five Volumes

I. POEMS
II. STUDIES AND APPRECIATIONS
III. PAPERS CRITICAL AND REMINISCENT
IV. LITERARY GEOGRAPHY AND TRAVEL SKETCHES
V. VISTAS: THE GIPSY CHRIST AND OTHER PROSE IMAGININGS

AND

A MEMOIR OF WILLIAM SHARP
(FIONA MACLEOD)
Compiled by MRS. WILLIAM SHARP
(In two volumes)

LONDON: WILLIAM HEINEMANN

From the original by D. Y. Cameron.

Isle of Skye

THE SILENCE OF AMOR

WHERE THE FOREST MURMURS

BY FIONA MACLEOD

"The murmur of woods is like a big psalm
it is the music of endless wanderings."
FIONA MACLEOD

LONDON
WILLIAM HEINEMANN
1912

THE SILENCE OF AMOR

WHERE THE FOREST MURMURS

BY
"FIONA MACLEOD"
(WILLIAM SHARP)

*"The network of words is like a big forest;
it is the cause of curious wanderings."*
INDIAN SAYING.

LONDON
WILLIAM HEINEMANN
1919

UNIFORM EDITION

First published 1910   New Edition 1912
Reprinted 1919

PR
5354
S48
1919

Copyright 1895, 1910

CONTENTS

	PAGE
THE SILENCE OF AMOR	1
TRAGIC LANDSCAPES	39
WHERE THE FOREST MURMURS	57
WHERE THE FOREST MURMURS	61
THE MOUNTAIN CHARM	72
THE CLANS OF THE GRASS	85
THE TIDES	96
THE HILL-TARN	107
AT THE TURN OF THE YEAR	116
THE SONS OF THE NORTH WIND	126
ST. BRIGET OF THE SHORES	136
THE HERALDS OF MARCH	148
THE TRIBE OF THE PLOVER	161
THE AWAKENER OF THE WOODS	175
THE WILD-APPLE	187
RUNNING WATERS	199
THE SUMMER HERALDS	209
THE SEA-SPELL	221
SUMMER CLOUDS	231
THE CUCKOO'S SILENCE	241
THE COMING OF DUSK	251

Contents

WHERE THE FOREST MURMURS—*Continued*

	PAGE
AT THE RISING OF THE MOON	263
THE GARDENS OF THE SEA	274
THE MILKY WAY	284
SEPTEMBER	295
THE CHILDREN OF WIND AND THE CLAN OF PEACE	305
STILL WATERS	318
THE PLEIAD-MONTH	328
THE RAINY HYADES	340
WINTER STARS. I	353
WINTER STARS. II	364
BEYOND THE BLUE SEPTENTRIONS. TWO LEGENDS OF THE POLAR STARS	376
WHITE WEATHER. A MOUNTAIN REVERIE	392
ROSA MYSTICA (AND ROSES OF AUTUMN)	402
THE STAR OF REST. A FRAGMENT	414
AN ALMANAC	415

BIBLIOGRAPHICAL NOTE . . . 416
By Mrs. William Sharp

THE SILENCE OF AMOR

FOREWORD

These prose rhythms, written a year or two earlier, were first published in 1896, at the end of the volume of verse *From the Hills of Dream*. They were taken by many reviewers to be prose-poems. I do not call them so, for I think the designation a mistake. Prose is prose, and poetry is poetry. The two arts are distinct, though they may lie so close in method and achievement as to seem to differ only in degree. But it is possible to widen the marches of the one, as it is possible for the rash to cross the frontiers of the other. I do not know who was the first to attempt the illusion of poetry in the signature of prose, but Turgéniev stands eminent, and Baudelaire added a subtler artifice to the simple emotional statement of the great Russian. The most famous user of "free verse" is, of course, Whitman. This is not the place or occasion to discuss these problems in detail. Each is either a real art or a fantastical and mistaken aberration from art—disordered prose or lawless verse— in accordance with the conviction of the critic

Foreword

that the artifice of prose and the artifice of prosody are as allied as the music of viola and violin, or the conviction that they are as different in kind as the art of the sculptor and the aquarellist.

As one does not care to hear a picture called a sonata, or a symphony a "great tone-poem," or to hear any form of art called by the title of another art's nomenclature, so it would be more scrupulous to avoid the literary use of "prose-poem."

It is obvious that there are emotions and intensified sentiments which, while they may or may not desire expression in that constrained utterance (the primary condition of music) we call poetry, must needs quiver for freedom under the reins of ordinary prose. In other words, there is, under the stress of emotion, an inevitable reversion to the impulse to chant. And as one of the characteristics of the primitive chant is repetition, either choric or in the narrative cadence—as in the sorrow of Oisìn :

Grey age of the rocks is on me, grey age of the rocks: I am old, I am old! so in that literary form the prose-rhythm of to-day, will commonly be found an iteration more or less insistent, more or less subtle and involved. It is this substitution of a calculated monotony and of a careful

Foreword

iteration—a recurrence either of order and cadence, or of a like cadence with an inverted order—which differentiates the brief and complete prose-rhythm from the dubious "prose-poem," so apt to be merely ornate prose crested with metaphor or plumed with hyperbole. . . .

The test of these forms is to read them aloud. If they have not the rise and fall of the wind upon the hill, the wave upon the shore, the murmur in the woods, they are not prose-rhythms in the sense indicated. They must come suddenly and silently as the twilight airs. In their coming and going they must not be as intervals of an inconstant wind, but must each be a wind, an air, a breath, that is as complete, as final, as a few brief sudden notes of song from the moonlit thickets of May, as the sound of a swallow's wing in the dusk.

Within the last few years others who have felt the charm of this subtle form—that has in it the atmosphere and music we know best when borne to us on the wings of metre, and the sinuous glide or swift march of an ordered and uplifted prose—have experimented with it. I believe that in America it has votaries: in France and Italy it certainly has. I daresay that to the Latin temperament—to which a little vagueness of form, with adumbration

Foreword

rather than limning of feature, comes with the charm of novelty—the temptation is more natural. We are makers first, and then artists when may be: they are artists first. The nuances of expression in any art can come only from an instinctive and trained mental and spiritual finesse. Of all who have tried this method systematically as a narrative form perhaps the best known is the author of the *Chants de Bilitis*, but I myself know of none who has so true an understanding and so deft a faculty as Paul Fort. I am sorry I knew nothing of his work till last year, when I read the fascinating *Roman de Louis XI*. In the prologue to that book I found this significant sentence—"J'ai cherché un style pouvant passer, au gré de l'émotion, de la prose au vers et du vers à la prose: la prose rhythmée fournit la transition."

After that I read all M. Fort's writings, from the first, *Ballades Françaises*, which was published so recently as 1897. Frankly I do not think his method suitable for narrative: if used narratively, then possibly the paragraphic and brief sectional method of *Bilitis* is better than that of the *Roman de Louis XI*. Probably the future of the prose-rhythm as a literary method is assured: for as the general impulse towards art widens so will the rarer individual impulse

Foreword

to subtlety deepen. If any think that the form may be adopted because easier than metrical composition, it should be left alone. No artist desires open gates or short cuts. The value of the form will lie in its adaptability to an emotional mood desiring a particular rhythm and a particular harmony that is something more than the lightest tread of prose, something less than the delicate or stately measures of verse. In a word, the desiderated form is the Chant, tamed now to a low and subtle modulation, in transition from the rude choric cry to the song wedded to viol or flute, or the lyric fashioned to charm the inward ear.

FIONA MACLEOD.

In the hollows of quiet places we may meet, the quiet places where is neither moon nor sun, but only the light as of amber and pale gold that comes from the Hills of the Heart. There, listen at times: there you will call, and I hear: there will I whisper, and that whisper will come to you as dew is gathered into the grass, at the rising of the moon.

TO ESCLARMOUNDO

There is one word never spoken in these estrays of passion and longing. But you, Flower of my dreams know it: for the rustle of the wings of Amor awakens you at dawn, and in the dark your heart is his secret haven.

For, truly, that wandering voice, that twilight-whisper, that breath so dewy sweet, that flame-wing'd luteplayer whom none sees but for a moment, in a rainbow-shimmer of joy, or a sudden lightning-flare of passion, this exquisite mystery we call Amor, comes, to some rapt visionaries at least, not with a song upon the lips that all may hear, or with blithe viol of a public music, but as one wrought by ecstasy, dumbly eloquent with desire, ineffable, silent.

For Amor is ofttimes a dreamer, and when he dreams it is through lovely analogies. He speaks not, he whispers not, who in the flight of the wild swan against the frosty stars, or in the interlaceries of black branches against the moonlight, or the abrupt song of a bird in the green-gloom of the forest, hears the voice that

To Esclarmoundo

is all Music for him, sees the face of his unattainable Desire. These things are his silences, wherein his heart and his passion commune. And being his, they are mine : to lay before you, Dear ; as a wind, that has lifted the blossoms of a secret orchard, stoops, and lays milk-white drift and honeyed odours at the opened window of one who within sleeps and dreams.

THE SHADOWY WOODLANDS

Above the shadowy woodlands I hear the voice of the cuckoo, sailing like a silver skiff upon the moonflood.

I hear the far-off plaint of the cuckoo sink deep through the moonshine above the shadowy woodlands. At last, in the dense shadow of the wood, the moonlight sleeps. Through the shadowy woodlands a voice rises on the moonflood, like a silver skiff: far off it sails, O dear and longed-for voice; far off it sinks, where the moonlit dusk becomes the woods, the woods become the dusk. Follow, O wayward bird, and call that voice, follow and hither lead that voice to the shadowy woodlands, here, where in the dense shadow of the wood, the moonlight sleeps.

AT THE RISING OF THE MOON

At the rising of the moon I heard the falling echo of a song, down by the linn where the wild brier hangs over the swirling foam. Ah, swirling foam, ah, poignant breath of the wild brier, now that I hear no haunting-sweet echo of a falling song at the rising of the moon.

NOCTURNE

By dim, mauve and dream-white bushes of lilac I pass to the cypress alley, and to the water which lies breathless in the moonshine. A fish leaps, a momentary flame of fire. Then all is still again on the moonlit water, where, breathless, it lies beyond the cypress alley. In the vague moonshine of the cypress alley I pass again, a silent shadow, by the dim, mauve and dream-white bushes of lilac.

LANCES OF GOLD

The afternoon has drowsed through the sun-flood. The green leaves have grown golden, saturated with light. And now, at the sudden whirling of the lances of gold, a cloud of wild-doves arises from the pines, wheels against the sunblaze, and flashes out of sight, flames of purple and rose, of foam-white and pink. I know the green hidden nests of the wild-doves, when ye come again, O whirling lances of gold!

THE NIGHTJAR

Low upon a pine-branch a nightjar leans and sings his churring song. He sings his churring song to his mate, who, poised upon a juniper hard by, listens with quivering wings.

The whirring of the nightjar fills the dusk, heavy with the fragrance of new-mown hay. There is neither star nor moon in the dim, flowing darkness, only the red and yellow wayfaring flames where the glow-worms are. Like a wandering wave, in the dewy dark, the churring note of the nightjar rises and falls against the juniper bush hard by.

THE TWILIT WATERS

Upon the dim seas in the twilight I hear the tide forging slowly through the husht waters. There is not a sound else : neither the scream of a sea-mew, nor the harsh cry of the heron, nor the idle song of the wind : only the steadfast forging of the tide through the husht waters of the twilit seas. O steadfast onward tide, O gloaming-hidden palpitating seas !

EVOË!

Oceanward, the sea-horses sweep magnificently, champing and whirling white foam about their green flanks, and tossing on high their manes of sunlit rainbow-gold, dazzling white and multitudinous far as sight can reach.

O champing horses of my soul, toss, toss, on high your sunlit manes, your manes of rainbow-gold, dazzling white and multitudinous : for I too rejoice, rejoice !

GREY AND ROSE

I watched the greying of the dawn. The grey leaf became a leaf of rose. Then a yellow ripple came out of a narrow corrie at the summit of the hill. The yellow ripple ran like the running tide through the flushed grey, and washed in among the sprays of a birch beside me and among the rowan-clusters of a mountain-ash. But at the falling of the sun the yellow ripple was an ebbing tide, and the sprays of the birch were as a perishing flame and the rowan-berries were red as drops of blood. Thereafter I watched the rose slow fading into the grey veils of dusk. O greying of my dawn slow flushing into rose: O grey veils of dusk that obscure the tender flushing of my rose-lit dawn!

HIGH NOON

To-day, as I walked at high noon, listening to the larks filling the April blue with a spray of delicate song, I saw a shadow pass me, where no one was, and where nothing moved, above me or around.

It was not my shadow that passed me, nor the shadow of one for whom I longed. That other shadow came not.

I have heard that there is a god clothed in shadow who goes to and fro among the human kind, putting silence between hearts with his waving hands, and breathing a chill out of his cold breath, and leaving a gulf as of deep waters flowing between them because of the passing of his feet.

Thus, thus it was that the shadow for which I longed came not. Yet, in the April blue I heard the wild aërial chimes of song, and watched the golden fulfilment of the day under the high, illimitable arch of noon.

THE WHITE MERLE

Long, long ago, a white merle flew out of Eden. Its song has been in the world ever since, but few there are who have seen the flash of its white wings through the green-gloom of the living wood—the sun-splashed, rain-drenched, mist-girt, storm-beat wood of human life.

But to-day, as I came through the wood, under an arch of tempest, and led by lightnings, I passed into a green sun-splashed place. There, there, I heard the singing of a rapt song of joy! there, ah, there I saw the flash of white wings!

THE IMMORTALS

I saw the Weaver of Dreams, an immortal shape of star-eyed Silence; and the Weaver of Death, a lovely Dusk with a heart of hidden flame: and each wove with the shuttles of Beauty and Wonder and Mystery.

I knew not which was the more fair: for Death seemed to me as Love, and in the eyes of Dream I saw Joy. Oh, come, come to me, Weaver of Dreams! Come, come unto me, O Lovely Dusk, thou that hast the heart of hidden flame!

THE WEAVER OF HOPE

Again I saw a beautiful lordly one. He, too, lifted the three shuttles of Beauty and Wonder and Mystery, and wove a mist of rainbows. Rainbow after rainbow he wrought out of the mist of glory that he made, and sent each forth to drift across the desert of the human soul, and over every high road of retreating faiths, and into every valley of defeated dreams.

O drifting rainbows of Hope, I know a hidden place of broken and scattered faiths, a haunted valley of defeated dreams.

THE GOLDEN TIDES

The moon lay low above the sea, and all the flowing gold and flashing silver of the rippling, running water seemed to be a flood going that way and falling into the shining hollow of the moon. O, that the tides of my heart, for ever flowing one way, might fall to rest in the hollow of a golden moon.

THE STARS OF DUSK

A pale golden flame illumes the moveless uplifted billows of the forest. Star after star steals softly through the moongold lapping the velvet-soft shores of dusk. Slowly the yellowing flame rises like smoke among the dark-blue depths. The white rays of the stars wander over the moveless, over the shadowless and breathless green lawns of the tree-tops. Oh, would that I were a star lost deep within the paling yellow flame that illumes the suspended billows of the forest.

THE REED PLAYER

I saw one put a hollow reed to his lips. It was a forlorn, sweet air that he played, an ancient forgotten strain learned of a shepherding woman upon the hills. The Song of Songs it was that he played: and the beating of hearts was heard, and I heard sighs, and a voice like a distant bird-song rose and fell.

"Play me a song of Death," I said. Then he who had the hollow reed at his lips smiled, and he played again the Song of Songs.

HY BRASIL

I heard the voice of the wind among the pines. It was as the tide coming over smooth sands. On the red pine-boles the sun flamed goldenly out of the west. In falling cadences the cuckoos called across the tides of light.

In dreams, now, I hear the cuckoos calling across a dim sea of light, there where a sun that never rose nor set flames goldenly upon ancient trees, in whose midst the wind goes sighingly, with a sound as of the tide slipping swift over smooth sands. And I hear a solitary voice singing there, where I stand beside the gold-flamed pine-boles and look with hungry eyes against the light of a sun that never rose nor set.

THE WILD BEES

There was a man, seeking Peace, who found a precious treasure in the heather, when the bells were sweet with honey-ooze. Did the wild bees know of it? Would that I could hear the soft hum of their gauzy wings.

Where blooms that heather, and what wind is it that moveth the bells that are sweet with the honey-ooze? Only the wild bees know of it; but I think they must be the bees of Magh-Mell, the bees that make a sweet sound in the drowsy ears of those who beneath the heather have indeed found rest by the dim waysides of Peace.

WHIRLED STARS

The rain has ceased falling softly through the dusk. A cool green wind flows through the deeps of air. The stars are as wind-whirled fruit blown upward from the tree-tops. Full-orbed, a sea of stilled pale fire, the moon leads a tide of quiet light over the brown shores of the world.

But here, here where I stand upon the brown shores of the world, in the shine of that quiet flame where, full-orbed, the moon uplifts the dark, I think only of the stars as wind-whirled fruit blown upward from the tree-tops. I think only of that wind that blew upon the tree-tops, where the whirling stars spun in a mazy dance, when, at last, the rain had ceased falling softly through the dusk. O wind-whirled stars, O secret falling rain!

ORCHIL

I dreamed of Orchil, the dim goddess who is under the brown earth, in a vast cavern, where she weaves at two looms. With one hand she weaves life upward through the grass; with the other she weaves death downward through the mould; and the sound of the weaving is Eternity, and the name of it in the green world is Time. And, through all, Orchil weaves the weft of Eternal Beauty, that passeth not, though her soul is Change.

This is my comfort, O Beauty that art of Time, who am faint and hopeless in the strong sound of that other Weaving, where Orchil, the dim goddess, sits dreaming at her loom under the brown earth.

FUIT ILIUM

I see the lift of the dark, the lovely advance of the lunar twilight, the miracle of the pale yellow flood—golden here and here white as frost-fire—upon sea and land. I see, and yet see not. I hear the muffled voice of ocean and soft recurrent whisperings of the foam-white runnels at my feet: I hear, and yet hear not. But one sound, one voice, I hear; one gleam, one vision, I see: O irrevocable, ineffable Desire!

THE SEA-SHELL

In the heart of the shell a wild-rose flush lies shut from wind or wave; lies close, and dreams to the unceasing lullaby that the sea-shell sings.

O would that I were that wild-rose flush, shut close from wind or wave: O would that I were that wild-rose flush to dream for ever to the unceasing song my sea-shell sings.

THE WHITE PROCESSION

One by one the stars come forth—solemn eyes watching for ever the white procession move onward orderly where there is neither height, nor depth, nor beginning, nor end.

In the vast stellar space the moonglow wanes until it grows cold, white, ineffably remote. Only upon our little dusky earth, upon our restless span of waters, the light descends in a tender warmth.

Deep gladness to me, though but the creature of an hour, that I am on this little moonlit dusky earth. Too cold, too white, too ineffably remote the moonglow in these vast wastes of Infinity where, one by one, the constellations roam—solemn witnesses watching for ever the white procession move onward orderly where there is neither height, nor depth, nor beginning, nor end.

AËRIAL CHIMES

Through the blue deeps of noon I heard the cuckoo tolling his infrequent peals from skiey belfries built of sun and mist.

And now, through the blue deeps of night, from skiey belfries built of dusk and stars, I hear the tolling of infrequent peals.

THE HILLS OF DREAM

The tide of noon is upon the hills. Amid leagues of purple heather, of pale amethyst ling, stand isled great yellow-lichened granite boulders, fringed with tawny bracken. In the vast dome of blue there is nought visible save a speck of white, a gannet that drifts above the invisible sea. And through the hot tide of noon goes a breath as of the heart of flame. Far off, far off, I know dim hills of dream, and there my heart suspends as a white bird longing for home: and there, oh there, is a heart of flame, and the breath of it is as the tide of noon upon these hills of dream.

THE TWO ETERNITIES

Time never was, Time is not. Thus I heard the grasses whisper, the green lips of the wind that chants the blind oblivious rune of Time, far in that island-sanctuary that I shall not see again.

Time never was ˙Time is not. O Time that was! O Time that is!

TRAGIC LANDSCAPES

Tragic Landscapes

I

THE TEMPEST

The forest undulated across the land in vast black-green billows. Their sombre solitudes held no light. The sky was of a uniform grey, a dull metallic hue such as the sea takes when a rainy wind comes out of the east. There was not a break in the appalling monotony.

To the north rose a chain of mountains. Connecting one to another were serrated scaurs, or cleft, tortured, and precipitous ridges. The wild-stag had his sanctuary here; here were reared the young of the osprey, the raven, the kestrel, and the corbie. On the extreme heights the eagles called from their eyries at sunrise; at sundown they might be seen whirling like minute discs around the flaming peaks.

An absolute silence prevailed. At long intervals there was the restless mewing of a

The Tempest

wind-eddy, baffled among the remote corries. Sometimes, far beneath and beyond, in the mid-most depths of the forest, a sound, as of the flowing tide at an immeasurable distance, rose, sighed through the grey silences, and sank into their drowning depths.

At noon, a slight stir was visible here and there. Two crows drifted inky-black against the slate-grey firmament. A kestrel, hovering over a rocky wilderness, screamed, and with a sudden slant cut the heavy air, skimmed the ground, breasted the extreme summits of the pines, and sailed slowly westward, silent, apparently motionless, till absorbed into the gloom. A slight mist rose from a stagnant place. On a black moorland tract, miles away from where the forest began, two small, gaunt creatures, human males, stooped continually, tearing at the peaty soil.

By the fourth hour from noon, there was nothing audible; not a thing visible, save the black-gloom overhead, the green-gloom of the vast pine-forest, the grey sterility of the hills, to the north.

Towards the fifth hour, a sickly white flame darted forkedly out of the slate-hued sky to the northwest. There was no wind, no stir of any kind, following. The same breathless silence brooded everywhere.

The Tempest

Close upon the sixth hour a strange shivering went through a portion of the forest. It was as though the flank of a monster quivered. A confused rustling arose, ebbed, died away. Thrice at long intervals the narrow, jagged flame lunged and thrust, as a needle thridding the two horizons. At a vast distance a wail, a murmur, a faint vanishing cry, might be heard, like the humming of a gnat. It was the wind, tearing and lashing the extreme frontiers, and screaming in its blind fury.

A raven came flying rapidly out of the west. Again and again in its undeviating flight its hoarse croak reëchoed as though it fell clanging from ledge to brazen ledge. At an immense height, three eagles, no larger than three pin-points, winging their way at terrific speed, seemed to crawl like ants along the blank slope of a summitless and endless wall.

In the southwest the greyness became involved. Dark masses bulged forward. A gigantic hand appeared to mould them from behind. The ponderous avalanches of rain were suspended, lifted, whirled this way and that, fused, divided, and swung low over the earth like horrible balloons of death.

Furtive eddies of wind moved stealthily among the forest-trees. The pines were motionless, though a thin song ascended spirally the columnar boles; but the near beeches were flooded with innumerable green wavelets of unquiet light. A constant tremor lived suspensive in every birk, in every rowan. On the hither frontier of the pines a few scattered oaks lifted their upper boughs, lifted and lapsed, slowly lifted again and slowly lapsed. These were silent, though a confused murmur as of bewildered bees came from the foliage midway and beneath Wan green tongues of air licked the fronds of the myriad bracken. Swift arrows of wind, narrow as reeds, darted through the fern and over the patches of grass, leaving for a moment a wake of white light. By a pool the bulrushes seemed to strain their tufty heads one way, listening; the tall, slim, fairy-lances beside them continually trembled.

Suddenly there was an obscure noise upon the hills. Far off, a linn roared hoarsely, whose voice had been muffled before. Many streams and hill-torrents called. Then the mountain-wind came rushing down the strath, with incoherent shouts and a confused tumult of tidings. Every green thing moved one way, or stood back upon itself as a javelin-thrower. In the tragic silence of the forest and the moorland, the pulse of the earth beat slowly, heavily. A suffocating grip was at the brown heart.

But the moment the hill-wind dashed through the swaying rowans and beeches, and leaped into the forest, a hurricane of cries arose. Every tree called to its neighbour; each pine shouted, screamed, moaned, or chanted a wild song; the more ancient lifted a deep voice, mocking and defiant. For now they knew what was coming.

The sea-tempest was climbing up over the back of the sun, and had already, with rolling thunders and frightful sulphurous blasts, with flame of many lightnings and vast volumes of cloud holding seas of rain and gravelly avalanches of hail, attacked, prostrated, trampled upon, mutilated, slain and twice slain, the far-off battalions of the forest! This was what the herald of the hills proclaimed, as with panic haste he leaped through the woods screaming wild warnings as he went.

For leagues and leagues he swept onward, then, suddenly swerving, raced up a rock-bastioned height that rose in the forest. For a while he swung suspensive, then, swaying blindly, fell back stumbling, and, as one delirious, staggered to the forest again, and once more flew like a flying deer, though no longer forward but by the way he had come.

The Tempest

"The Tempest! The Tempest!" he screamed: "The Tempest comes!"

Soon all the forest knew what he had seen. Distant lines of great trees were being mowed down as by a scythe; gigantic pines were being torn from the ground and hurled hither and thither; the Black Loch had become a flood; the river had swollen into a frightful spate, and raged and ravened like a beast of prey. He had seen cattle fall, slain by lightning; a stag had crashed downwards as he leaped from boulder to boulder; the huts of some humans had been laid low, and the sprawling creatures beneath been killed or mutilated; sheep had been dashed up against stone-dykes and left lifeless. The air in places was thick and dark with whirling grouse, snipe, wild-doves, lapwings, crows, and a dust of small birds.

A moan went up from the forest—a new sound, horrible, full of awe, of terror, of despair. In the blank grey hollows of the mountains to the north the echo of this was as though the Grave were opened, and the Dead moaned.

Young and old moved near to each other, with clinging boughs, and tremulous sprays and branches. The fluttering leaves made a confused babble of tongues. The males

The Tempest

swirled their upper boughs continuously, inclining their bodies now this way and now that. The ancient pines spread their boles as far as they could reach, murmuring low to their green offspring, and to the tender offspring of these. Sighs and sobs, swift admonitions, and sudden, passionate heart-break cries resounded. Death would be among them in a few moments; all could not survive, many must perish, patriarch and sapling, proud bridegroom and swaying bride, the withered and the strong.

From the extreme edge there was a constant emigration of living things. The birds sang among the bracken.

Some deer, three human males and a female, some foxes and stoats came out into the open, hesitated, and slowly retreated.

The first thunder-chariot now hurtled overhead. The charioteer leaned low, and thrust hither and thither with his frightful lance. A deer was killed, also the human female and one of the males. A scorching smell came from a spruce-fir; the next moment it hung in tongues of flame.

Then—silence: awful, appalling. Suddenly, the heaven opened in fire: the earth became a hollow globe of brass wherein an excruciating

The Tempest

tumult whirled ruin against ruin. The howl of desolation seemed to belch at once from the entrails of the mountains and from the bowels of the bursting sky.

The Tempest was come!

II

MIST

A dense white mist lay upon the hills, clothing them from summit to base in a dripping shroud. The damp spongy peat everywhere sweated forth its overwelling ooze. Not a living thing seemed to haunt the desolation, though once or twice a faint cry from a bewildered curlew came stumblingly through the sodden atmosphere.

There was neither day nor night, but only the lifeless gloom of the endless, weary rain, thin, soaking, full of the chill and silence of the grave.

Hour lapsed into hour, till at last the gradual deepening of the mists betokened the dreary end of the dreary day. Soaked, boggy, treacherous as were the drenched and pool-haunted moors, no living thing, not even the restless hill-sheep, fared across them. But towards the late afternoon a stooping figure passed from gloom to gloom—wan, silent, making the awfulness of the hour and the place take on a new desolation.

Mist

As the shadow stole slowly across the moor, it stopped ever and anon. It was a man. The heavy moisture on his brow from the rain passing through his matted hair mixed with the great drops of sweat that gathered there continually. For as often as he stopped he heard footsteps anigh, footsteps in that lonely deserted place—sometimes following, sometimes beyond him, sometimes almost at his side. Yet it was not for the sound of those following feet that he stopped, but because on the rain-matted cranberry-bushes or upon the glistening thyme or on the sodden grass, he saw now bloody foot-marks, now marks of bloody fingers. When he looked, there was nothing below or beyond him but the dull sheen of the rain-soaked herbage; when he looked again, a bloody footstep, a bloody finger-mark.

But at last the following feet were heard no more, the bloody imprints were no more seen. The man stood beside a deep tarn, and was looking into it, as the damned in hell look into their souls.

At times a faint, almost inaudible sigh breathed behind the mist in one direction. It was the hill-wind stirring among the scaurs and corries at a great height on a mountain to the north. Here and there, a slight drifting of the vapour disclosed a shadowy boulder:

then the veils would lapse and intervolve, and the old impermeable obscurity prevail.

It was in one of these fugitive intervals that a stag, standing upon an overhanging rock, beheld another, a rival with whom it had fought almost to the death the day before. This second stag stood among the wet bracken, his ears now laid back, now extended quiveringly, his nostrils vibrating, as he strove to smell the something that moved through the dense mist by the tarn.

The upper stag tautened his haunches. His lips and nostrils curled, and left his yellow teeth agleam. The next moment he had launched himself upon his enemy. There was a crash, a sound as of a wind-lashed sea, sharp cries and panting breaths, groans. Then a long silence. Later, a single faint, perishing bleat came through the mist from the fern far up upon the hill.

The restless wind that was amid the summits died. Night crept up from glen and strath; the veils of mist grew more and more obscure, more dark. At last, from the extreme peaks to where the torrent crawled into hollows in the sterile valley, there was a uniform pall of blackness.

In the chill, soaking silence not a thing stirred, not a sound was audible.

III

SUMMER-SLEEP

The high-road sinuated like a white snake, along the steeper slope of the valley. The vast expanse of the lowland lay basking in the July sunlight. In all directions woodlands, mostly of planes and oaks, swelled or lapsed in green billows.

The cuckoo had gone; the thrush was silent; blackbird and shilfa and linnet were now songless. But every here and there a lark still filled the summer air, as with the cool spray of aerial music; in the grain the corncrakes called; and, in shadowy places, in the twilight, the churring of the belated fern-owl was still a midsummer sweetness upon the ear.

The gloom of July was upon the trees. The oaks dreamed of green water. The limes were already displaying fugitive yellow banners. A red flush dusked the green-gloom of the sycamores. But by far the greater mass of the woodlands consisted of planes; and these were now of a black green darker than that of

Summer-Sleep

north-wind waves on a day of storm. The meadows, too, lay in the shadow, as it were, even when the sunflood poured upon them.

From the low ranges to the south a faint wind drifted leisurely northward. The sky was of a vivid blue, up whose invisible azure ledges a few rounded clouds, dazzling white or grey as swan's-down, climbed imperceptibly.

In the air was a pleasant murmur of the green world. The wild-bee and the wasp, the dragon-fly and the gnat, wrought everywhere a humming undertone. From copse and garth and water-meadow suspired an audible breath.

The lowing of kine from many steadings blended with the continuous murmur of a weir, where the river curved under ancient alders and slipped into a dense green shaw of birches beyond an old water-mill, whose vast black wheel, jagged and broken, swung slowly, fanning the hot air so that it made a haze as of faint-falling rain.

Peace was upon the land, and beauty. The languor of dream gave the late summer a loveliness that was all its own—as of a fair woman, asleep, dreaming of the lover who has not long left her, and the touch of whose lips is still warm upon her mouth and hair.

Along the high-road, where it made a sweep southwestward, and led to a small hamlet of thatched, white-walled cottages, three men walked. The long fantastic shadows which they cast were pale blue upon the chalky dust of the road, and leaped and contracted and slid stealthily forward with wearisome, monotonous energy. Two of the men were tall and fair: one dark, loosely built, and of a smaller and slighter build.

"There is my home," said the tallest wayfarer suddenly, after what had been a long silence; and as he spoke he pointed to a small square house set among orchard-trees, a stone's throw from the hamlet.

"It is a beautiful place," replied his comrade, slowly, "and I envy you."

"Yes, indeed," added the other.

"I am glad you think so," the owner of the house answered quietly.

But the three shadows leapt to one side, moved with fantastic steps, and seemed convulsed with laughter.

Perhaps the tall shiver-grsss that rose by the wayside out of the garth of campions and purple scabious could catch the attenuated sounds and understand the speech of the shadows. If so, it would know that the taller of the two strangers said in his heart :—

"There is something of awe, of terror about that house; nay, the whole land here is under a tragic gloom. I should die here, stifled. I am glad I go on the morrow."

It would know that the smaller and darker of the two strangers said in his heart:—

"It may be all beautiful and peaceful, but something tragic hides behind this flooding sunlight, behind these dark woodlands, down by the water-course there, past the water-mill, up by that house among the orchard-trees."

It would know that the tallest of the three men, he who lived in that square cottage by the pleasant hamlet, said in his heart:—

"It may be that the gate of hell is hidden there among the grass, or beneath the foundations of my house. Would God I were free! O my God, madness and death!"

Then, after another long silence, as the three wayfarers drew near, the dark man murmured his pleasure at the comely hamlet, at the quiet land lying warm in the afternoon glow. And his companion said that rest and coolness would be welcome, and doubly so in so fair and peaceful a home. And the tallest of the three, he who owned the house in the orchard, laughed blithely. And all three moved onward, with quickened steps, through the hot, sweet, dusty afternoon, golden now with the waning sun-glow.

WHERE THE FOREST
MURMURS
NATURE ESSAYS

"There through the branches go the ravens of unresting thought."

W. B. YEATS.

TO
MR. P. ANDERSON GRAHAM

DEAR MR. GRAHAM—To whom so fittingly as to you could I inscribe this book? It was you who suggested it; you who in *Country Life* published at intervals, longer or shorter as the errant spirit of composition moved me, the several papers which make it one book; you without whose encouragement and good counsel this volume would probably not have been written. Then, perchance, it might have gone to that Y-Brasil Press in the Country of the Young wherefrom are issued all the delightful books which, though possible and welcome in Tir-na-n'Og, are unachieved in this more difficult world, except in dreams and hopes. It would be good to have readers among the kindly Shee . . . do not the poets there know an easy time, having only to breathe their thought on to a leaf and to whisper their music to a reed, and lo the poem is public from the caverns of Tir-fo-tuinn to the hills of Flatheanas! . . . but, till one gets behind the foam yonder, the desire of the heart is for comrades here. These hours of beauty have meant so much to me, somewhat in the writing, but much more in the long, incalculable hours and days out of which the writing has risen like the blue smoke out of woods, that I want to share them with others, who may care for the things written of as you and I care for them, and among whom may be a few who, likewise, will be moved to garner from each day of the eternal pageant one hour of unforgettable beauty.

FIONA MACLEOD.

Many runes the cold has taught me,
Many lays the rain has brought me,
Other songs the winds have sung me;
Many birds from many forests
Oft have sung me lays in concord;
Waves of sea, and ocean billows,
Music from the many waters,
Music from the whole creation,
Oft have been my guide and master.
The Kalevala.

Where the Forest Murmurs

It is when the trees are leafless, or when the last withered leaves rustle in the wintry air, creeping along the bare boughs like tremulous mice, or fluttering from the branches like the tired and starving swallows left behind in the ebbing tides of migration, that the secret of the forest is most likely to be surprised. Mystery is always there. Silence and whispers, still glooms, sudden radiances, the passage of wind and idle airs, all these inhabit the forest at every season. But it is not in their amplitude that great woodlands reveal their secret life. In the first vernal weeks the wave of green creates a mist or shimmering veil of delicate beauty, through which the misselthrush calls, and the loud screech of the jay is heard like a savage trumpet-cry. The woods then are full of a virginal beauty. There is intoxication in the light air. The cold azure among the beech-spaces or where the tall elms sway in the east wind, is, like the sea, exquisitely desirable, exquisitely unfamiliar, inhuman, of another world. Then follow the days when the violets creep through the mosses

Where the Forest Murmurs

at the base of great oaks, when the dust of snow-bloom on the blackthorn gives way to the trailing dog-rose, when myriads of bees among the chestnut-blossoms fill the air with a continuous drowsy unrest, when the cushat calls from the heart of the fir, when beyond the green billowy roof of elm and hornbeam, of oak and beech, of sycamore and lime and tardy ash, the mysterious bells of the South fall through leagues of warm air, as the unseen cuckoo sails on the long tides of the wind. Then, in truth, is there magic in the woods. The forest is alive in its divine youth. Every bough is a vast plume of joy: on every branch a sunray falls, or a thrush sways in song, or the gauzy ephemeridæ dance in rising and falling aerial cones. The wind moves with the feet of a fawn, with the wings of a dove, with the passing breath of the white owl at dusk. There is not a spot where is neither fragrance nor beauty nor life. From the tiniest arch of grass and twig the shrew-mouse will peep: above the shallowest rainpool the dragon-fly will hang in miraculous suspense, like one of the faery javelins of Midir which in a moment could be withheld in mid-flight. The squirrel swings from branch to branch: the leveret shakes the dew from the shadowed grass: the rabbits flitter to and fro like brown beams of life: the robin, the chaffinch, the ousel, call through the warm green-glooms: on' the bramble-spray and from the fern-garth the yellow-hammer reiterates his gladsome single song: in the cloudless blue fields of the sky the swifts weave a maze of shadow, the rooks rise and fall in giddy ascents and descents like black galleys surmounting measureless waves and sinking into incalculable gulfs.

Then the forest wearies of this interminable exuberance, this daily and nightly charm of exultant life. It desires another spell, the enchantment of silence, of dreams. One day the songs cease: the nests are cold. In the lush meads the hare sleeps, the corncrake calls. By the brook the cattle stand, motionless, or with long tails rhythmically a-swing and ears a-twitch above the moist amber-violet dreamless eyes. The columnar trees are like phantom-smoke of secret invisible fires. In the green-glooms of the forest a sigh is heard. A troubled and furtive moan is audible in waste indiscoverable places. The thunder-time is come. Now in the woods may be seen and heard and felt that secret presence which, in the spring months hid behind songs and blossom, and later clothed itself in dense veils of green and all the magic of June. Something is now evident, that was not evident;

Where the Forest Murmurs

somewhat is entered into the forest. The leaves know it: the bracken knows it: the secret is in every copse, in every thicket, is palpable in every glade, is abroad in every shadow-thridden avenue, is common to the spreading bough and the leaning branch. It is not a rumour; for that might be the wind stealthily lifting his long wings from glade to glade. It is not a whisper; for that might be the secret passage of unquiet airs, furtive heralds of the unloosening thunder. It is not a sigh; for that might be the breath of branch and bough, of fern-frond and grass, obvious in the great suspense. It is an ineffable communication. It comes along the ways of silence; along the ways of sound: its light feet are on sunrays and on shadows. Like dew, one knows not whether it is mysteriously gathered from below or secretly come from on high: simply it is there, above, around, beneath.

But the hush is dispelled at last. The long lances of the rain come slanting through the branches; they break, as against invisible barriers, and fall in a myriad pattering rush. The hoarse mutterings and sudden crashing roar of the thunder possess the whole forest. There are no more privacies, the secrecies are violated. From that moment the woods are renewed, and with the renewal the secret spirit that dwells within them withdraws, is not to be surprised, is inaudible, indefinitely recedes, is become remote, obscure, ineffable, incommunicable. And so, through veils of silence, and hot noons and husht warm midnights, the long weeks of July and August go by.

In the woods of September surely the forest-soul may be surprised, will be the thought of many. In that month the sweet incessant business of bird and beast lessens or is at an end. The woodpecker may still tap at the boles of gnarled oaks and chestnuts; the squirrel is more than ever mischievously gay; on frosty mornings, when the gossamer webs are woven across every bramble, and from frond to frond of the bronze-stained bracken, the redbreast tries and retries the poignant new song he has somehow learned since first he flaunted his bright canticles of March and April from the meadow-hedge or the sunned greenness of the beech-covert. But there is a general silence, a present suspense, while the lime yellows, and the birch takes on her pale gold, and oak and sycamore and ash slowly transmute their green multitudes into a new throng clad in russet or dull red or sunset-orange. The forest is full of loveliness: in her dusky ways faint azure mists gather.

Where the Forest Murmurs

When the fawn leaps through the fern it is no longer soundlessly: there is a thin dry rustle, as of a dove brushing swiftly from its fastness in an ancient yew. One may pass from covert to covert, from glade to glade, and find the Secret just about to be revealed . . . somewhere beyond the group of birches, beside that oak it may be, just behind that isolated thorn. But it is never quite overtaken. It is as evasive as moonlight in the hollows of waves. When present, it is already gone. When approached, it has the unhasting but irretrievable withdrawal of the shadow. In October this bewildering evasion is still more obvious, because the continual disclosure is more near and intimate. When, after autumns of rain and wind, or the sudden stealthy advent of nocturnal frosts, a multitude of leaves becomes sere and wan, and then the leaves strew every billow of wind like clots of driven foam, or fall in still wavering flight like flakes of windless snow, then, it is surely then that the great surprise is imminent, that the secret and furtive whisper will become a voice. And yet there is something withheld. In November itself there are days, weeks even, when a rich autumn survives. The oaks and ashes will often keep their red and orange till after St. Luke's Peace; in sheltered parts of the forest even the plane, the sycamore, and the chestnut will flaunt their thin leopard-spotted yellow bannerets. I remember coming upon a Spanish chestnut in the centre of a group of all but leafless hornbeams. There seemed to be not a leaf missing from that splendid congregation of scarlet and amber and luminous saffron. A few yards on and even the hardy beeches and oaks were denuded of all but a scattered and defeated company of brown or withered stragglers. Why should that single tree have kept its early October loveliness unchanged through those weeks of rain and wind and frosts of midnight and dawn? There was not one of its immediate company but was in desolate ruin, showing the bare nests high among the stark boughs. Through the whole forest the great unloosening had gone. Even the oaks in hollow places which had kept greenness like a continual wave suspended among dull masses of seaweed, had begun to yield to the vanishing call of the last voices of summer. Day by day their scattered tribes, then whole clans, broke up the tents of home and departed on the long mysterious exile. Yet this sentinel at the Gate of the North stood undaunted, splendid in warrior array. The same instinct that impels the soul from its outward home into the incalculable void moves the leaf with the imperious desire of the grey wind. But as, in human life, there are some who retain a splendid youth far into the failing regions of grey hair and broken years, so in the forest life there are trees which seem able to defy wind and rain and the consuming fect of frost.

The most subtle charm of the woods in November is in those blue spaces which lie at so brief a distance in every avenue of meeting boughs, under every enclosing branch. This azure mist which gathers like still faint smoke has the spell of silent waters, of moonlight, of the pale rose of serene dawns. It has a light that is its own, as unique as that unnameable flame which burns in the core of the rainbow. The earth breathes it; it is the breath of the fallen leaves, the moss, the tangled fern, the undergrowth, the trees; it is the breath also of the windless grey-blue sky that leans so low. Surely, also, it is the breath of that otherworld of which our songs and legends are so full. It has that mysteriousness, that spell, with which in imagination we endow the noon silences, the eves and dawns of faery twilights.

Still, the silence and the witchery of the forest solitudes in November are of the spell of autumn. The last enchantment of mid-winter is not yet come.

Where the Forest Murmurs

It is in "the dead months" that the forest permits the last disguises to fall away. The forest-soul is no longer an incommunicable mystery. It is abroad. It is a communicable dream. In that magnificent nakedness it knows its safety. For the first time it stands like a soul that has mastered all material things and is fearless in face of the immaterial things which are the only life of the spirit.

In these "dead months" of December and January the forest lives its own life. It is not asleep as the poets feign. Sleep has entered into the forest, has made the deep silence its habitation: but the forest itself is awake, mysterious, omnipresent, a creature seen at last in its naked majesty.

One says lightly, there is no green thing left. That, of course, is a mere phrase of relativity. There is always green fern somewhere, even in the garths of tangled yellow-brown bracken. There is always moss somewhere, hidden among the great serpentine roots of the beeches. The ilex will keep its dusty green through the harvest winter: the yew, the cypress, the holly, have no need of the continual invasion of the winds and rains and snows. On the ash and elm the wood-ivy will hang her spiked leaves. On many of the oaks the lovely dull green of the mistletoe will droop in graceful clusters, the cream-white berries glistening like innumerable pleiads of pearls. But these are lost in the immense uniformity of desolation. They are accidents, interludes. The wilderness knows them, as the grey wastes of tempestuous seas know a wave here and there that lifts a huge rampart of jade crowned with snow, or the long resiliency of gigantic billows which reveal smooth falling precipices of azure. The waste itself is one vast desolation, the more grey and terrible because in the mass invariable.

To go through those winter-aisles of the forest is to know an elation foreign to the melancholy of November or to the first fall of the leaf. It is not the elation of certain days in February, when the storm-cock tosses his song among the wild reefs of naked bough and branch. It is not the elation of March, when a blueness haunts the myriad unburst buds, and the throstle builds her nest and calls to the South. It is not the elation of April, when the virginal green is like exquisite music of life in miraculous suspense; nor the elation of May, when the wild rose moves in soft flame upon the thickets and the returned magic of the cuckoo is an intoxication; nor the elation of June, when the merle above the honeysuckle and the cushat in the green-glooms fill the hot noons with joy, and when the long fragrant twilights are thrilled with the passion of the nightjar. It has not this rapture nor that delight; but its elation is an ecstasy that is its own. It is then that one understands as one has never understood. It is then that one loves the mystery one has but fugitively divined. Where the forest murmurs there is music: ancient, everlasting. Go to the winter woods: listen there, look, watch, and "the dead months" will give you a subtler secret than any you have yet found in the forest. Then there is always one possible superb fortune. You may see the woods in snow. There is nothing in the world more beautiful than the forest clothed to its very hollows in snow. That is a loveliness to which surely none can be insensitive. It is the still ecstasy of Nature, wherein every spray, every blade of grass, every spire of reed, every intricacy of twig, is clad with radiance, and myriad form is renewed in continual change as though in the passionate delight of the white Artificer. It is beauty so great and complex that the imagination is stilled into an aching hush. There is the same trouble in the soul as before the starry hosts of a winter night.

THE MOUNTAIN CHARM

A famous writer of the eighteenth century declared that to a civilised mind the mountain solitude was naturally abhorrent. To be impressed was unavoidable, he allowed; to love barrenness and the wilderness, to take delight in shadow and silence, to find peace in loneliness, was unnatural. It is humanity that redeems nature, he added in effect. The opinion is not one commonly held now, or not admitted. But many hold it who would not admit that they so felt or thought. I have often asked summer wanderers if they have no wish to see the solitudes in early spring, when the ptarmigan's wing begins to brown; in November, when the rust of the bracken can loom through the hill-mist like the bronze shields of the sleeping Fianna; in December, when the polar wind frays the peaks into columns of smoke, the loose, dry snow on the northward foreheads of ancient summits; in January, when there is white silence, and the blue flitting shadow of the merlin's wing; in March, when in the south glens the cries of lambs are a lamenting music, and the scream of the eagle is like a faint bugle-call through two thousand feet of flowing wind. Few, however, would really care "to be away from home" in those months when snow and wind and cloud and rain are the continually recurrent notes in the majestic Mountain Symphony. "To see in a picture, to read of in a story or poem, that is delightful; but . . . well, one needs fine weather to enjoy the hills and the moorlands." That, in effect, is what I have commonly heard, or discerned in the evasive commonplace. It is not so with those who love the mountain-lands as the cushat loves the green twilight of beech or cedar, as the mew loves troubled waters and the weaving of foam. I remember, a year or so ago, being impressed by the sincerity of a lowlander whom I met on the road among the Perthshire mountains, in a region where the hills frowned and there was silence save for the hoarse sea-murmur of pines and the surge of a river hidden under boughs of hornbeam and leaning birch. I forget whence he had come, but it was from a place where the low lineaments of the fields were hardly more than long wave-lines on a calm sea; the only heights were heaps of "shag" by old mines, scattered columnar chimney-stacks. The man had trod

The Mountain Charm

far afoot, and was eager for work. I told him to go on toward the pass for about a mile, and then to a big farm he would see to his right, and ask there, and probably he would get work and good pay. Some three hours later I was returning by the same road, and again met the wayfarer, but southward set. I asked him why he had turned, for I knew labour was wanted at the farm, and the man was strong, and seemed willing, and was of decent mien. "No" he said, "he had not got work up yonder." I knew he prevaricated, and he saw it. With sudden candour he added: "It's no the good man at the farm—nor the work—nor the pay. It's just this: I'm fair clemmed at the sight o' yon hills . . . eh, but they're just dreidful. I couldna' abide them. They're na *human*. I've felt it all along since I cam up beyont the Ochils, but it's only the now I've kent weel I couldna' live here amang them." "Weel, first and foremost," he added, when I pressed him further, "it's the silence. It fair kills me. An' what's more, it *would* kill me if I stayed. The wife up yonder gave me a sup o' milk an' a bannock, an' when I was at them I sat on a bench an' looked about me. Naething but hills, hills, hills; hills an' black gloom an' that awfu' silence. An' there was a burd—a

The Mountain Charm

whaup we ca' it in the southlands—which fair shook my mind. It went lamentin' like a grave-bell, an' I heard it long after it was out o' sicht. Then there wasn't another sound. Na, na, wark or no wark, I'm awa' south."

And so the wayfarer set foot to the white road again, the south spelling home and human solace to him. Those dreary coallands, where the green grass is wan and the thorn hedge sombre, and any wandering water illucid and defiled, those hideous heaps of "shag," those gaunt mine-chimneys, those squalid hamlets in a populous desolation— these meant "human comfort" to him. Or, if they did not, at least they gave him somewhat which the mountain silence denied, which the gathered hills withheld, which the moorland solitudes overbore and refuted.

An extreme case, no doubt. But the deep disquietude of hill silence, of the mountain solitude, is felt by most habitual dwellers in towns and thronged communities. There is no mountain charm for these except the charm of release, of holiday, of novelty, of an imagined delight, of contrast, of unwonted air, of unfamiliar aspect. One of the popular excursion resorts in the near highlands of Argyll and Dunbarton is Loch Goil Head. A dweller there told me last autumn that of the

The Mountain Charm

hundreds who land every week, and especially on Saturdays and Fair holidays, and generally with an impatient eagerness, by far the greater number soon tire of the loneliness of the hills a brief way inland, and become depressed, and with a new and perhaps perturbing eagerness seek again the house-clad ways and the busy shore; and seem content, an hour or two before their steamer sails, to sit where they can see the movement of familiar life, and turn their back upon the strangely oppressive loneliness, so perturbingly remote, so paralysingly silent.

But for those who love the hills as comrades, what a spell, what enchantment! To wander by old grassy ways, old "pack-road" or timeless mountain path; to go through the bracken, by grey boulders tufted with green moss and yellow lichen, and see nothing but great rounded shoulders or sudden peaks overhead or beyond, nothing near but the yellow-hammer or wandering hawk or raven: to feel the pliant heather underfoot, and smell the wild thyme, and watch a cloud trail a purple shadow across the grey-blue slope rising like a gigantic wave from a sea of moors, rising and falling against the azure walls, but miraculously suspended there, a changeless vision, an eternal phantom: to go up into

The Mountain Charm

solitary passes, where even the June sunshine is hardly come ere it is gone, where the corbie screams, and the stag tramples the cranberry scrub and sniffs the wind blowing from beyond the scarlet-fruited rowan leaning from an ancient fallen crag: to see slope sinking into enveloping slope, and height uplifted to uplifting heights, and crags gathered confusedly to serene and immutable summits: to come at last upon these vast foreheads, and look down upon the lost world of green glens and dusky forests and many waters, to look down, as it were, from eternity into time . . . this indeed is to know the mountain charm, this is enchantment.

For the mountain-lover it would be hard to choose any pre-eminent season. The highland beauty appeals through each of the months, and from day to day. But, for all the glory of purple heather and dim amethystine slopes, it is perhaps not the early autumnal mountain charm, so loved of every one, that ranks first in one's heart. For myself I think midwinter, June, and the St. Martin's Summer of late October, or early November, more intimately compel in charm. And of these, I think June is not least. In midwinter the mountains have their most ideal beauty. It is an austere charm, the charm of whiteness and stillness.

The Mountain Charm

It is akin to the ineffable charm of a white flood of moonshine on a stilled ocean; but it has that which the waters do not have, the immobility of trance. There is nothing more wonderful in dream-beauty than vast and snow-bound mountain-solitudes in the dead of winter. That beauty becomes poignant when sea-fjords or inland waters lie at the sheer bases of the white hills, and in the luminous green or shadowy blue the heights are mirrored, so that one indeed stands between two worlds, unknowing the phantom from the real.

There is a dream-beauty also in that lovely suspense between the last wild winds of the equinox and "the snow-bringer," that period of hushed farewell which we call St. Martin's Summer. The glory of the heather is gone, but the gold and bronze of the bracken take on an equal beauty. The birch hangs her still tresses of pale gold, "that beautiful wild woman of the hills," as a Gaelic poet says. The red and russet of rowan and bramble, the rich hues of the haw, the sloe, the briony, all the golds and browns and delicate ambers of entranced autumn are woven in a magic web. In the mornings, the gossamer hangs on every bush of gorse and juniper. Through the serene air, exquisitely fresh with

The Mountain Charm

the light frosts which from dayset to dawn have fallen idly, rings the sweet and thrilling song of the robin, that music of autumn so poignant, so infinitely winsome. In what lovely words our Elizabethan Chapman wrote of the robin, of which we also of the North speak lovingly as " St. Colum's Friend," " St. Bride's Sweetheart," and the " little brother of Christ ":

" . . . . . the bird that loves humans best,
 That hath the bugle eyes and ruddy breast,
 And is the yellow autumn's nightingale."

But it is in June, I think, that the mountain charm is most intoxicating. The airs are lightsome. The hill-mists are seldom heavy, and only on south-wind mornings do the lovely grey-white vapours linger among the climbing corries and overhanging scarps. Many of the slopes are blue as a winter sky, palely blue, aerially delicate, from the incalculable myriad host of the bluebells. The green of the bracken is more wonderful than at any other time. When the wind plays upon it the rise and fall is as the breathing of the green seas among the caverns of Mingulay, or among the savage rock-pools of the Seven Hunters, or where the Summer Isles lie in the churn of the Atlantic tides. Everything is alive in joy.

The Mountain Charm

The young broods exult. The air is vibrant with the eddies of many wings, great and small. The shadow-grass sways with the passage of the shrewmouse or the wing's-breath of the darting swallow. The stillest pool quivers, for among the shadows of breathless reeds the phantom javelin of the dragon-fly whirls for a second from silence to silence. In the morning the far lamentation of the flocks on the summer shielings falls like the sound of bells across water. The curlew and the plover are not spirits of desolation, but blithe children of the wilderness. As the afternoon swims in blue haze and floating gold the drowsy call of the moorcock stirs the heather-sea. The snorting of trampling deer may be heard. The land-rail sweeps the dew from the tall grass and sends her harsh but summer-sweet cry in long monotonous echoes, till the air rings with the resonant *krek-crake*. And that sudden break in the silences of the dusk, when—beyond the blossoming elder, or the tangle of wild roses where the white moths rise and fall in fluttering ecstasy, or, yonder, by the black-green juniper on the moorland — the low whirring note of the nightjar vibrates in a continual passionate iterance! There, in truth, we have the passionate whisper of the heart of June, that

The Mountain Charm

most wonderful, that most thrilling of the voices of summer.

It is in June, too, that one mountain charm in particular may be known with rapt delight. It is when one can approach mountains whose outlying flanks and bases are green hills. The bright green of these under-slopes, these swelling heights and rolling uplands, is never more vivid. Near, one wonders why grasses so thick with white daisy and red sorrel and purple orchis and blue harebell can be green at all! But that wonderful sea-green of the hills near at hand gives way soon to the still more wonderful blue as the heights recede. The glens and wooded valleys grow paler. Rock and tree and heather blend. "What colour is that?" I asked a shepherd once. "The blueness of blueness," he answered in Gaelic. It is so. It is not blue one sees, but the bloom of blue; as on a wild plum, it is not the purple skin we note, but the amethyst bloom of purple which lies upon it. It is beauty, with its own loveliness upon it like a breath. Then the blue deepens, or greys, as the hour and the light compel. The most rare and subtle loveliness is when the grey silhouette of the mountain-ridge, serrated line, or freaked and tormented peaks, or vast unbroken amplitude, *sinks* into the

The Mountain Charm

sudden deep clearness of the enveloping sky.

Even in June, however, the mountain charm is not to be sought, as in a last sanctuary, on the summits of the hills. I believe that to be a delusion, a confusion, which asserts the supreme beauty of the views from mountain summits. I have climbed many hills and not a few mountains, and, except in one or two instances (as Hecla in the Hebrides), never without recognition that, in beauty, one does not gain, but loses. There are no heights in Scotland more often climbed by the holiday mountaineer than Ben Nevis in Argyle and Goat Fell in the Isle of Arran. Neither, in beauty or grandeur of view, repays the ascent. Goat Fell is a hundred times lovelier seen from the shores or glens of its own lower slopes, or from a spur of the Eastern Caisteall Abhaill: the boatmen on the waters of Lorne, the shepherd on the hills of Morven, the wayfarer in the wilds of Appin, they know the beauty of "the Sacred Hill" as none knows it who thinks he has surprised the secret on the vast brows overhanging the inchoate wilderness. At its best, we look through a phantasmal appearance upon a phantasmal world, and any artist will tell us that the disappointment is because every object is seen in its high light, none in its shadowed portion; that the direct sunlight being over all is reflected back to us from every surface; that the downward vision means a monotony of light and a monotony of colour.

The supreme charm of the mountain-lands in June is their investiture with the loveliest blue air that the year knows, and the entrancement of summer cloud. Small feathery cirrus or salmon-pink and snow-white cumulus emerging behind the shoulder of a mountain or drifting above the vast silent brows have an infinite beauty. We should be cloud-climbers rather than mere mountain-climbers; we should climb to see the heights recede in continual fold of loveliness, and the clouds lift their trailing purple shadows and sail slowly or hang motionless beyond the eternal buttresses. And it is but an added poignancy to the sense of infinite beauty to know that this word "eternal" is, even for those ancient "changeless" hills, but the idlest hyperbole—as though one were to call the breaking wave everlasting, or the blowing seed of the meadows as timeless as the wind. There is not a vast and lonely mountain that has not a fallen comrade among the low undulating ridges of the continual lowland; not one of these that has not in turn to feed the white dust of the

The Mountain Charm

plain or the sea-gathered sand of ancient or as yet unformed shores. For the hills pass, even as we or the green leaf become sere, or the fruit that ripens to its fall; though we speak of them as everlasting, and find the subtlest spell of their incalculable charm in the overwhelming sense of their imagined eternity.

THE CLANS OF THE GRASS

Of all the miracles of the green world none surpasses that of the grass. It has many names, many raiments even, but it is always that wonderful thing which the poets of all time have delighted in calling the green hair of earth. "Soft green hair of the rocks," says a Breton poet. Another Celtic poet has used the word alike for the mosses which clothe the talons of old trees and for the forests themselves. No fantastic hyperbole this: from a great height forests of pine and oak seem like reaches of sombre grass. To the shrewmouse the tall grasses of June are green woods, and the slim stems of the reddening sorrels are groves of pine-trees. I remember having read somewhere of a lovely name given to the grass by the Arabs of the desert . . . "the Bride of Mahomet." What lovelier and more gracious thing in the world, in their eyes, than this soft cool greenness of the oasis, this emerald carpet below the green shadowy roof of waving palms; and as of all women in the world there could be but one,

The Clans of the Grass

according to the old legend, worthy to be the supreme bride of the Prophet, what poetic name for her so fitting as this exquisite apparition of the desert, so beautiful, so ever-new in itself, so welcome for its association with sweet waters and shade and coolness. A Gaelic poet calls the grass the Gift of Christ, literally slender-greenness of Christ (*uaineachd-caol Chriosde*), and another has written of how it came to be called Green-Peace —both from an old tale (one of the many ebbed, forgotten tales of the isles) that, when God had created the world, Christ said: "Surely one thing yet lacks, my Father: soft greenness for the barren mountain, soft greenness for rocks and cliffs, soft greenness for stony places and the wilderness, soft greenness for the airidhs of the poor." Whereupon God said, "Let thy tenderness be upon these things, O my Son, and thy peace be upon them, and let the green grass be the colour of peace and of home"—and thereafter, says the taleteller, the Eternal Father turned to the Holy Spirit and said of the Son that from that hour He should be named the Prince of Peace, *Prionnsa na Siolh-cainnt canar ris.*

Grass is as universal as dew, as commonplace as light. That which feels the seawind in the loneliest Hebrides is brother to that

The Clans of the Grass

which lies on Himalaya or is fanned by the hot airs of Asian valleys. That which covers a grey scarp in Iceland is the same as that on Adam's Peak in Ceylon, and that which in myriad is the prairie of the north is in myriad the pampas of the south; that whose multitude covers the Gaelic hills is that whose multitude covers the Russian steppes. It is of all the signature of Nature that which to us is nearest and homeliest. The green grass after long voyaging, the grass of home-valley or hillside after long wayfaring, the green grass of the Psalmist to souls athirst and weary, the grass of El Dorado to the visionary seeking the gold of the spirit, the grass of the Fortunate Isles, of the Hills of Youth, to the poets and dreamers of all lands and times . . . everywhere and ever has this omnipresent herb that withereth and yet is continually reborn, been the eternal symbol of that which passes like a dream, the symbol of everlasting illusion, and yet, too, is the symbol of resurrection, of all the old divine illusion essayed anew, of the inexplicable mystery of life recovered and everlastingly perpetrated.

When we speak of grass we generally mean one thing, the small slim green herb which carpets the familiar earth. But there are many grasses, from the smooth close-set herb

The Clans of the Grass

of our lawns or the sheep-nibbled downy greenness of mountain-pastures, to the forest-like groves which sway in the torrid winds of the south. Of these alone much might be written. I prefer, however, that name I have placed at the head of this article—taken, if I remember rightly, from a poem by the Gaelic mountain-poet, Duncan Ban Macintyre—and used in the sense of the original. In this sense, the Clans of the Grass are not only the grasses of the pasture, the sand-dune, the windy down, not only the sorrel-red meadow-grass or the delicate quaking-grass, but all the humbler greengrowth which covers the face of the earth. In this company are the bee-loved clover, the trailing vetch, the yellow-sea clover and the sea-pink; the vast tribe of the charlock or wild mustard which on showery days sometimes lights up field or hill-meadow with yellow flame so translucent that one thinks a sudden radiant sunflood burns and abides there. In it too are all the slim peoples of the reed and rush, by streams and pools and lochans; of the yellow iris by the sea-loch and the tall flag by the mountain-tarn: the grey thistle, the sweet-gale, and all the tribe of the bog-cotton or canna *ceann-bàn-a-mhonaidh* the white head of the hillside, as we call it in Gaelic), those lovers

The Clans of the Grass

of the wilderness and boggy places. With these is the bind weed that with the salt bent holds the loose shores. With these are all the shadow-loving clans of the fern, from the bracken, whose April-glow lightens the glens and whose autumnal brown and dull gold make the hillsides so resplendent, to the stonewort on the dykes, the lady-fern in the birch-woods, the maidenhair by springs and falls, the hart's-tongue in caverns, the Royal fern whose broad fronds are the pride of heather-waste and morass. The mosses, too, are from this vast clan of the earth-set, from the velvet-soft edging of the oak-roots or the wandering greenness of the swamp to the ashy tresses which hang on spruce or hemlock or the grey fringes of the rocks by northern seas. And with them are the lichens, that beautiful secret company who love the shadow-side of trees, and make stones like flowers, and transmute the barrenness of rock and boulder with dyes of pale gold and blazing orange and umber, rich as the brown hearts of tarns, and pearl-grey delicate as a cushat's breast, and saffron as yellow-green as the sunset-light after the clearing of rains. To all these, indeed, should be added the greater grasses which we know as wheat and oats, as rye and maize. Thus do we come to

The Clans of the Grass

"the waving hair of the ever-wheeling earth," and behold the unresting mother as in a vision, but with the winds of space for ever blowing her waving tresses in a green gladness, or in a shimmer of summer-gold, or in the bronze splendour of the columnal passage.

But the grasses proper, alone: the green grass itself—what a delight to think of these, even if the meaning of the title of this paper be inclusive of them and them only. What variety, here, moreover. The first spring-grass, how welcome it is. What lovely delicacy of green. It is difficult anywhere to match it. Perhaps the first greening of the sallow, that lovely hair hung over ponds and streams or where sloping lawns catch the wandering airs of the south: or the pale green-flame of the awakening larch: or the tips of bursting hawthorn in the hedgerows —perhaps, these are nearest to it in hue. But with noonlight it may become almost the pale-yellow of sheltered primroses, or yellow-green as the cowslip before its faint gold is minted, and in the mellowing afternoon it may often be seen as illuminated (as with hidden delicate flame) as the pale-emerald candelabra of the hellebore. How different is the luxuriant grass in hollows and combes and along watered meadows in June, often

The Clans of the Grass

dark as pine-greens or as sunlit jade, and in shadowy places or a twilight sometimes as lustrously sombre-grey as the obsidian, that precious stone of the Caucasus now no longer a rarity among us. How swiftly, too, that changes after the heats of midsummer, often being threaded with grey light before the dog-days are spent.

Moreover, at any season there is a difference between down-grass and mountain-grass, between sea-grass and valley-grass, between moor-grass and wood-grass. It may be slight, and not in kind but only in shadowy dissemblances of texture and hue; still one may note the difference. More obvious, of course, is the difference between, say, April-grass and the same grass when May or June suffuses it with the red glow of the seeding sorrel, or between the sea-grass that has had the salt wind upon it since its birth, the bent as it is commonly called, and its brother among the scarps and cliff-edges of the hills, so marvellously soft and hairlike for all that it is not long since the snows have lifted or since sleet and hail have harried the worn faces of boulder and crag. Or, again, between even the most delicate wantonness of the seeding hay, fragrant with white clover and purple vetch, and the light aerial breathfulness, frail as thistledown,

The Clans of the Grass

of the quaking-grass. How it loves the wood's-edge, this last, or sheltered places by the hedgerows, the dream-hollows of sloping pastures, meadow-edges where the cow-parsley whitens like foam and the meadow-sweet floats creamwhite and the white campions hang in clotted froth over the long surge of daisies: or, where, like sloops of the nautilus on tropic seas, curved blossoms of the white wild-rose motionlessly suspend or idly drift, hardly less frail, less wantonly errant than the white bloomy dust of the dandelion.

Caran-cheann-air-chrith, "little friend of the quaking-grass," is one of the Gaelic names of the wagtail, perhaps given to it because of a like tremulous movement, as though invisible wings of gossamer shook ever in a secret wind. Or given to it, perhaps, because of a legend which puts the common grass, the quaking-grass, the wagtail, the cuckoo, the aspen, and the lichen in one traditional company. In the Garden of Gethsemane, so runs the Gaelic folk-tale as I heard it as a child, all Nature suddenly knew the Sorrow of Christ. The dew whispered it: it was communicated in the dusk: in pale gold and shaken silver it stole from moon and star into the green darkness of cypress and cedar. The grass-blades put all their

The Clans of the Grass

green lips into one breath, and sighed *Peace, Brother!* Christ smiled in His sorrow, and said, *Peace to you for ever.* But here and there among the grasses, as here and there among the trees, and as here and there among the husht birds, were those who doubted, saying, "It is but a man who lies here. His sorrow is not our sorrow." Christ looked at them, and they were shaken with the grief of all grief and the sorrow of all sorrow. And that is why to this day the quaking-grass and the aspen are for ever a-tremble, and why the wagtail has no rest but quivers along the earth like a dancing shadow. But to those mosses of Gethsemane which did not give out the sympathy of their kin among the roots of cedar and oak, and to the cuckoo who rang from her nest a low chime of *All's well! All's well!* Christ's sorrowful eyes when He rose at dawn could not be endured. So the cuckoo rose and flew away across the Hill of Calvary, ringing through the morning twilight the bells of sorrow, and from that day was homeless and without power anywhere to make a home of her own. As for the mosses that had refused love, they wandered away to desolate places and hung out forlorn flags of orange-red and pale-yellow and faded-silver along the grey encampments of the rocks.

The Clans of the Grass

Often I have thought of this when lying in the mountain-grass beside one of those ancient lichened boulders which strew our hill-sides. The lichen is the least of the grasses—and let us use the term in its poetic sense—but how lovely a thing it is; almost as lovely in endless variety of form as the frost-flower. In a sense they are strangely akin, these two; the frost-flower, which is the breath of Beauty itself, lasting a briefer hour than the noon-tide dew, and the moss-flower which the barren rock sustains through all the changing seasons.

Who is that Artificer who has subtly and diversely hidden the secret of rhythm in the lichen of the rock and in the rock's heart itself; in the frost-flower, so perfect in beauty that a sunbeam breathes it away; in the falling star, a snowflake in the abyss, yet with the miraculous curve in flight which the wave has had, which the bent poplar has had, which the rainbow has had, since the world began? The grey immemorial stone and the vanishing meteor are one. Both are the offspring of the Eternal Passion, and it may be that between the æon of the one and the less than a minute of the other there shall not, in the divine-reckoning, be more than the throb of a pulse. For who of us can measure even

The Clans of the Grass

Time, that the gnat measures as well as we, or the eagle, or the ancient yew, or the mountain whose granite blows are white with ages— much less Eternity, wherein Time is but a vanishing pulse?

THE TIDES

I remember that one of the most strange and perturbing pleasures of my childhood was in watching, from a grassy height, the stealthy motions of the tides. The fascination never waned, nor has it yet waned: to-day, as then, I know at times the old thrill, almost the old fear, when through a white calm or up some sea-loch I watch those dark involutions, in sudden twists and long serpentine curves, as the eddies of the tide force their mysterious way. For one thing my childish imagination was profoundly impressed by the words of an old islander whom I had asked where the tides came from and what they were and had they names. We were on the steep slope of a small grassy hill, and overlooked the eastern end of an island where the troubled waters of a *caoileas* or strait to the south met the vast placid reach of ocean on the north. Through the lustrous green of the Sound, fleckt with long mauve shadows or clouded here and there with great splatches of purple-brown; and, again, to the

The Tides

left through the near calm heave of deep water so blue that as a child I could not understand why the shells which were washed up from it were not blue also : to right and to left I saw the sudden furtive motions of the flowing tide. I had often watched the blindworm move thus through the coarse seagrasses, and again and again had seen the adder dart through the bracken like one of those terrible living arrows of Faerie of which I had heard : often, too, I had followed the shadow-swift underwave glide of the hunting seal : and once, in a deep brown pool in Morven, when I was looking with trembling hope for the floating hair or dim white face of a kelpie, I had seen an otter rise from the depths—rise like a fantastic elfin face and half-human figure in a dream—make a soundless sinuous plunge and in less than a moment vanish utterly, still without sound or the least ruffling of the brown depths. So, it was natural that I should associate those mysterious gliding things of the sea with these sinuous things of the grass and heather and the shadowy pool. They, too, I thought, were furtive and sinister. There was something as of the same evil enchantment in their abrupt and inexplicable appearing and in their soundless departures. Thus it was I felt no surprise when my old island-friend Seumais remarked to me:

"They are creatures of the sea."

"What are they, Seumais?" I urged; "are they great eels, or adders, or what? Can they put death on a swimmer? Have you ever caught one? Have——"

"Ay, for sure they might put death on a swimmer: and by the same token I will be remembering that Rùaridh Stewart, the Appin poet, has a *rann* about them as the Hounds of the Sea."

"And have they names?"

"For sure, that: *Luath* (Swift) and *Gorm-Dhu* (Blue-Black), *Luath-Donn* (Fleet-brown-one) and *Braco* (Speckled), *Rùn-folninne* (Underwave Secret) and *Cu-Bhais* (Hound of Death), and others that I will be forgetting."

"But, Seumais," I persisted, "are they male-seafolk and women-seafolk like the seals, and have they little ones, and where do they go, and where do the big tides come from?"

"Well, well, I will not be knowing that, though, for sure, it is likely. But as to where they come from, and where they go, there will be none in all the world who can tell that; no, not one. They will be just like the

The Tides

wind, that no one knows the road of, behind or before. Ay, the sea's just like the grey road: the green road an' the grey road, they show no tracks. The wind an' the tides, they just come an' they just go. "Blind as the wind," "blind as the tide" . . . ay, it may be; but not so blind as we are, for they know their way, an' brightest noon an' darkest night, an' summer an' winter, an' calm an' storm, are one an' the same to them."

It is long ago now since I heard these words from old Seumais Macleod, but I am certain (so deeply did they impress my childish imagination, and sink into a child's mind) that I repeat them almost exactly. I had no hesitation in believing in *Gorm-Dhu* and *Luath-Donn*, and the rest, and took these names to be real names of actual creatures, as *Daoine-Vhara* (folk of the sea) for seals, or as *piocach* for the brown saithe I was wont to watch swimming amid the fronds of the seaweed, or as *sgàdan* for the flashing herring whose shoals so often made a dazzle in the offing beyond the strait, and whose radiant scales glorified as with gems the nets hauled up in the moonshine or in the pale rose and cowslip-yellow of August dawns.

The Tides

And, in truth, I am not much the wiser now. There is no great gain in wisdom in the knowledge that the tides are not mysterious creatures of the deep, and are nameless as the winds, as homeless as they, as silent, furtive, as formless, as incalculable almost, as variable. The old islander knew how to turn into service their comings and goings, how to meet them when friendly, how to evade them when hostile, how to wonder continually at their strange beauty, how to reverence the terrible order of their rhythmic flow and ebb. What matter if, also, his old-world Gaelic imagination imaged to him these dark forces of the sea as living creatures; not of flesh and blood as the slim brown seals who, too, can glide not less swiftly and secretly through dusky green water-ways; not even of such consistency as the tide-wrack floating on the wave, or the dim, wandering medusæ which drift like pale, quenchless fires in the untroubled stillness of the twilit underworld; but at least of the company of lightning, of fire, of the wind, of dew, of shadow—creatures without form as we know form, but animate with a terrible and mysterious life of their own—a secret brotherhood among the visible and invisible clans of the world. What matter if, remembering songs and old tales and in-

The Tides

calculable traditions, he thought of them with names, as the "fleet-brown-one," as "swift-darkness," as "the dark-courser," as "the untameable," as "the hound of death?" These tell us neither more nor less (to many of us more, not less) than the abstruse algebraical formulæ of Newton and Laplace. The imagination does not move like flame among intricate calculations, though the mind may be compelled and convinced; and some of us at least would learn more of the tides and their occult nature and laws from an old islesman telling of *lionadh* and *srùth-mara* than from the bewildering maze of the five-and-fifty columns which the *Encyclopædia Britannica* devotes to the subject.

Everywhere this tidal mystery, this beauty of flood and ebb, is to be seen; along whatever coasts sea-waters move or wherever they penetrate. The "tideless Mediterranean" is but a phrase. Even along the shores of Malta and Sicily there is a perceptible rise and fall, and at a thousand points between Marseilles or Tangier and Venice or Cape Matapan the tidal movement is as mysterious and impressive as among the shoals of Ushant or in the Norsk fjords. There are few places where the trained eye could not perceive a

The Tides

difference of rise or fall. I recollect being shown a spot on the Argive coast of the Peloponnesus where, it was said, the tidal difference was non-existent. On that very day, a day of windless calm, I noticed a fall of over a foot in depth. Dark, steep rocks shelved to deep waters, and to all ordinary appearance there was nothing to indicate the slightest variance between flow and ebb. Even a Morean Greek declared "there is no flood, no ebb, here."

But, in our own home-waters, what marvellous changes take place under the strong continuous pull of the lunar reins. Think of wind and flood-tide on the Channel coasts, with the strange sound as of a murmurous host confusedly marching: think of the daily two-fold flooding of estuaries, and the sinuous invasion of the sea past curving banks and among remote inland meadows. Are rivers not enhanced in mystery when through the downward flow a salt serpentine envoy from the distant sea forces its way, revealing itself in circuitous eddies, in dark revolving rings, in troubled surface-seethe: bringing to the flags and rushes, to the leaning grasses and gold kingcup and purple mallow that salt lip, which a score or half-score miles away had been laid on the sea-grapes of the bladder-

The Tides

wrack, or on the slow-involving tresses of the twisting long-weed? Then there is that miraculous halt, when the cold hand of the tide can reach no farther: when at a boat's helm a curl of dark brackish water will indolently lapse, while at the prow the clear-brown rippling rush will be fresh with gathered rains and dews and the unsullied issues of wellsprings and sunlit sources.

The tide-flow may be more beautiful and obvious seen from the high shores of certain estuaries, as, say, from the Falmouth uplands, or from the hillsides of our narrow Highland sea-lochs, but the mind is deeplier impressed and the imagination compelled by the more obscure, menacing, and almost terrifying swift arrivals along vast shallow estuaries, such as The Wash or the inner reaches of Solway Firth or by the Sands o' Dee. With what abrupt turbulence the calms are violated, with what a gathering sound the invisible host is marshalled, with what impetuous surge the immeasurable sortie advances! Of a sudden those little shallows in the sands, those little weed-hung pools below slippery rocks covered with mussel and dog-whelk, shiver. A faint undulation thrills the still small world. A shrimp darts from a sand-mound: a blood-red

The Tides

anemone thrusts out feathered antennæ : now one, now another shell-fish stirs, lifts, gapes. It is the response of the obscure, the insignificant, and the silent, to that mighty incalculable force which is hastening from the fathomless depths and across countless leagues of the great Sea. Soon the flood will come : perhaps in furtive swiftness and silence, perhaps with a confused multitudinous noise among which are inchoate cries and fragmentary bewildering echoes of muffled songs and chants, perhaps as in charging hordes of wild sea-horses where the riders are not seen in the dazzle of spray nor their shouting heard in the tumult of wave dashed against wave and billow hurled on billow.

To be in some such place—say, again, where the Breton tide races against the flank of Normandy and in a few minutes isolates Mont St. Michel from the mainland ; or where the Northumbrian flood pours across the narrow sands of Lindisfarne ; or, more than everywhere else, I think, where the fierce Atlantic tides leap with bewildering surge and clamour across the vast sea-gates of Uist and rush like a cataract into the Hebrid Sea—to be in some such place and at the first mysterious signals of the oncoming flood, by night, is to meet the unforgettable, and, as

The Tides

Blake says, to be at one with the eternal mystery.

Flow and ebb, ebb and flow . . . it is that ancient inexplicable mystery, the everlasting and unchanging rhythm which holds star to star in infinite procession, which lifts and lowers the poles of our sun-wheeling world, which compels the great oceans to arise and follow the mysterious bidding of the moon. It is wonderful that the moon travels along the equator at the rate of a thousand miles an hour: but more wonderful that these loose, formless, blind and insensate waters should awake at the touch of that pale hand, should move to it and follow it as the flocks on the hills to the voice of the shepherd.

Flow and ebb, ebb and flow . . . it is the utterance of the divine law, the eternal word of Order. It is life itself. What life is there, from the phosphorescent atom in the running wave to the enfranchised soul stepping westward beyond the twilights of time, that is not subject to this ineffable rhythmic law. The tides of the world, the tides of life: the grey sap, the red blood, the secret dews, the tameless seas, birth and death, the noons and midnights of the mind of man, the evening dusk and the morning glory of the soul: one

The Tides

and all move inevitably, and in one way : in one way come, and go, and come again.

" *Mar a bha,*	*As it was,*
Mar a tha,	*As it is,*
Mar a bhitheas	*As it shall be*
Gu brath	*Evermore*
. . . .	. . . .
Ri tràgadh,	*With the ebb,*
'S ri lionadh."	*With the flow."*

THE HILL-TARN

Isolated, in one of the wildest and loneliest mountain-regions of the Highlands of Ross, I know a hill-tarn so rarely visited that one might almost say the shadow of man does not fall across its brown water from year's end to year's end. It lies on the summit of a vast barren hill, its cradle being the hollow of a crater. Seven mountains encircle Maoldhu from north, south, east, and west. One of these is split like a hayfork, and that is why it is called in Gaelic the Prong of Fionn. Another, whose furrowed brows are dark with the immemorial rheum of the Atlantic, is called the Organ of Oisin, because at a height of about two thousand feet it shows on its haggard front a black colonnade of basalt, where all the winds of the west make a wild and desolate music. I have heard its lamentation falling across the hill-solitudes and down through the mountain-glens with a sound as of a myriad confused sobs and cries, a sound that is now a forlorn ecstasy and now the voice of the abyss and of immeasurable desolation. Another, that on the east, is an unscalable cone, from whose crest, when sunrise flames the serrated crags into a crown of burning bronze, the golden eagle sways like a slow-rising and slow-falling meteor. All day, save for a brief hour at noon, shadow dwells about its knees, and never lifts from the dark grassy lochan at its feet. It is called Maol Athair-Uaibhreach, the Hill of the Haughty Father: I know not why. "The Haughty Father" is a Gaelic analogue for the Prince of Darkness—son of Saturn, as he is called in an old poem: "God's Elder Brother," as he is named in a legend that I have met or heard of once only—a legend that He was God of this world before "Mac Greinne" (lit.: Son of the Sun) triumphed over him, and drove him out of the East and out of the South, leaving him only in the West and in the North two ancient forgotten cities of the moon, that in the West below the thunder of grey seas and that in the North under the last shaken auroras of the Pole.

It is not easy to reach this tarn of Maoldhu even when the hillways are known. The mountain-flanks have so vast a sweep, with such wide tracts of barren declivity, where the loose stones and boulders seem to hang in the air like a grey suspended fruit though

The Hill-Tarn

the first tempest will set them rolling in avalanche. There are so many hidden ravines, and sudden precipices that lean beneath tangled brows like smooth appalling faces; on the eastern slopes the mountain-sheep cannot climb more than halfway; on the south and west the wailing curlews are in continual flight above wide unfrontiered reaches of peat-bog and quaking morass; so many crags lead abruptly to long shelving ledges shelterless and slippery as ice, and twice an abyss of a thousand feet falls sheer from loose rock covered by treacherous heather for a yard or more beyond the last gnarled, twisted roots.

But, when it is once reached, is there any solitude in the world more solitary than here. The tarn, or lochan rather—for if it is not wide enough to be called a loch it is larger than the ordinary tarn one is familiar with on high moorlands and among the hills—has no outlook save to the lonely reach of sky just above it. A serrated crest of herbless and lifeless precipice circles it. On the lower slopes a rough grass grows, and here and there a little bog-myrtle may be seen. At one end a small dishevelled array of reed disputes the water-edge, in thin, straggling, disconsolate lines. There is nothing else. Sometimes the ptarmigan will whirr across it, though

The Hill-Tarn

they do not love crossing water. Sometimes the shadow of an eagle's wing darkens the already obscure depths. But the mountain-sheep never reach this height, and even the red deer do not come here to drink these still, brown waters: "One sees no antlers where the heather ceases," as the shepherds say. The clouds rise above the crests of the west and pass beyond the crests of the east: snow, the steel-blue sleet, the gray rains, sweep past overhead. In summer, a vast cumulus will sometimes for hours overlean the barren crater and fill the tarn with a snowy wonderland and soft abysses of rose and violet: sometimes a deep, cloudless azure will transmute it to a still flame of unruffled, shadowless blue. At night, when it is not a pit of darkness to which the upper darkness is twilight, it will hold many stars. For three hours Arcturus will pulsate in it like a white flame. Other planets will rise, and other stars. Their silver feet tread the depths in silence. Sometimes the moon thrusts long yellow lances down into its brooding heart, or will lie on its breast like the curled horn of the honeysuckle, or, in autumn, like a floating shell filled with fires of phosphorescence. Sunset never burns there, though sometimes the flush of the afterglow descends as on soft

The Hill-Tarn

impalpable wings from the zenith. At dawn, in midsummer, long scarlet lines will drift from its midmost to the south and west, like bloodstained shafts and battle-spears of a defeated aërial host.

Few sounds are heard by that mountain-tarn. The travelling cloud lets fall no echo of its fierce frost-crashing shards. Dawn and noon and dusk are quiet-footed as mist. The stars march in silence. The springing Northern Lights dance in swift fantastic flame, but are voiceless as the leaping shadows in a wood. Only those other wayfarers of the mountain-summit, tempest, thunder, the streaming wind, the snow coming with muffled rush out of the north, wild rains and whirling sleet, the sharp crackling tread of the hosts of frost: only these break the silence; or, at times, the cries of "the eldest children of the hill" as the mountain-Gael calls the eagle, the hill-fox, and the ptarmigan—the only creatures that have their home above the reach of the heather and in the grey stony wildernesses where only the speckled moss and the lichen thrive.

When I was last at this desolate and remote tarn I realised the truth of that hill-saying. After the farthest oaks on Sliabh Gorm, as the ridge to the south-west is called

The Hill-Tarn

and up which alone is a practicable if rough and often broken way, came scattered groups and then isolated trees of birch and mountain-ash. Thereafter for a long way the heather climbed. Then it gave way more and more to bracken. In turn the bracken broke like the last faint surf against huge boulders and waste stony places. The grouse called far below. The last deer were browsing along their extreme pastures, some five hundred to eight hundred feet below the precipitous bastions of Maoldhu. Higher than they I saw a circling hawk and three ravens flying slowly against the wind. Then came the unpeopled wilderness, or so it seemed till I heard the wail of a solitary curlew (that spirit of the waste, for whom no boggy moors lie too low and desolate, for whom no mountain-ranges are too high and wild and solitary), and once, twice, and again in harsh response but faint against the wind, the barking of a hill-fox and its mate. All life had ceased, I thought, after that, save an eagle which in a tireless monotony swung round and round the vast summit of Maoldhu. But suddenly, perhaps a hundred feet above me, six or seven ptarmigan rose with a whirr, made a long sailing sweep, and settled (slidingly and gradually as flounders in shallow waters among

The Hill-Tarn

grey pebbles and obscuring sand-furrows) among the lichened boulders and loose disarray of speckled granite and dark and grey basalt and trap—an ideal cover, for even a keen following gaze could not discern the living from the inanimate.

Truly the eagle, the hill-fox, and the ptarmigan are "the eldest children of the hill." The stag may climb thus high too at times, for outlook, or for the intoxication of desolation and of illimitable vastness; sometimes the hawks soar over the wilderness; even the mountain-hares sometimes reach and race desperately across these high arid wastes. But these all come as men in forlorn and lonely lands climb the grey uninhabitable mountains beyond them, seeking to know that which they cannot see beneath, seeking often for they know not what. They are not dwellers there. The stag, that mountain-lover, cannot inhabit waste rock; the red grouse would perish where the ptarmigan thrives and is content.

How little has been written about these birds of the mountain-brow. What poetry is in their name; for those who know the hills. They dwell higher than the highest June-flight of the tireless swift, higher than the last reaches of the sunrise-leaping larks.

The Hill-Tarn

Cities might crumble away in pale clouds of dust, floods might whelm every lowland, great fires might devour the forests and the red insatiable myriad of flame lap up the last high frontiers of bracken and climbing heather, and the ptarmigan would know nothing of it, would not care. Their grey home would be inviolate. No tempest can drive them forth. Even the dense snows of January do not starve them out. Do they not mock them by then taking the whiteness of the snow for their own? They have nothing to fear save the coming of a black frost so prolonged and deathly that even the sunfire in the eagle's blood grows chill, and the great pinions dare no more face the icy polar breath. "They'll be the last things alive when the world is cold," said an old gillie to me, speaking of these storm-swept lichen-fed children of the upper-wild.

The same old gillie once saw a strange sight at my mountain-tarn. He had when a youth climbed Maoldhu to its summit in midwinter, because of a challenge that he could not do what no other had ever done at that season. He started before dawn, but did not reach the lochan till a red fire of sunset flared along the crests. The tarn was frozen deep, and for all the pale light that dwelled upon it

The Hill-Tarn

was black as basalt, for a noon-tempest had swept its surface clear of snow. At first he thought small motionless icebergs lay in it, but wondered at their symmetrical circle. He descended as far as he dared, and saw that seven wild-swans were frozen on the tarn's face. They had alit there to rest, no doubt: but a fierce cold had numbed them, and an intense frost of death had suddenly transfixed each as they swam slowly circlewise as is their wont. They may have been there for days, perhaps for weeks. A month later the gillie repeated his arduous and dangerous feat. They were still there, motionless, ready for flight as it seemed.

How often in thought have I seen that coronal of white swans above the dark face of that far, solitary tarn: in how many dreams I have listened to the rustle of un-loosening wings, and seen seven white phantoms rise cloud-like, and like clouds at night drift swiftly into the dark; and heard, as mournful bells through the solitudes of sleep, the *honk-honk* of the wild-swans traversing the obscure forgotten ways to the secret country beyond sleep and dreams and silence.

AT THE TURN OF THE YEAR

When one hears of "the dead months," of "dead December" and "bleak January," the best corrective is to be found in the coppice or by the stream-side, by the field thicket, in the glens, and even on the wide moors if the snow is not everywhere fallen, a coverlet so dense and wide that even the juniper has not a green spike to show, or the dauntless bunting a clean whin-branch to call from on the broomie-knowe. Even the common sayings reveal a knowledge hidden from those to whom winter is "a dead season"—and it is a continual surprise to find how many people believe that from the fall of the leaf or the first sleet and snow, till the thrush doubles and trebles his note in the February wet-shine, that bird and insect and all green life have gone, that all Nature is dead or asleep. Thus, for example, "as keen in the hearing as a winter-plover" must have been uttered, when first said, by a watcher of the multi-form bird-life of our winter-fields and fallow lands, one who knew that the same drama of

At the Turn of the Year

life and death is enacted in midwinter as in midspring or midsummer, a drama only less crowded, less complex and less obvious, but not less continual, not less vital for the actors. Who that has watched the peewits seeking worms on ploughed lands at midwinter, and seen them poise their delicate heads and listen for the phantom rustle of a worm in this clod or under yonder fallow, while the greedy but incapable seamews, inland come from frost-bound coasts or on the front of prolonged gales, hear nothing of "the red people" and trust only to bulk and fierce beak to snatch the prey from hungry plover-bills—who that has seen this can fail to recognise the aptness of the saying, "as keen in the hearing as a winter-plover"? Who that has watched the ebb and flow of lark-life, resident and immigrant; the troubled winter-days of the field-travellers (as the familiar word "fieldfare" means) and the wandering thrushes; the vagrant rooks, the barn-haunting hoodie; the yellowhammer flocks and tribes of the finch; the ample riverside life, where heron and snipe, mallard and moor-hen, wren and kingfisher, and even plover and the everywhere adaptable starling are to be found with ease by quick eyes and careful ears: who that has seen the sudden apparition of the bat, or the columnar dance of the ephemeridæ, or the flight of the winter-moth along the dishevelled hedgerows: or who that, besides the mistletoe and the ivy, the holly and the fir, the box and the late-flowering clematis, and many other of the green and flowering clans of the forest and the garden, has noted the midwinter-blooming shepherd's purse, healing groundsel, bright chickweed, and red deadnettle, can think of Nature as lifeless at this season?

When amid the rains and storms of December an old gardener, instead of saying that spring was on the move, remarked to me that "'Twill be starling days soon," he gave voice to a truth of observation as impressive as it is beautiful. For often December has not lapsed before the mysterious breeding-change of the Vita Nuova, the New Life that spreads like a flowing wave so early in the coming year, will begin to be obvious on the dun-hued lapwing, on the inland-wandering gull, and even on one or other of the small "clan of the bushes" more dear and familiar to us. On none, however, is the change so marked as on the blithe starling, surely the bird of cheerfulness, for he will sing (does he ever cease that ever-varying call or flute or whistle of his?) when the lark cannot rise in the polar air, when the missel-thrush will not throw a challenge on the wet wind, and long before the most jubilant great-tit in the forest will ring his early tinkling bell under leafless boughs. For, even at Christmastide, though rarely perhaps quite so early, the dark bill will suddenly yellow, and a green and purple sheen will come over the russet plumage. Already Nature has looked northward again. And, when she looks, there is at once a first movement of the infinite sweet trouble of the New Life once more. The Creative Spirit is come again from the sunways of the South. "'Twill be starling days soon"—what is that but a homely way of saying that the old year has not lapsed before the new year has already stirred with the divine throes of rebirth. "The King is dead: Long live the King!" is the human analogue. There is no interregnum. The cuckoo may have fled before the swallow, the landrail before the wild swan, but during the grey ebb of Autumn ten thousand wings have rustled in the dawn as the migrants from oversea descend at last on our English and Scottish shores. A myriad host may have fled at the equinox, or lingered till the wet winds of the west and the freezing blasts of the north swept them from November; but on those east winds from Norway and the Baltic, from Jutland and Friesland, on those south winds leaping upward from the marshes of Picardy and the Breton heathlands and from all of the swarm-delivering South behind, on those southwest gales warm with the soft air of the isles of the West, and wet with the foam over lost Ys and sunken Lyonesse— what an incalculable host has come hitherward! Like great fans, the invisible pinions of the Bird-God, that Winged Spirit whom a Finnish legend images in continual suspense at the Crossways of the Four Winds, beat this way and that: so that when already the lament of the wild-geese in storm-baffled flight from the South ululates in our norland dawns, clouds of larks are gathered like dust from the North-Sea lands and are blown upon our shores, a multitude of thrush turn westward, the rook and the hoodie rise on the Danish wind, and yonder shadow drifting over the woods of Norway is none other than ten thousand fieldfares whose congregation will soon be spilt like rain upon our fields and pastures.

When is the turn of the year? We have certainly not to wait till the missel-thrush calls down the wind on the moist southwester that comes in February. The changing

At the Turn of the Year

seasons are indifferent to our calendars. Autumn may burn the lime and chestnut while Summer is still in her glory; Summer may steal back upon us through the September haze, or even after we have heard the dry rustle in the woods of October. We are familiar with the return of halcyon days when St. Luke's Peace follows the wind Euroclydon, or when St. Martin's Summer gleams like a quiet sunset on the stormy brows of Winter. In mid-December the gnat may still be seen spinning her dance by the hedgerow, the warmth-loving bat may still wheel through silent afternoon dusks, the robin will pitch his blithe song from holly to holly, the hedgesparrow will chase the winter moth, the chaffinch will challenge the marauding tit. In January, when the snow-lids open and the blue is seen, a lark will spray his sudden music from far up in the pale azure, and as the long notes tinkle and the interwoven song falls down the blue invisible ways, we almost imagine that sky-glimpse to be the very face of Spring.

Thus we have to wait for no day on which to note from the calendar that the New Year is come, or on which to exclaim that Winter is gone and Spring has arrived. A day may come, in February, perhaps, when, suddenly

At the Turn of the Year

one will realise, as after sleep one realises one is awake, that the hands of the South are in the woods, that the eyes of the South are looking into the white sleep of blossom and flower, that the breath of the South has awakened love, has stirred music in the hearts of all the clans of song. But if we had not ourselves been asleep we should not have waited thus long for the exquisite surprise. We should have known the divine conspiracy by which the North and South are lovers, and the West comrade to the East. The conspiracy of the eternal passion by which power desires power, and dominion lusteth after dominion: so that all the effort of the North is to touch the lips of the South, all the dream of the East is to reach the sunset-gardens of the West We should have known, when out of December frost or January snow the redbreast thrilled a canticle of joy, or the russet moth sought his wingless love in windless flame-set twilights, that the Grey Lover already felt the breath from those ardent lips. We should have realised that when across the snow-silence the fieldfares no longer edged southward, that when on the upland-pasture the lapwing began his bridal change and in the bare orchard the starling began to glisten as though he had bathed at the edge of the

At the Turn of the Year

rainbow, or to wonder, in some ice-set mirror, at his dun beak now grown yellow as the sheltered crocus he knows of under the garden-yew . . . we should have realised that while this dark-browed barbarian from the North slept, the fair woman of the South had passed smiling by, and kissed him as she passed.

The breeding-change that may be seen even before Christmas, the January stir that becomes so obvious a week or so, or any day, after the New Year is come, here and now we are at the turn of the year. By mid-January, even, here and there, the song-thrush and the missel may have begun to build, and even the great-tit's bell may tinkle in the coppice or wind-spared russet oak-glade. Already the snowdrop and the Christmas-rose, the green-white aconite and the pale winter-iris are become old acquaintances: many a primrose may have adventured in shy retreats: any day a wandering minstrel will spill a tinkle of music from among the first yellow spray of hazel catkins, the hedgesparrow may unloosen song under the early-opening woodbine-buds, the corn-bunting may crack his fairy-hammer or the wren try his new-year flute among the yellowing gorse: any day, at the sight of the first nomad daisies or the first gay vagrant dandelion, the yellow-hammer may become a lover and a poet. It is this unchanging "any-day" element that redeems even the longest and dreariest midwinter; the sense of the ever-moving ichor in the eternal veins; the inward exultation at the ever-quickening and ever-slowing, but never-ceasing fans of life and death.

Yesterday, rain-fog; to-day, frost-mist. But how fascinating each. How vast and menacing the familiar oaks looked, leaning gigantic over dim lapsing hedgerows. How phantom-like and processional, the elms, stealing into view one after the other; the birches disclosing tresses wet with dews from the secret woods they are gliding from to regain the secret lauds beyond the misty river where I can hear the mallard call, like a sudden tocsin among the falling towers and silent avalanches of Cloudland.

It is so desolate here, where I stand.

"*Cinnidh fcanntag 's a ghàradh*
'*N uair thig faillinn 'san ròs.*"
"*Nettles grow in the garden,*
While the roses decay."

A long way off yet till the wood-thrush rings his falling chime from the April-Tree

At the Turn of the Year

or French-Broom, as the laburnum is called in some parts of the Highlands. I know a wood where a great *Bealaidh Fhrangach* sleeps, to awake months hence in sun-gold beauty. The wood-thrush will be its flute. Already I have to-day cut a slip from a garden-laburnum, for a friend who wants "a flute of the April-Tree" (*feadan na Craobh Abraon*) . . . for there is no timber better for the whistlewood of the bagpipe than this. And what more fit for the Strayed Pan, if perchance he follow the phantom Call in the Hills of the North? But see . . . the mist has gone like a haze from blue water. I hear starling-music over yonder in the *Talamh nan Ramh*, as Oisìn calls the Country of the Woods. *The Flute of the April-Tree*, and snow at my feet! "The Flute of the April-Tree": it has the yellow and white magic of Spring in it.

THE SONS OF THE NORTH WIND

> Down thro' the Northlands
> Come the White Brothers,
> One clad in foam
> And one mailed in water—
> Foam white as bear-felt,
> Water like coat of mail.
> *Snow is the Song of Me,*
> Singeth the one;
> *Silence the Breath of Me,*
> Whispers the other.

So sings a Swedish poet, a lineal descendant of one of the Saga-men whose songs the Vikings carried to the ends of the world of that day. The song is called "The Sons of the North Wind," and the allusion is to an old ballad-saga common in one form or another throughout all the countries of both the Gall and the Gael . . . from Finland to the last of the island-kingdoms between Ultima Thule and the Gaelic West. The White Brothers are familiar indeed, though with us they come oftener clothed with beauty than with terror, with strange and beautiful new

The Sons of the North Wind

life rather than with the solemnity and dread aspect of death.

Among the Gaelic hills we have a prose variant of "The Sons of the North Wind," which I suppose is still told to children by the fireglow on winter evenings, as, when a child, the present writer was told it and retold it by the fireglow on many a winter evening when the crackling fall of icicles from fir-sprays near the window could be heard, or the sudden shuffle of snow in the declivities of the steep glen hard-by. The story is generally told as a tale, but sometimes the teller chants it as a *duan* or poem. For it is more a poem than a prose narrative on the lips of Gaelic speakers.

The North Wind had three sons. These Sons of the North Wind were called White-Feet and White-Wings and White-Hands. When White-Feet and White-Wings and White-Hands first came into our world from the invisible palaces, they were so beautiful that many mortals died from beholding them, while others dared not look, but fled affrighted into woods or obscure places. So when these three sons of the Great Chieftain saw that they were too radiant for the eyes of the earth-bound, they receded beyond the gates of the sunset and took counsel with the

The Sons of the North Wind

Allfather. When, through the gates of dawn, they came again they were no longer visible to men, nor, in all the long grey reaches of the years, has any since been seen of mortal eyes. How are they known, these Sons of the North Wind? They were known of old, they are known still, only by the white feet of one treading the waves of the sea; and by the white rustle and sheen of a myriad tiny plumes as the other unfolds great pinions above hills and valleys, woodlands and garths, and the homes of men; and by the white silence of dream that the third lays upon moving waters, and the windless boughs of trees, upon the reed by the silent loch, upon the grass by the silent tarn, upon the bracken by the unfalling hill-stream hanging like a scarf among the rock and mountain-ash. We know them no more by their ancient names or in their immortal body, but only thus by the radiance of their passing, and we call them the Polar Wind, and Snow, and Ice.

It is at this season, in all northern lands, that the miracle of the snow-change, the new beauty of the snow-world, is transcendent. Truly, it is miraculous, that change: that new world, what a revelation it is, showing us the familiar as we have never known it or have of it but a dream-like remembrance, showing

The Sons of the North Wind

it to us at times as we can hardly conceive it. To the continual element of surprise much has to be attributed, in our country at least. In lands like Scandinavia and Russia the periodicity and uniformity of the snow-raiment of earth take much from this element of surprise. Hardly have the inhabitants grown used to the greenness of grass and sprouting grain and fluttering leaf, after the long months of a silent whiteness become dreadful as a shroud, when a grey pall is spun out of the east once more and out of the north comes the wind of death, and the leaf is gone away on the polar air, the grain is gathered or withered, the sere grass fades like wintry grey-green seas fading into continual foam.

Not so with us, who have those visitors, who can be so dread even here, for so short a time. The dark sword-thrust of the ice, compelling moving waters to silence and the blue rigour of steel, may reign for weeks in the Anglian fen-lands. Dense mantles of snow may cover the hills of the north for months, and the foreheads of Nevis and Schiehallion be white from the autumnal equinox till cuckoo-cry: for weeks the hill-fox and the mountain-hare may not drink at the frozen tarns, the moor-pastures may be

The Sons of the North Wind

lost to deer and sheep, and only the ptarmigan survive in the waste white places: for a week or two the boughs of the oak and chestnut, the plumes of the spruce and hemlock, the tresses of the larch and birch, may bend with the unmelting snowfall. But, at the worst, it is never long before a wind out of the south, or from the wet mouth of the west, breathes upon the fens, and the silence is become a faint stir, a whisper, a rustle; till the moveless steel is become a film, to be gathered some noon, like May-dew from the thickets, the autumn-frost from the whin and gorse. It is never long till the *meh-ing* of the sheep is again a sweet lamentation upon the hill-pastures, or till the fox dusts the last snow from his root-roof in the wintry glen, or till the jay screams in the woodlands as from fir-plume and oak-bough slip or fall with heavy thump their unloosened burthens. True, the Sons of the North Wind, as in the Highland West and North we know so well and often to such bitter cost, may come to us with suddenness of tempest, raging in their mysterious wrath, and may long endure, trampling upon life, as, in the old legend, the gigantic phantom-men of the Northern Lights trample the souls of the dead condemned to Ifurin, the Gaelic hell. Every year there is sorrow upon some strath, grief in the glens, lamentation by hillside and moor. From the Ord of Sutherland to Land's End there may be a tale of disaster. Snow-drift, snow-storm, snow-fog may paralyse communications and bring deep anxiety or irremediable grief to an incalculable number. Yet, we must admit that even our severest winter is but a fierce reminder of times long past for us, the times of the mail-coach, the rude cart, the mountain-pony, that the worst we ever have is tolerable beside the bleak wretchedness of Pomerania, the frightful cold of Esthonia, the death-in-life of Muscovy—to say nothing of lands still more wild and remote.

One cannot say, here is snow at its loveliest, here is ice in a unique beauty. Frozen lochs by moonlight, frozen fens under the pale azure of cloudless noons, dark winding rivers, lifeless seemingly in the grip of frost, traversed by starshine under overhanging boughs, lagoons where the dark-blue or steel-blue ice mirrors the drifting cloud or the flying skater, village-ponds, canals, the water-ways of towns and cities, in all, in each, the radiant miracle is evident. Like moonshine, this beauty of ice or snow may be omnipresent. If it inhabits the wilderness, it is fulfilled also in the streets of cities. Who has not looked out on the sordid thoroughfares of a town, and seen the poor ignoble disarray of chimney-tops and slated roofs and crude angles and ornamentations take on a new and entrancing aspect, so that even the untidy shops and tawdry dwellings assume a crown of loveliness, and the long, dull, perspectives of monotonous roads might be the trampled avenues about the gates of fairyland? The most sordid hamlet in the dreariest manufacturing-region may, suddenly, awake to a dawn so wonderful in what it reveals that the villagers might well believe, as in the old folktale, that Christ had passed that way in the night and left the world white and husht, stainlessly pure.

But, of course, we have each of us our preferences. Some love best to see the long swelling reaches of ploughed lands covered with new fallen snow not too heavy to hide the wave-like procession of the hidden furrows. Some love best to look on wide interminable wolds, a solitude of unbroken whiteness, without even the shadow of a cloud or the half-light of a grey sky: some, upon familiar pastures now changed as though in the night the fields had receded into the earth, and the fields of another world had silently sunk into their place: some, upon mountain-slopes, on

The Sons of the North Wind

whose vast walls the shadows of wheeling hawks and curlews pass like pale blue scimetars: some, on woodlands, where from the topmost elm-bough to the lowest fir-plume or outspread bough of cedar the immaculate soft burthens miraculously suspend. For myself—after the supreme loveliness of snowy mountain-ranges at dawn or sunset or moonglow—I am most entranced by snow in a pine-forest. The more so if, as in one my mind recreates for me as I write, there are glades where I can come to a rock whence an overleaning white hill may be seen as though falling out of heaven, with white mountains beyond, white shoulders lapsing on white shoulders, white peaks rising beyond white peaks, white crests fading into further snowy crests, and, nearer, it may be, glens sinking into glens, no longer a sombre green, but as though stilled avalanches awaiting a magician's unloosening spell.

Once, just there, in just such a place, I saw a wonderful sight. The January frosts had gone, and February had come in with the soft sighing of a wind out of the south. The snows faded like morning-mists. But after three days the north wind came again in the night. At dawn it veered, and a light snow fell once more, then thick and moist and flaky, and by noon had changed to rain. But an hour or so later the polar breath once more came over the brows of the hill, and with midwinter intensity. The rain was frozen on every bough, on every branch, on every spray, on every twig, on every leaf, on every frond of bracken, on every spire of reed, on every blade of grass. The world had become cased in shining ice, crystalline, exquisite in radiant beauty, ineffable, as in a trance, the ecstacy of the Unknown Dreamer. At sundown the vast orb of blood-red flame sank over the glens and burned among the aisles of the forest. Looking at the ice-mailed wilderness of bole and bough and branch between me and the sun I saw a forest of living fire, wherein, as a wind stirred and threw sudden shadows, phantoms of flame moved to and fro, or stood, terrible children of light, as though entranced, as though listening, as though looking on Life or on Death. When at last the flame was all gathered up out of the west, and an aura of faint rose hung under the first glittering stars, an extraordinary ocean of yellow spread from the horizons serrated with immense mauve peninsulas and long narrow grass-green lagoons. But the mass of the western firmament was yellow, from the orange-yellow of lichen and the orange-red of the dandelion to the faint vanishing yellows of cowslip and primrose. How lovely then were the trees which had been set on fire by the unconsuming flames of the sunset: what a fairyland, now, of delicate amber and translucent topaz. What mysterious colonnades, what avenues of lovely light! And then, later, to turn, and see the chill-grey blue ice-bound trees behind one filling slowly with moonshine, as the immensity of ocean fills, wave after wave, at moonrise, when a cloud is slowly uplifted by mysterious withdrawing airs! Then, truly, was Dreamland no longer a phantasy of sleep, but a loveliness so great that, like deep music, there could be no words wherewith to measure it, but only the breathless unspoken speech of the soul upon whom has fallen the secret dews.

ST. BRIGET OF THE SHORES

I have heard many names of St. Briget, most beloved of Gaelic saints, with whom the month of February is identified—the month of "Bride min, gentle St. Bride"—*Brighid boidheach Muime Chriosd*, Bride the Beautiful, Christ's Foster Mother . . . but there are three so less common that many even of my readers familiar with the Highland West may not know them. These are "the Fair Woman of February," "St. Bride of the Kindly Fire," and "St. Bride (or Briget) of the Shores." They are of the Isles, and may be heard in some of the *sgeulachdan gàidhealach*, or Gaelic tales, still told among seafaring and hill folk, where the curse of cheap ignoble periodicals is unknown and books are rare. True, in several of the isles—Colonsay, Tiree, the Outer Hebrides—"St. Bride of the Shores" is not infrequent in songs and seasonal hymns, for when her signals are seen along the grey beaches, on the sandy machars, by the meadow path, the glen-track, the white shore-road,

St. Briget of the Shores

the islanders know that the new year is disclosed at last, that food, warmth, and gladness are coming out of the south. As "the Fair Woman of February," though whatever other designation St. Bride goes by, she is often revealed. Her humble yellow fires are lit among the grasses, on the shore-ways, during this month. Everywhere in the Gaelic lands "Candlemas-Queen" is honoured at this time. *Am Fheill Bhride*, the Festival of St. Briget, was till recently a festival of joy throughout the west, from the Highland Line to the last weedy shores of Barra or the Lews: in the isles and in the remote Highlands, still is.

It is an old tale, this association of St. Briget with February. It goes further back than the days of the monkish chroniclers who first attempted to put the disguise of verbal Christian raiment on the most widely-loved and revered beings of the ancient Gaelic pantheon. Long before the maiden Brigida (whether of Ireland or Scotland matters little) made her fame as a "daughter of God"; long before to Colum in Iona or to Patrick "the great Cleric" in Ireland "Holy St. Bride" revealed in a vision the service she had done to Mary and the Child in far-away Bethlehem in the East; before ever the first

St. Briget of the Shores

bell of Christ was heard by startled Druids coming across the hills and forest lands of Gaul, the Gaels worshipped a Brighde or Bride, goddess of women, of fire, of poetry. When, to-day, a Gaelic islesman alludes to Briget of the Songs, or when a woman of South Uist prays to Good St. Bride to bless the empty cradle that is soon to be filled, or when a shennachie or teller of tales speaks of an oath taken by Briget of the Flame, they refer, though probably unconsciously, to a far older Brighid than do they who speak with loving familiarity of *Muime Chriosd*, Christ's Foster Mother, or *Brighid-nam-Bratta*, St. Bride of the Mantle. They refer to one who in the dim, far-off days of the forgotten pagan world of our ancestors was a noble and great goddess. They refer to one to whom the women of the Gael went with offerings and prayers, as went the women of ancient Hellas to the temples of Aphroditê, as went the Syrian women to the altars of Astarte, as went the women of Egypt to the milk-fed shrines of Isis. They refer to one whom the Druids held in honour as a torch bearer of the eternal light, a Daughter of the Morning, who held sunrise in one hand as a little yellow flame, and in the other held the red flower of fire without

St. Briget of the Shores

which men would be as the beasts who live in caves and holes, or as the dark *Fómor* who have their habitations in cloud and wind and the wilderness. They refer to one whom the bards and singers revered as mistress of their craft, she whose breath was a flame, and that flame song: she whose secret name was fire and whose inmost soul was radiant air, she therefore who was the divine impersonation of the divine thing she stood for, Poetry.

"St. Bride of the Kindly Fire," of whom one may hear to-day as "oh, just *Bhrighde min Muim* (gentle St. Bride the Foster Mother), she herself an' no other," is she, that ancient goddess, whom our ancestors saw lighting the torches of sunrise on the brows of hills, or thrusting the quenchless flame above the horizons of the sea: whom the Druids hailed with hymns at the turn of the year, when, in the season we call February, the firstcomers of the advancing Spring are to be seen on the grey land or on the grey wave or by the grey shores: whom every poet, from the humblest wandering singer to Oisin of the Songs, from Oisin of the Songs to Angus Òg on the rainbow or to Midir of the Under-world, blessed, because of the flame she put in the heart of poets. as well as the red life she put in the flame that springs from wood and peat. None forgot that she was the daughter of the ancient God of the Earth, but greater than he, because in him there was but earth and water, whereas in her veins ran the elements of air and fire. Was she not born at sunrise? On the day she reached womanhood did not the house wherein she dwelled become wrapped in a flame which consumed it not, though the crown of that flame licked the high unburning roof of Heaven? In that hour when, her ancient divinity relinquished and she reborn a Christain saint, she took the white veil, did not a column of golden light rise from her head till no eyes could follow it? In that moment when she died from earth, having taken mortality upon her so as to know a divine resurrection to a new and still more enduring Country of the Immortal, were there not wings of fire seen flashing along all the shores of the west and upon the summits of all Gaelic hills? And how could one forget that at any time she had but to bend above the dead, and her breath would quicken, and a pulse would come back into the still heart, and what was dust would arise and be once more glad.

The Fair Woman of February is still loved,

St. Briget of the Shores

still revered. Few remember the last fading traditions of her ancient greatness: few, even, know that she lived before the coming of the Cross: but all love her, because of her service to Mary in Her travail and to the newborn Child, and because she looks with eyes of love into every cradle and puts the hand of peace on the troubled hearts of women: and all delight in her return to the world after the ninety days of the winter-sleep, when her heralds are manifest.

What, then, are the insignia of St. Briget of the Shores? They are simple. They are the dandelion, the lamb, and the sea-bird, popularly called the oyster-opener. From time immemorial, this humble, familiar yellow plant of the wayside has been identified with St. Bride. To this day shepherds, on *Am Fheill Bhrighde*, are wont to hear among the mists the crying of innumerable young lambs, and this without the bleating of ewes, and so by that token know that Holy St. Bride has passed by, coming earthward with her flock of the countless lambs soon to be born on all the hillsides and pastures of the world. Fisherfolk on the shores of the west and on the far isles have gladdened at the first prolonged repetitive whistle of the oyster-

St. Briget of the Shores

opener, for its advent means that the hosts of the good fish are moving towards the welcoming coasts once more, that the wind of the south is unloosened, that greenness will creep to the grass, that birds will seek the bushes, that song will come to them, and that everywhere a new gladness will be abroad. By these signs is St. Briget of the Shores known. One, perhaps, must live in the remote places, and where wind and cloud, rain and tempest, great tides and uprising floods are the common companions of day and night, in order to realise the joy with which things so simple are welcomed. To see the bright sunsweet face of the dandelion once more—*an dealan Dhé*, the little flame of God, *am bearnan Bhrighde*, St. Bride's forerunner—what a joy this is. It comes into the grass like a sunray. Often before the new green is in the blade it flaunts its bright laughter in the sere bent. It will lie in ditches and stare at the sun. It will climb broken walls, and lean from nooks and corners. It will come close to the sands and rocks, sometimes will even join company with the sea-pink, though it cannot find footing where later the bind-weed and the horned poppy, those children of the sea-wind who love to be near and yet shrink from the spray of

St. Briget of the Shores

the salt wave, defy wind and rain. It is worthier the name "Traveller's Joy" than the wild clematis of the autumnal hedgerows: for its bright yellow leaps at one from the roadside like a smile, and its homeliness is pleasant as the gladness of playing children.

It is a herald of Spring that precedes even the first loud flute-like calls of the misselthrush. When snow is still on the track of the three winds of the north it is, by the wayside, a glad companion. Soon it will be everywhere. Before long the milk-white sheen of the daisy and the moon-daisy, the green-gold of the tansy, the pale gold of the gorse and the broom, the yellow of the primrose and wild colchicum, of the cowslip and buttercup, of the copse-loving celandine and meadow-rejoicing crowsfoot, all these yellows of first spring will soon be abroad: but the dandelion comes first. I have known days when, after midwinter, one could go a mile and catch never a glimpse of this bright comrade of the ways, and then suddenly see one or two or three, and rejoice forthwith as though at the first blossom on the blackthorn, at the first wild-roses, at the first swallow, at the first thrilling bells of the cuckoo. We are so apt to lose the old

St. Briget of the Shores

delight in familiar humble things. So apt to ignore what is by the way, just because it is by the way. I recall a dour old lowland gardener in a loch-and-hill-set region of Argyll, who, having listened to exclamations of delight at a rainbow, muttered, "Weel, I juist think naethin ava' o' yon rainbows; ye can see one whenever ye tak the trouble to look for them hereaboots." He saw them daily, or so frequently that for him all beauty and strangeness had faded from these sudden evanescent Children of Beauty. Beauty has only to be perceptible to give an immediate joy; and it is no paradoxical extravagance to say that one may receive the thrilling communication from "the little flame of God" by the homely roadside, as well as from these leaning towers built of air and water which a mysterious alchemy reveals to us on the cloudy deserts of heaven. "Man is surprised," Emerson says, "to find that things near and familiar are not less beautiful and wondrous than things remote." Certainly no Gaelic lover of St. Bride's Flower, of the Flower of February, but rejoices to see its welcome face after the snow and sleet of winter have first sullenly receded, if only for a time, and to know that St. Bride of the Shores wears it at her breast, and that when

St. Briget of the Shores

she throws it broadcast the world is become a green place again and the quickening sunlight a gladsome reality.

In these desolate far isles where life is so hard, where the grey winds from the north and east prevail for weeks at a time on the grey tempestuous seas, and where so much depends on such small things—a little driftwood, a few heaps of peat, a few shoal of fish now of one kind now of another, a few cartloads of seaweed, a rejoicing sound is that in truth when the *Gille-Bhride* is heard crying along the shores. Who that has heard its rapid whirling cry as its darts from haunt to haunt but will recognise its own testimony to being "Servant of Breed" (the common pronunciation of the Gaelic Brighid or Bride) —for does it not cry over and over again with swift incessant iterance, *Gilly-breed, gilly-breed, gilly-breed, gilly-breed, gilly-breed?*

"White may my milking be,
  White as thee;
Thy face is white, thy neck is white,
Thy hands are white, thy feet are white,
For thy sweet soul is shining bright—
  O dear to me,
  O dear to see,
  St. Briget White!

St. Briget of the Shores

Yellow may my butter be,
    Firm, and round:
Thy breasts are sweet,
Firm, round, and sweet,
So may my butter be:
So may my butter be, O
    Briget Sweet!
Safe thy way is, safe, O
    Safe, St. Bride:
May my kye come home at even,
None be fallin', none be leavin',
Dusky even, breath-sweet even,
Here, as there, where O
    St. Bride thou
Keepest tryst with God in heav'n,
Seest the angels bow
And souls be shriven—
Here, as there, 'tis breath-sweet even
    Far and wide—
Singeth thy little maid
Safe in thy shade
    Briget, Bride!"

When the first lambs appear, many are the invocations among the Irish and Hebridean Gaels to good St. Bride. At the hearth-side, too, the women, carding wool, knitting, telling tales, singing songs, dreaming—these know her whether they name her in thought, or have forgotten what was dear wisdom to their mothers of old. She leans over cradles, and when babies smile they have seen her face. When the *cra'thull* swings in the twilight the

St. Briget of the Shores

slow rhythm, which is music in the mother's ear, is the quiet clapping of her hushing hands. St. Bride, too, loves the byres or the pastures when the kye are milked, though now she is no longer "the Woman of February," but simply "good St. Bride of the yellow hair."

THE HERALDS OF MARCH

Under this heading I had meant to deal with the return of the Plover and Lapwing, having in mind a Galloway rhyme,

"Whaup Whimbrel, an' Plover,
Whan these whustle the worst o' t's over!"

But on consideration it was evident that March has so complicated an orchestral prelude that the name could hardly be given to any one group of birds. Does not another rhyme go,

"The Lavrock, the Mavis,
The Woodlark, the Plover,
March brings them back
Because Winter is over."

But March brings back so many birds! There is another bird rhyme . . .

"When the Song-Thrush is ready to laugh,
Ye'll hear the Woodlark an' the Wheatear an' the Chaff."

Well, the Song-Thrush has been "ready to laugh" a good while back, now: his "laughter" has already whirled the flute-notes of Spring, amid branches swelling to leaf-break, but not yet at the greening. The Chiff-Chaff has been heard on many a common, or on the ridge of a stone-dyke, or calling from the blackthorn thickets. The Wheatear has by this time delighted many a superstitious yokel who has caught his first glimpse of it sitting on a grassy tuft, or on a low spray of gorse or juniper, or depressed him sorely if he has come upon it for the first time when seen perched on a stone. But all three are birds which are with us long before the real Spring is come. With the missel-thrush on the elmbole, the song-thrush in the copses, the blackbird calling from the evergreens, it does not follow, alas! that, as in the fairytale, the north wind has become a feeble old man and the east wind a silly old wife. Frost and snow and sleet, rain and flood, and the dull greyness of returned winter, may only too likely succeed these blithe heralds, have so succeeded, this year, as we know to our cost. There was jubilation in some places at January-end because of the early singing of the larks, which here and there had been heard soon after the New Year; but those who rejoiced untimely at the advent of spring-weather must have forgot the north-country proverb, "As long as the laverock sings before Candlemas it will greet after it."

The lark and the blackbird are, in truth, such irresponsible singers, have such glad irrepressible hearts, that they will sing in the dead of winter, if only the wind slides through a windless air and the sunshine is unclouded. Tens of thousands have gone oversea, but thousands remain; and these are not to be chilled into silence if but the least excuse be given for the unsealing of the founts of joy. In green Decembers one may hear the merle's note fluting down the wet alleys as though Christmas were still a long way off; but the wary will recall another north-country saying akin to that just quoted concerning the laveroch—"When the blackbird sings before Christmas she will cry before Candlemas."

So now I shall leave the Tribe of the Plover to a succeeding article, and, speaking of the skylark and his spring comrades, allude to that Mysterious March wayfaring of the winged people which is so enthralling a problem in the psychology of birdlife.

The whole problem of Migration is still a mystery, but an enhancement of this mystery

The Heralds of March

is in the irregularity and incompleteness of the working out of this all but universal instinct, this inscrutable rhythmic law. Both the skylark and the blackbird, for example, are migratory birds, and yet larks and merles by the thousand remain in our northlands through the winter, and even come to us at that season. The skylark in particular puzzles the ornithologist. While certain birds appear and disappear with an astonishing regularity, as though they heard the pealing of aërial chimes afar off and knew the bells of home—the swallow, for example; or, again, the tiny gold-crested wren, in some parts called "the woodcock-pilot" because in two or at most three days after its appearance the first woodcocks are invariably seen —there are others, like the song-thrush, which will pass away in the great migratory clouds that like withdrawing veils every autumn carry the winged clans oversea; which will pass so absolutely that for a hundred miles not one of its kind will be observed, not even a straggler: and yet, in some other direction, others will be seen weeks later and perhaps even through the winter. We are all familiar with the homestay of the redbreast, and many people believe that it is not a migrant because of its frequency

The Heralds of March

about our garden-ways even in the hardest winter: and yet, in incalculable myriads, the redbreast migrates as far south as the Sahara, and its sweet home-song of the north may be heard in Greece, by the banks of the Nile, throughout Palestine even, from the cedars of Lebanon to the valleys about Jerusalem.

It is the skylark, however, more than any other bird which so often upsets rules and calculations. Even people who do not observe the ways of birds must be struck by the numbers of larks which may be met with in the course of several midwinter walks, by the occasional outbreak of brief song, even, though snow be upon the wolds and a grey wind blow through the sere leaves of the oak-coppice or among the desolate hedgerows; must be the more struck by this, or by mention of it on the part of others, when they read of the hundreds, sometimes thousands, of dead larks found on nights of storm or bitter frost, on the rocks below lighthouses, along the great lines of migration during the season of the vast inscrutable ebb or of the as vast and inscrutable vernal arrival. Incalculable hosts leave our shores every autumn, and along the bleak fen-lands by wave-set lighthouses, on isles such as Ushant

The Heralds of March

or Heligoland, thousands of wings flutter and fail; and the host passes on; and the sea-wave, the fierce gull, the shore-hawk, all the tribe of the owl, all the innumerable foes which prey upon the helpless, give scant grace to the weaklings and the baffled and weary. But why should all this immense congregation have listened to the ancestral cry, and from meadow and moor and the illimitable dim-sea of the fallowlands come singly and in flocks and in immense herds and in a cloudlike multitude, as sheep at the cry of the herdsman, as hounds at the long ululation of a horn, while thousands of their clan remain deaf to the mysterious Voice, the imperative silent mandate from oversea? Of these, again, countless numbers merely move to another region, and mayhap some cross the salt straits only to return; or as many, it may be, leave not at all the familiar solitudes, and at most show by cloudy flights and wild and fluctuating gyrations the heritage of blind instinct, which, if it cannot be satiated by far pilgrimage, must at least shake these troubled hearts with sudden inexplicable restlessness. It is calculated again, that myriads of skylarks merely use our coasts as highways on their journey from the far south to the far north—in this, too, exemplify-

The Heralds of March

ing another strange law or manifestation of the mystery of migration, that the birds which move farthest north in their vernal arrival are those which penetrate farthest south when they turn again upon the autumnal wind of exile. Naturalists have proved, however, that countless hordes of skylarks actually arrive from Northern Europe to winter in our country. Are these birds moved by a different instinct from that which impels the majority of their kind? Have they, through generations following one another in the path of an accident, forgotten the sunlands of the common ancestral remembrance, and, having found Britain less snowbound and frostbound than the wastes of Esthonia and Pomerania, been content, when driven before the icy east wind, to fare no farther than our bleak, and yet, save in the worst winters, relatively habitable inlands? Again, naturalists have observed a like movement hitherward in winter from Central Europe. There may be observed in the early spring as regular an emigration as, on a perhaps not vaster scale, an incalculable immigration. Apparently, most if not all of the myriads of skylarks which are undoubtedly with us throughout the winter are these immigrants from Northern and Central Europe. Those who

The Heralds of March

come in February and in still greater numbers in March and April (and the later the arrivals the farther north the goal, it is said) are the "strayed revellers" from the South, the homebred birds home again. In our remote Hebrides the nesting season is hardly over before the island-bred skylarks, so late in coming, are on the Great South Road once more. What with the habitual two and the not infrequent three broods raised in a single season, particularly in Southern England, South-West Scotland, and Ireland, and the enormous influx of aliens from Northern and Central Europe, our skylark population is at its highest, not, as most people might think, in May, or even about the season of the autumnal equinox, but at the beginning of November, when already the great tides of migration have ebbed.

Another puzzling problem is the rhythmic regularity of the arrivals and departures of the incomers and the outgoers. For, while the latter will not take the high-road of the upper air till nightfall or at least until dusk, the former travel by day: and the goings and comings are so timed, or to observation appear so timed, that about four o'clock on a late October day the first cohort of the invaders may in the wide lonely desert overhead pass

The Heralds of March

the first caravans of exiles. In March, again, the two currents may once more meet: the homebred birds are on their return, the aliens are on the wing for the hill-pastures and the vales and uplands of their native countries. This will account for how, say in the Hebrides, one observer will chronicle the departure of the skylarks before Summer-end, at the early close there of the nesting season, and how another, not less accurate, will note the presence weeks later of larks in apparently as great a number as ever. The islanders have gone, to seek the south: the newcomers from Scandinavia have taken their place. But here also, as elsewhere, the conditions of the weather will be more potent than even the summons of the spirit of migration: a severe frost will for a time clear a whole region of the tufted birdeens, a prolonged frost will drive them away from that region for the winter.

The Lark, then, so often apostrophised as the first voice of Spring, is by no means specifically the Herald of March. When we see his brown body breasting the air-waves of the March wind, it may not be the welcome migrant from the South we see, with greenness in his high aërial note and the smell of hay and wild roses in the o'er-

The Heralds of March

come of his song, but a winter-exile from a far mountain-vale in Scandinavia or from the snowbound wastes of Courland or Westphalia.

The Woodlark, the Chiff-Chaff, and the rest, all are heralds of March. But as we identify certain birds with certain seasons and certain qualities—as the Swallow with April, and the Cuckoo with May, and the Dove with peace—so we have come to think of the Mavis and the Merle, but, above all, of the Skylark as the true heralds of March, the month when the Flutes of Pan sound from land's end to land's end, for all that tempest and flood, sleet and the polar blast and the bitter wind of the east, may ravage the coverts of the winged clans.

To write of all the birds who come back to us in the Spring, even so early as the front of March, would be, here, a mere catalogue, and then be incomplete. For the hidden places in the woods, in the meadows, in the hedgerows, on the moors, in the sandy dunes, in the hollowed rocks, on the ledges over green water and on the wind-scooped foreheads of cliffs and precipices; everywhere, from the heather-wilderness on the unsnowed hills to the tangled bent on the little wind-swept eyot set in the swing of the tides,

The Heralds of March

the secret homes are waiting, or are already filled, and glad with that everlasting and unchanging business of the weaving anew of life which has the constancy of sunrise, the rhythmic certitude of day and night.

The spiritual secret of our delight in the joyousness of the lark's song, or in that of mavis or merle, is because the swift music is a rapture transcending human utterance. There is not less joy in the screech of the jay, in the hoarse cry of the cormorant, in the scream of the gannet poised like a snowflake two thousand feet above the turbulent surge of blue and white, or green and grey, to its vision but a vast obscurity of calm filled with phantom life, a calm moveless seen from that great height, wrinkled only with perplexing interplay of wave and shadow. These have their joy, and to the open ear *are* joy; not less than the merle singing among wet lilac, the mavis calling from the swaying poplar, the lark flinging the largesse of his golden music along the high devious azure roads. Can one doubt that this is so —that, listening with the inward ear, we must hold as dear the wail of the curlew, the mournful cry of the lapwing, when on the hill-slope or in the wild grass these call

The Heralds of March

rejoicingly in life and love and the mute ecstasy of implicit duty?

As long, however, as we impose our own needs and our own desires on the indifferent tribes of the earth and air, so long shall we take this or that comrade of the elements and say it is the voice of Peace, or War, or Love, or Joy. March, we say, is the month of gladness. A new spirit is awake, is abroad. The thrush and the blackbird are *our* clarions of rejoicing. The lark, supremely, is *our* lyric of joy.

Joy, the poet tells us, is the Mother of Spring, and of Joy has it not been said that there is no more ancient God? What fitter symbol for this divine uplift of the year than this bird whose ecstasy in song makes the very word Spring an intoxication in our ears? We have a Gaelic legend that the first word of God spoken to the world became a lark . . . the eternal joy translated into a moment's ecstasy. But farther back has not Aristophanes told us that the lark existed, not only before the green grass where it nests or the blue lift into which it soars, but before Zeus and Kronos themselves, before the Creation, before Time. It is but a symbol of the divine Joy which is Life: that most ancient Breath, that Spirit whose least thought

The Heralds of March

is Creation, whose least motion is Beauty, whose least glance is that eternal miracle which we, seeing dimly and in the rhythmic rise of the long cadence of the hours, call by a word of outwelling, of measureless effluence, the Spring.

THE TRIBE OF THE PLOVER

In the preceding paper I alluded to a Galloway rhyme—

"Whaup, Whimbrel, an' Plover,
Whan these whustle the worst o' 't 's over."

By this time the neatherd by Loch Ken and the shepherd among the wilds of Kirkcudbright, like their kin from the Sussex downs, to the last *sliabh* or *maol* in Sutherland, may repeat the rhyme with safety. "The worst o' 't 's over." For to-day the curlews cry above the moors, the whimbrel's warning note echoes down the long sands o' Solway, and everywhere, from the salt bent by the coasts to the loneliest inlands, the lapwing wails. The Tribe of the Plover is in the land once more, and so Spring is with us. Not, perhaps, the Spring of the poets, who look (as Ailil in the old Celtic tale) under boughs of white blossom as to where the sunlight moves like a fawn of gold in a windless land, where the songs of birds turn to flowers, and where flowers change in the twilights of dawn into singing birds. Not thus does Spring come to us in the north. The black-headed gull screaming on the east wind, restless before his long flight to the wilderness and the grassy homes of the mating season: the hoodie-crow, weary of the south, heard on grey mornings when sleet whips the uplands: the troubled fieldfares, eager for lands oversea: the curlews crying along the Anglian fens and lamenting over Solway Moss: the mallard calling to his mate in the chill waters: the shadow of harrier and peregrine from Surrey upland to the long braes of Lammermuir—these, rather, are the signals of our bleak northern Spring. What though the song-thrush and the skylark have long sung, though the wheatear and chiff-chaff have been late in coming, though the first swallows have not had the word passed on by the woodpecker, and somewhere in the glens of Greece and Sicily the cuckoo lingers? How often the first have called *Spring* to us, and, while we have listened, the wind has passed from the south to the north and the rains have become sleet or snow: how often the missel-thrush has rung-in the tides of blossom, and the woods have but grown darker with gloom of the east while the first yellow clans along the hedgerows have been

The Tribe of the Plover

swept by hail. How often, again, the wind of the west has been fragrant with cowslip and ox-eye, with daffodil and wallflower, with the pungent growing-odours of barbery and butcher's broom and the unloosening larch, when, indeed, the swallow-blooms have put on their gold, and the green woodpecker is calling his love-notes in the copses, and yet the delaying swallow has not been seen north of the Loire or where the Loiny winds between Moret and the woods of Fontainebleau. How often the wild-rose has moved in first-flame along the skirts of hornbeam-hedge or beech-thicket, or the honeysuckle begun to unwind her pale horns of ivory and moongold, and yet across the farthest elm-tops to the south the magic summons of the cuckoo has been still unheard in the windless amber dawn, or when, as in the poet's tale, the myriad little hands of Twilight pull the shadows out of the leaves and weave the evening dark. But when the cry of the plover is abroad we know that our less ideal, yet hardly less lovely, and welcome Spring is come at last: that Winter is old and broken and shuffling north, clinging to the bleak uplands and windygates: and this, even though Summer tarries still among the fields of France.

The Tribe of the Plover

Because of their association with solitary and waste places it is not strange that these harbingers of Swallow-time should everywhere have an evil repute. Even amid the unimaginative Sussex or Wilts peasants, the cry of the curlew, the wail of the lapwing, forbode sorrow, cover a vague menace: heard, at least, at dusk or at night, or in the grey gloaming at the edge of day.

The Cornish or Devon moorlander has many wild tales of the whimbrel, whose swift-repeated whistle hurtling suddenly in lonely places has given rise to innumerable legends of the Seven Whistlers, the Demon Huntsmen, the Hunted Souls. In Iona and along the Earraid of Mull, where the whimbrel or "little curlew" is rarely heard till May, though it is generally called *Guilbinnach*, a diminutive of the Gaelic name of the curlew, *Guilbin* (pronounced sometimes *Kooley-pin* or *guley-pin* and sometimes *gwilley-pin*), a compound word signifying wailing music, I have heard it called *Guilbhròn* (Kwillyvrone), Wail of Sorrow, and again *Keenyvàs* or Death-Cry, and once, either in a tale or poem, by the singular name *Guilchaismeachd*, the Wail of Warning. Any lowland cottar, from west of Lammermuir to east of Ballantrae, will "ken a wheen strange tales o' the whaup,"

The Tribe of the Plover

as the curlew is commonly called north of the Tweed and south of the Highland Line: and in some parts it is not only the children who shudder at its cry in lonely places at dusk, fearing "the bogle wi' the lang neb" like a pair of tongs, emissary of the Evil One, who gave this bird his long curved beak so that in the dark he might, like tongs lifting a stray coal or a nightjar snatching a wandering moth, carry off wrongdoers, unrepentant sinners, truants, and all naughty children generally. As for the lapwing, though more familiar than the curlew, and for many of us associated only with pastures and pleasant wilds, in the countries of the Gael dark things are whispered of the *Adharcan-luachrach*, or Little Horn of the Rushes —thus poetically called from the pretty tuft of the male *weep* or *peaseweep*, curving like a horn over the delicately poised head, and from the bird's fondness for nesting in rushy places or among tangled grasses. Is he not said to be one of the bitter clan who mocked on the day of the Crucifixion, and so was made homeless for ever, with a cry that should be for ever like the cry of wandering sorrow? It is of little avail to say that love among the rushes is as sweet as elsewhere, that the wilderness can be home

The Tribe of the Plover

and that the wailing of repentant souls may be no more than angry vituperations against the hoodie-crow or laughing-gull or other marauders after lapwing-eggs Is the *weep* not a spirit of the waste that was once human, but lost his soul, and so can never reach heaven nor yet dwell on earth, but must night and day be restless as the sea, and wail the long hours away from grey dawn to moonrise, from darkness to the paling of the stars? So they say, they who know: and who know with the unshakable surety of the unlettered peasant? In the Gaelic imagination the lapwing is something stranger and wilder still: a bird of the ancient world, of the dispossessed gods, nameless in truth because in truth a god nameless and homeless. The Gaelic poet hears in its lament the lamentation of what is gone never to come again, of what long since went away upon the wind, of what is going away on the wind: and he has called the *weep* the Birds of the Sorrowful Past. Is not the lapwing the bird of Dalua, that unknown mysterious god, that terrible Shadow who is the invisible, inaudible, secret, and dread divinity of weariness, separation, gloom, sadness, decay, desolation, madness, despair?

It is not only in our own land that the

The Tribe of the Plover

lapwing and all the tribe of the plover bear so evil a repute. Not always thus, however: for in some parts of Germany this plover, I do not know why, is called the Virgin Mary's Dove, and is greeted with welcome. Even in Argyll there is a lost or confused kindly legend, for sometimes when children run along the moorland mocking the Pibhinn *(pee-veen* ... the Gaelic equivalent of the lowland *peaseweep* and the southern pee-*weet)* they cry:

"*Welcome back, welcome back, Pēe-vcen, Pee-vēen!
But keep the wind and the rain behind your tail,
Or you'll never see the fields of heaven again! ...*"

or words to that effect. In the East the Mohammedan women have a beautiful name for this bird—the Sister of the Brother: and, says the authority whence in some forgotten reading I took this note, "when these women hear the cry in the evening, they run from their houses and throw water in the air, that the bird may use it to assuage the pain of the burn on the top of the head, still marked by some black feathers." This is in allusion to an oriental legend that the lapwing was once a princess. This princess had a passionate love for a brother who had long been absent, and when one day she heard that he was on his return and close at hand and weary, she snatched a bowl of hot milk from the fire and hastened to meet him. But an evil-wisher, knowing her great love and how she would not rest till she found her brother, had misinformed her, and for all the pain on her head caused by the heated bowl, she ran now this way and now that, continually crying *Brother! O Brother!* Hours passed, and then days, and week after week and month after month the girl vainly sought her loved one. At last, feeling her strength ebbing, she cried aloud to Allah. Allah, moved by compassion, gave her wings and changed her into a lapwing or black-plover, the better to accomplish her purpose. Hence, when the little brown children on the desert or on the sun-scorched ways of the East look up and see the lapwings wheeling overhead in long circling flights and sudden dashes, they hear, in the wailing voices, either the long yearning or the sudden eager hope in the cry which to their ears sounds as *Brother! O Brother!*

Perhaps the German name of the Virgin Mary's Dove is merely a variant of the Swedish folk-legend concerning the lapwing. The tale goes that this bird was once one of

The Tribe of the Plover

Mary's handmaidens, but lost place and honour because of her theft of a pair of scissors. The punishment was transformation into a bird with a forked scissors-tail, and to go out across the fjords and above all the meadows and pastures and keep crying incessantly *Tyvit-Tyvit-Tyvit (i.e.,* I stole them! I stole them!). I think, however, I have heard or read the same story in connection with the wagtail. In his interesting book on the *Manners and Customs of the Russian People*, Mr. Ralston has the following Slavonic plover-legend. When God had created the earth, and wished to supply it with seas and lakes and rivers, He ordered the birds to convey the waters to their appointed places. All obeyed except the lapwing, whose reason for this indolence and impiety was that it had no need of seas, lakes, or rivers, to slake its thirst. At that the Lord waxed wroth, and forbade it and its posterity ever to approach a sea or stream, and that it might quench its thirst only with that water which remains in hollows and among stones after rain. So from that time this sorrowful plover has never ceased its wailing cry of *Peet-peet! (i.e.,* Drink! Drink!). In another northern book (Thiel's *Danish Traditions*, vol. ii.) there are two lapwing-legends not

The Tribe of the Plover

less homely than the Russian and the Swedish.

When Christ, says one, was a bairn, He took a walk one day and came to an old crone who was busy baking. She said she would give Him a new cake for His trouble, if He would go and split her a little wood for the oven. Christ did as she wanted, and the old wife put aside a small bit of dough for the promised cake. When the batch was drawn from the oven, however, she saw to her surprise and chagrin that the wee bit cake was equally large with the rest. So again she broke off a small bit of dough; but again the same thing happened. Hereupon she broke out with, "That's a vast oure-muckle cake for the likes o' thee; thee's get thy cake anither time." At this injustice Christ was angered, so He said to the old crone, "I split your wood as you asked me, and you would not give me the little cake you promised. Now you in turn shall go and cleave wood, and that, too, as long as the world shall last!" And with that our Lord turned her into a *vipa* (a weep). "So the weep fares betwixt heaven and earth as long as the world lasts; and fare where she will she says no other words than *Klyf ved! Klyf ved!*" (*i.e.*, Cleave wood! Cleave wood!).

The Tribe of the Plover

The other Danish plover-tale given by Thiel is one of the familiar Crucifixion legends. While Christ still hung upon the Cross, three birds came flying towards Calvary, the Styrkham (the Stork), the Svalham (the Swallow), and the Pün-ham (Pee-weet). As they flew overhead each cried a cry. The stork cried, *Styrk ham! Styrk ham! (i.e.,* Strengthen Him !), and so has this bird called ever since, and been under God's blessing and man's care. The swallow cried, *Sval ham! Sval ham! (i.e.,* Cool or refresh Him!), and so is evermore known by that name, and likewise is loved by man and guided by God. But the weep wheeled about the Cross, shrieking derisively, *Pün ham! Pün ham! (i.e.,* Pine Him, make Him suffer !), and so is not only accursed by men from then till now, but is under God's ban till the Last Day, after which the lapwing's wail will never be heard again.

Although *Guilbinn*, or Wailing Music, is, as I have said, the common Gaelic name for the Curlew, as the Whaup in the lowlands, it is also often called the *Crann-toch*, the long-beaked one, or Coulter-neb, as they say in Dumfries and Galloway. Of the mythical origin of the name Crann-toch (a very obvious designation, and needing no mythical legend one would think) I remember hearing a year or so ago from a boatman of Lismore a wild and romantic legend, but it is too long to quote now. Few Gaelic tales, few poems, in which are not to be heard the voices of the wind or the sea or the wailing curlew. We have perhaps no bird more wild and solitary: a Highland saying places it with the herons and wild-geese. "When a man has shot six herons, six wild-geese, and six curlews, he may call himself a sportsman."

When the Golden Plover, or Grey Plover as he is sometimes called, wheels in Spring above the fallowlands of the North the ploughman hears in his cry *Plough weel! Sow weel! Harrow weel!* This beautiful bird —of whom no poet has written a finer line than Burns in

"The deep-toned plover grey, wild whistling on the hill"—

is not exempt from the common tradition of uncanniness. He, too, is classed with the dreaded "Seven Whistlers": and from Cornwall to Iceland he is often vituperated as one of these, or as of the spectral pack called Gabriel's Hounds, or as of Odin's Phantom Chase. I spoke of a name I had heard in

The Tribe of the Plover

Iona and Mull for the whimbrel, but applicable also to any plover or curlew . . . the *Guilchaismeachd* or Wail of Warning, the Alarm Bird so to say: and this repute is held by the plover in many mining parts of England, where it is said that the miners will not descend a pit if the "Whistlers" be heard lamenting overhead. To this day there are many regions not only in our own country but abroad where the plovers are called the Wandering Jews, from an old legend that the first of the clan were the transmuted souls of those Jews who assisted at the Crucifixion. An old woman who gave me some plovers' eggs told me in all good faith that the *feadag* (the Gaelic name, equivalent to flute-note or mellow whistle) neither ate nor drank but fed upon the wind . . . a superstition said to have been almost universal in the Middle Ages.

As for many of us, surely they are birds of our love. The cry of the curlew on the hill, the wail of the lapwing in waste places, have not these something of the same enthralling spell, the same entrancing call—the summons to the wilderness, whether that be only to solitude, or to wild loneliness, or to the lonelier solitudes, the dim limitless wilderness of the imagination—that the wind has,

The Tribe of the Plover

at night, coming with rain through woods, or that the sea has, heard in inland hollows, or when athwart a long shore or among fallen rocks the tide rises on the breast-swell of coming storm? They call us to the wild.

THE AWAKENER OF THE WOODS

The Spirit of Spring is abroad. There is no one of our island coasts so lone and forlorn that the cries of the winged newcomers have not lamented down the wind. There is not an inland valley where small brown birds from the South have not penetrated, some from Mediterranean sunlands, some from the Desert, some from the hidden homes on unknown isles, some from beyond the foam of unfamiliar shores. Not a backwater surely but has heard the flute of the ouzel, or the loud call of the mallard. The wren, that sweet forerunner of "the little clan of the bushes," as we say in Gaelic, *clann bheag' nam preas*, the robin, the mavis, the merle, have been heard in every coppice and wildgrowth from the red combes of the winding Dart to the granite-ledges by the rushing Spey. From the last Cornish upland to the last brown moor on the Ord of Sutherland the curlew and the lapwing have wheeled with wailing cry or long melancholy

The Awakener of the Woods

flutelike whistle. The gorse, whose golden fires have been lit, has everywhere heard the prolonged sweet plaintive note of the yellow-hammer. From the greening boughs the woodpeckers call.

The tides of Blossom have begun to flow. The land soon will be inundated. Already a far and wide forethrow of foam is flung along the blackthorn hedges. Listen . . . that chaffinch's blithe song comes from the flowering almond! . . . that pipit's brief lay fell past yonder wild-pear! In the meadows the titlarks are running about looking in the faces of the daisies, as children love to be told. On the fenlands and mosses the windy whimper of the redshank is heard like the cry of a phantom: and like a "bogle," too, is the perturbing drumming of the snipe falling swiftly on sloping wings back to the marsh.

The shores, the meadows, the uplands, on each there is a continual rumour. It is the sound of Spring. Listen . . . put your ear to the throbbing earth that is so soon to become the green world: you will hear a voice like the voice which miraculously evades in the hollow curves of a shell. Faint, mysterious, yet ever present, a continual rhythm. Already that rhythm is become a

The Awakener of the Woods

cadence: the birds chant the strophes, flower and blossom and green leaf yield their subtler antiphones, the ancient yet ever young protagonist is the heart of man. Soon the cadence will be a song, a pæan. The hour of the rose and the honeysuckle will come, the hour of the swallow hawking the grey gnat above the lilied stream, the hour when the voice of the cuckoo floats through ancient woods rejoicing in their green youth, that voice which has in it the magic of all springs, the eternal cry of the renewal of delight.

True, one may as yet more universally see the feet of Spring, or the blossom-touch of her hands, in the meadows and by the shores, than in the woods. She passes by the hedgerows or along the pastures, and her trail has the sheen of gold. Do not the celandine and the flaming dandelion, the pale cowslip and delicate crowsfoot, the jonquil and daffodil, the yellow of the broom and the bee-loved gorse, everywhere show it? She goes by the upland meadows, and touches the boughs of the wild-apple or leaning pear, stoops by the quince or the wild-cherry, and the white foam of the miraculous wind that is in the hollow of her hand is left upon the branches. The slim gean at the edge of the woodland catches the spray, the twisted crab is an old

The Awakener of the Woods

woman suddenly become a lovely girl cream-white and rose-flusht. Or she goes down the island-shores, or by the brackened coasts of inland lochs, or along the overhanging brows of streams, or where brooks glide between grassy banks; or, facing northward, she wanders where the hill-burn falls from ledge to ledge, or leaps past the outswung roots of mountain-ash or birch, or steals between peaty grasses where the wren has her nest in the pendant bramble and the greenfinch calls across the fern. And wherever she goes the yellow iris is left by her feet, the yellow-white willow-catkins have become musical with a myriad bees, dust of gold has fallen into the milk-white snow of the countless clans of the daisy, tides of an invisible flood have foamed along the hawthorns, the wild crocus has shone like the spear of Pisarr, the buttercup is brimmed with golden wine, and even the kingcup-ingots are melted in the waters—for whence else can come that flowing gold which is blent with yonder moving emerald that is as the breath of the grass, yonder floating azure as of drowned speedwells, yonder wandering violet, child of shadow and the wind, yonder mysterious phantom of pale mauve which tells that a becalmed cloud-ship drifts on the deeps of heaven.

The Awakener of the Woods

Nevertheless, it is in the woods that the miracle may be more intimately seen. The Presence perchance is not universally abroad so much as immediately evident. A hand touched that larch yonder: for why is it so suddenly green, with a greenness as of a sea-wave, or as the wet emerald crystal one finds on the sands of Iona, or, rather, with the softer, moister, the indescribable greenness of the rainbow's breast? A foot leaned upon the moss beneath that vast oak, on whose southern slopes the russet leaves still hang like a multitude of bats along dark ragged cliffs: for why has the cyclamen suddenly burned in a faint flame, there; why has the sky suddenly come up through the moss, in that maze of speedwells? Who rose, yonder, and passed like a phantom westward? Some one, surely, of the divine race, for the tips of the sycamore-boughs have suddenly burned with a bronze-hued fire. Who went suddenly down that mysterious alley of dim columnar pines, stirring the untrodden silent ways? For, look, the air is full of delicate golden dust. The wind-wooer has whispered, and the pine-tree has loved, and the seed of the forests to come floats like summer-dust along the aerial highways.

But what of the Forest-Awakener? Who

The Awakener of the Woods

is he? Her name, is it known of men? Who can it be but the Wind of the South, that first-born of the wooing Year and sweetheart Spring? But what if the name be only that of a bird? Then, surely, it must be the woodthrush, or perchance the cushat, or, no, that wandering Summer-herald, the Cuckoo! Not the skylark, for he is in the sunlight, lost above the pastures: not the merle, for he is flooding the wayside elms with ancient music of ever-young love: not the blithe clans of the Finch, for one and all are gypsies of the open. Perchance, then, the Nightingale? No, he is a moon-worshipper, a chorister of the stars, the incense-swinger before the altars of the dawn: and though he is a child of the woods, he loves the thickets also. Besides, he will not come far north. Are there not deep woods of silence and dream beyond the banks of the Tyne? Are there no forest sanctuaries north of the green ramparts which divide Northumbria from the glen of Tweed and the Solitudes of the shadowy Urr? Are there no inland valleys buried in sea-sounding woods beyond the green vale of Quair? Alas, the sweet Songmaker from the South does not think so, does not so dream. In moon-reveries in the woods of Surrey, in starry serenades along the lanes of Devon, in lonely

The Awakener of the Woods

nocturnes in the shadowy groves of the New Forest, he has no thought of more vast, more secret and impenetrable woods through which move mountain-airs from Schiehallion, chanting winds from the brows of the Grampians: he has no ancestral memory of the countless battalions of the red pine which throng the wilds of Argyll or look on the grey shoreless seas of the west; these green pillars which once covered the barren braes of Balquhidder, the desolate hill-lands of the Gregara, and, when the world was young, were wet with the spray of the unquiet wastes wherein are set the treeless Hebrides.

No, in the north at least, we cannot call the nightingale the Forest-Awakener. In truth, nowhere in our land. For he comes late when he comes at all. The great awakening has already happened. Already in the south the song-thrush, the dandelion, the black thorn-snow are old tales: far in Ultima Thule to the north-west the gillebride has whistled the tidings to Gaelic ears, far in Ultima Thule to the north-east the Shetlander has rejoiced in that blithest thicket-signal of spring, the tossed lilt of the wren.

It is of the green woodpecker I speak.

The Awakener of the Woods

We do not know him well, most of us: but then most of us are alien to the woods. Town-dwellers and homestayers know little or nothing of the secret signals. It is only the obvious that they note, and seldom read in the great Script of Nature anything more than the conventional signature of certain loved and familiar names and tokens.

It was in the Forest of Fontainebleau I first heard the green woodpecker called by this delightful name, the Awakener of the Woods, *le Réveilleur de la Forêt*. My French friend told me it was not a literary name, as I fancied, but one given by the foresters. And how apt it is. In the first weeks of March—in the first week of April, it may be, as the scene moves northward—there is no more delightful, and certainly no more welcome, sound than the blithe bugle-call of the green woodpecker calling through the woods for love, and, after long expectant pauses, hearing love call back in thrilling response, now a flute-note of gladness, now a challenging clarion-cry. True, whether in the vast forest of Fontainebleau or in our northern woods the woodpecker is not so readily to be heard in the inward solitudes. He loves the open glades, and commonly the timbered park-land

The Awakener of the Woods

is his favourite resort. Still, save in the deepest and darkest woods, that delightful rejoicing note is now everywhere to be heard fluting along the sunlit ways of the wind. It awakes the forest. When the voice of the woodpecker is heard it is the hour for Nature to celebrate her own Ides of March. Elsewhere the song-thrush and the skylark have been the first heralds. Even in the woods the missel-thrush may have flung a sudden storm of song out on the cold tides of the wind swaying the elm-tops like dusky airweed of the upper ocean. But, in the glades themselves, in the listening coverts, it is the call of the green woodpecker that has awakened the dreaming forest.

And what an ancient old-world tale Picus could tell. For, in the long ago, was he not Picus the antique Italiot God? A forest-god he was, son of ancient Saturn, and himself the father of that beautiful being of the woods, Faunus. And how far he wandered from Thracian valley and Sabine oak-grove—for in that far northern Finland, which to the Latins was but an unknown remote waste under the star Septentrion, he and his son reappear, though now his name is Tapio and Faunus is become Nyyrikki:

The Awakener of the Woods

"O Nyyrikki, mountain-hero,
Son of Tapio of forests,
Hero with the scarlet headgear,
Notches make along the pathway,
Landmarks upward on the mountain,
That the hunter may not wander."

Still does Nyyrikki, or Pikker as he was called by the northmen long before the *Kalevala* was wrought into Finnish runes, make notches along the pathways of the woods, still the huntsman on the hillside sees his signals on the oak-boles. Perhaps to this day the Esthonian peasant offers in his heart a prayer to Pikker the woodpecker-god, god of thunder and storm, so god too of the glades and fields where these can devastate—a prayer such as that which Johann Gutsloff, a Finnish author of the seventeenth century, cites as the supplication of an old Esthonian farmer: " . . . Beloved Pikker, we will sacrifice to thee an ox with two horns and four hoofs, and want to beg you as to our ploughing and sowing that our straw shall be red as copper and our grain as yellow as gold. Send elsewhere all thick black clouds over great swamps, high woods, and wide wastes. But give to us ploughmen and sowers a fertile season and sweet rain."

In Gaelic lands many an old name has been

The Awakener of the Woods

dropped from common use, because thus associated with some shy and yet never-far divinity, and so too the Finn and the Esth ceased to call the woodpecker Pikker (a word so strangely like Picus) and thus it is that now the peasant knows him only as *Tikka*. With the Romans, Picus the god was figured with a woodpecker on his head, and all of us who have read Pliny will remember the great store laid by the auspices of Rome on the flight and direction and general procedure of this forest-traveller. Recently a sculptor, I know not of what nationality, exhibited in Paris a statue of the Unknown Pan, and on his shoulder perched a woodpecker. Was this a reminiscence, or ancestral memory, or the divining vision of the imagination? I have some fifty pages or more of MS. notes dealing with the folklore and legendary names and varying ways and habits of the fascinating woodlander, from his Greek appearance as Pelekas, the axe-hewer (Aristophanes calls him the oak-striker)—whence no doubt "Picus" and "Pikker" and "Peek" and the rest—to Latin Tindareas, mortal father of Leda, to the White Woodpecker, the magic bird of mediæval legend, to "der olle Picker," the horrible laughing god of human sacrifice in ancient Prussia, to Pak-a-Pak,

The Awakener of the Woods

"the lost lover of the woman in the oak," in a strange tale I heard once in the woods of Argyll. But of all this I would recall to-day only that tradition of the woodpecker which describes her (she is a wise-woman in the folk-tales) as knowing where the spring-wurzel grows, that mysterious plant of Pan and the sun with which one may open the faces of cliffs with a breath, as did the deer-mother of Oisin of the Songs, with which too one may find the secret ways of Venusberg and behold incalculable treasure.

For hark! . . . *Pak-a-Pak*, and the long cry of love! It is answered from the listening woods! Here must "the spring-wurzel" grow . . . here, for sure, are the green palaces of Venusberg, here, at very hand, are the incalculable treasures of the awakened Forest.

THE WILD-APPLE

The foam of the White Tide of blossom has been flung across the land. It is already ebbing from the blackthorn hedges; the wild-cherry herself is no longer so immaculately snow-white. It drifts on the wind that has wooed the wild-apple. The plum is like a reef swept with surf. Has not the laurustinus long been as cream-dappled as, later, the elder will be in every hedgerow or green lane or cottage-garden? Not that all the tides of blossom are like fallen snow: is not the apple-bloom itself flushed with the hearts of roses? Think of the flowering almond, that cloud of shell-heart pink: of the delicate bloom of the peach that lives on the south wind: of the green-gold of the sallow catkins: of the blazing yellow of the gorse: of the homely flowering-currant, which even by mid-March had hung out her gay tangle of pinky blooms: of the purple-red of the deadnettle in the ditch, and of the ruddy-hued fallaways of the poplar overhead. I wonder if in most places the flowering-currant is no more than an ordinary shrub. Here, where I write, there are several small trees of it, taller than the general growth of the lilac, tall as the laburnum, though at the time of their unloosening the one had not revealed her delicate mauve and white, while the other was still a miser of the countless gold he will now soon be spreading upon the wind. The pink blooms, carmine-ended where the five or six unfolded blossoms hang like fruit, droop in a roseal shower, as innumerous as the golden drops of the laburnum-rain or the suspended snowflakes of the white lilac themselves. The brown bees have long discovered this flusht Eden; their drowsily sweet murmurous drone is as continuous as though these slow-swaying pastures were of linden-bloom and the hour the heart of Summer.

Everywhere the largesse of Spring has followed her first penury in the scanty snow of the blackthorn on bare boughs. What, by the way, is the origin of the phrase "blackthorn-sorrow"? I heard it again recently, as though to say that Summer was safely at hand so that now there was no more fear of the blackthorn-sorrow. However, as later I hope to deal with the complex folklore of the Thorn, I need not let the subject delay me now, except to say that in the North-West

The Wild-Apple

Highlands I have heard the blackthorn called *Bròn Lochlannach*, the Northman's woe, literally Norse or Norland-sorrow or mourning, ... a legendary designation to which there is, I believe, a North-German analogue. The idea here is that the blackthorn sprang from the blood of the slain Norse invaders, the "pagans from Lochlin" of mediæval Gaelic story. In many parts of the kingdom it is looked on askance, and cut sprays of it brought into a house are considered as a menace of ill, as a death-token even; and it has been surmised that this is due to some confused memory of a druidical or other early symbolism of the commingling of winter and summer, in other words of life and death, in the blackthorn's blossom-strewn leafless branches. It may be so, but does not seem to me likely, for by far the greater part of flower and tree folklore has little to do with such subtle conceptions. Too many of these are as vague and fantastical as that legend which says that one must not taste of the root of the peony if a woodpecker be in sight, or else the penalty may be blindness: a safe prognostication!

It is that other thorn which holds us now, that lovely torch of blossom which has taken to itself the name of the lovers'-month. Not

The Wild-Apple

that the hawthorn has unchallenged use of May as a name. In Devon the white lilac is often called the May, and elsewhere, too, the "laylock" is spoken of as May-bloom. The laurustinus, again, is thus named in some parts of Somerset, and I have heard lilies-of-the-valley called May-blossoms. In Scotland I have often heard the hawthorn-in-bloom called Queen of the May and even Queen of the Meadow, though neither name properly belongs to it, and the latter is the inalienable title of the meadowsweet. But of all wild-blossom nothing surpasses in mass that of the hawthorn. It, truly, is the foam of the groves and hollows. From the south to the north it flows in a foaming tide. "Bride of the world" I have heard it called in a Gaelic song, and long ago an ancient Celtic bard spoke of it lovingly . . . "white is every green thorn, and honeysweet."

But it is of the Apple I want to write just now, she whose coronal of blossom is surely loveliest of all fruitbearers: Bride of the Wind we may say—"Persephone herself" as a modern Italian poet calls her.

In the Highlands to-day the Apple *(Ubhal)*, or the Wild-Apple or Crab-Apple *(Ubhal-fiadhaich)*, is still common in woods and by stream-sides. The bitter juice of the

The Wild-Apple

fruit is still used for sprains and bruises, and to-day as of old the Gaelic poet has no more frequent comparison of his sweetheart's charm than to the delicate-hued, sweet-smelling apple—*e.g.*,

> "*Iseabail òg*
> *An òr-fhuilt bhuidhe—*
> *Do ghruaidh mar ròs*
> *'S do phòg mar ubhal,*"

where the poet praises his Isabel of the yellow tresses and rose-flusht cheek and kissing-mouth sweet as an apple. Once the apple was far more common in Scotland than it is now. An old authority, Solinus, says that Moray and all the north-east abounded in the third century with fruit-bearing apple-trees, and Buchanan even speaks of Inverness-shire as being unsurpassed for the fruit. Visitors to Iona, to-day, who see it a sandy treeless isle, may hardly credit that it was once famous for its apple-orchards, and that, too, as late as the ninth century, till the monks of Iona were slain and the orchards destroyed by the ravaging vikings out of Norway. Beautiful Arran, too, was once lovelier still, so lovely with apple-blossom and ruddy yellow fruit that it was called Emhain Abhlach, the Avalon of the Gael.

The Wild-Apple

To come in a waste piece of tangled woods, or on some lapwing-haunted pasture-edge, or in the healthy wilderness, on the wild-apple in bloom, is to know one of the most thrilling experiences of the Spring. As a rule the wild-apple stands solitary. Seen thus, it has often something of the remote element of dreamland. I came once, in the heart of a beechwood, on a single tree of laburnum, in full glory of dense unfallen gold. How did it come to be there, what wind had first brought it on the tides of birth, what friendly nurture had led the seedling to the sapling and the sapling to lovely youth? I wondered; but most I wondered at the sudden beauty, at the unexpected revelation of vistas other than those of the woodland, at the unloosening of the secret gates of dreams and the imagination. Faerie stood open. Angus Òg, the Celtic Apollo Chrusokumos, the golden Balder of the Gael, stood yonder just a moment ago, surely? Yonder, in the sunlit greenness, Midir of the Dew it was who passed swiftly among the bat-wings of disguising shadows? Was that Findabair going like a moonbeam, there in the sea-caverns of the green leaf? Or was it Fand, whose laughter the storm-thrush caught, long, long ago? Surely that was an echo of old forgotten song in the

The Wild-Apple

gloom of the beeches? Could it be Fedelm of the *Sidhe*, "the young girl of the mouth of red berries, with voice sweeter than the strings of a curved harp, and skin showing like the snow of a single night"? And there, vanishing in the sunlit cataract of gold itself, like a rainbow behind falling water, was not that Niamh of the Golden Tresses? . . . Niamh, whose beauty was so great that the poets of the Other-world and those who died of love for her called her Love Entangled, she whose beauty filled three hundred years in the single hour that Fionn thought he was with her, in the days when the ancient world had suddenly grown old, and the little bell of Patrick the Christ-Bringer had tinkled sorrow and desolation and passing away across the Irish hills. Up among the devious green pathways of the travelling wood what lost king's voice was that? . . .

> "Say, down those halls of Quiet
>   Doth he cry upon his Queen?
> Or doth he sleep, contented
>   To dream of what has been?"

. . . what poet of long ago, living in a flame of passion still, a wandering breath for ever, went by on that drowsy wind?—

The Wild-Apple

> "Across the world my sorrow flies,
> A-hunger for the grey and wistful
> Beauty of Feithfailge's eyes."

Something of that emotion as of ancestral memories, as of an awakened past, of an unloosening of the imagination, may well come to any imaginative nature encountering suddenly a wild-apple in blossom in some solitary place. To people of a Celtic race or having a dominant Celtic strain, in particular, perhaps; for to the Gael, the Cymru and the Breton the apple-tree is associated with his most sacred traditional beliefs. Of old it was sacrosanct. It was the Celtic Tree of Life, what Yggdrasil was to the ancient dreamers of Scandinavia. He cannot think of it, but of the kingdom of eternal youth: of Emhain Abhlach, of Y-Breasil, of Avalon, of drowned Avillion. It waves over the lost Edens. In Tir-na-n'Og its boughs, heavy with blossom, hang above the foam of the last pale waters of doom. The tired islander, who has put away hunger and weariness and dreams and the old secret desire of the sword, lays himself down below its branches in Flatheanas, and hears the wild harpers of Rinn in a drowsy hum like the hum of wild bees. Grey-haired men and women on the shores of Connemara look out across the dim wave and see

The Wild-Apple

the waving of its boughs. The Breton peasant, standing at twilight on the rock-strewn beaches of Tregastèl, will cross himself as he smells the fragrance of apple-blossom coming from sunken isles across the long rolling billows, and remember, perhaps, how of old in moonlit nights he has seen his keel drive through the yielding topmost branches of the woods of Avalon. Many poets have wandered in the secret valleys of Avillion, and have passed under boughs heavy with foam of dreams, and have forgotten all things and been uplifted in joy. In the glens of the Land of Heart's Desire the tired singers of the world have become silent under the windless branches, snow-white in the moonshine, having found the Heart of Song.

The cross and death-coffer of apple-wood, the crown of wild-apple, the apple-staff, the poet's tablets of apple-wood, all the apple-myths and apple-legends, how could one tell of them in a few words. They are in old songs and old tales of all lands. Our Gaelic literature alone is fragrant with apple-bloom, is lovely with the flickering shadow of the apple-leaf, mysterious with symbol of fruit and the apple-wood, that holds life and death in one embrace. Many readers will at once recall that lovely old tale of Bailê the Sweet-

The Wild-Apple

spoken and Ailinn Honeymouth, whose love was so great that when in their beautiful youth they died and were buried, one in a grave to the north and one in a grave to the south, grave-wood grew into grave-wood, and green branches from the north and the south became one overhanging branch, under which the winds murmured of passion that winter-death could not kill nor the hot noons of summer lull into forgetfulness. There is an older and less-known *sgeul* of how Ana, that most ancient goddess, the Mother, after she had fashioned all the gods, and had made man out of rock and sand and water and the breathing of her breath, made woman out of the body of a wave of the sea and out of foam of apple-blossom and out of the wandering wind. And there are many tales that, in this way or a like way, have in them the mysterious wind of the wild apple, many poems on whose shadowy waters float the rose-flusht snow of the scattered blossoms of dreams and desires. Was not the apple-blossom first stained through the inappeasable longing of a poet-king, who, yet living, had reached Y Breasil? Ulad saw there a garth of white blossom, and of this he gathered, and warmed all night against his breast, and at dawn breathed into them. When the sunbreak slid

The Wild-Apple

a rising line along the dawn he saw that what had been white blooms, made warm by his breath and flusht by the beating of his heart, was a woman. And how at the end Fand became once more a drift of white blossom upon the deerskin. For, when the longing and the sorrow of all sorrows in the heart of Ulad wrapt his heart in flame, suddenly a wind-eddy scattered the blossoms upon the deerskin, so that they wavered hither and thither, but some were stained by the wandering fires of a rainbow that drifted out of the rose-red thickets of the dawn.

How far back do these apple-legends go? I know not. But when Aphrodite was born of the Idalian foam she held an apple in her hand, as Asia or Eve looked long upon the fruit of life and death in Eden. In Hades itself was it not the lure and the bitterness of Tantalus? All old poems and tales, as I have said, have it, whether as legend, or dream, or metaphor, or as a simile even, as in the seventh-century MS. of the *Caïn Adamnain*, where Adamnan's old mother cries *mo maccansa suut amail bis ubull fo' tuind* . . . "my dear son yonder is like an apple on a wave": [*i.e.*] little is his hold on the earth. And those of us who have read, and remember, the *Prose Edda*, will recall how Iduna " keeps in a box,

The Wild-Apple

apples, which the gods, when they feel old age approaching, have only to taste to become young again."

Is that too a dream, or is there no Ragnarök for the gods to fear? This at least we know, that as the winter-tide, the death-tide, eternally recurs, so is the foam-white Dream continually rewoven, so everlastingly does Spring come again in the green garment that is the symbol of immortality and wearing the white coronals of blossom which stand for the soul's inalienable hope, for the spirit's incalculable joy. For Avalon is not a dream. It is with us still. It is here indeed, though set within no frontiers, and unlimned in any chart. And even the apples of Iduna grow within reach: the least of us may eat of the fruit—till the coming of Ragnarök.

RUNNING WATERS

Is it because the wild-wood passion of Pan still lingers in our hearts, because still in our minds the voice of Syrinx floats in melancholy music, the music of regret and longing, that for most of us there is so potent a spell in running waters? We associate them with loneliness and beauty. Beauty and solitude . . . these are still the shepherd-kings of the imagination, to compel our wandering memories, our thoughts, our dreams. There is a story of one snatched from the closing hand of death, who, when asked if he had been oppressed by dark confusion and terror, answered that he had known no terror and no confusion, but only an all-embracing and intensifying silence, till at the last, deep within it as in a profound chasm, he had caught the low, continuous sound of running waters. That I can well believe. At the extremes of life thought naturally returns to the things that first communicated to the shaken mind of childhood the sense of mystery,

Running Waters

the summons and the elation of that which reveals in beauty and utters the vibration of wonder. The first coming of snow, the noise of wind in trees, the gathering murmur of the tide heard in the night's darkness and silence, music or songs borne across water, the first falling meteors with their terrifying suggestion that all these familiar stellar fires may likewise at any time be blown abroad by some obscure and awful wind, the furtive whisperings and inexplicable confused speech of running waters, of such are these primitive and unforgettable experiences.

The burn, the brook, the rivulet, what memories of them are possessed by those whose childhood has not been wholly spent in towns, or at those thronged seaside resorts where the bounteous green life of Nature is even more absent than in many cities, at least in those which have their wooded parks, in which there may be flowing or still waters, where the cushat may be heard among the cedars or beeches, and where, above the tall elms, the noisy coming and going of rooks seems to the exile the very voice of the countryside. The linn of brown foaming water, the amber surge of the hill-stream, the stealthy if swift rush of the brown flood beloved of the salmon, or the curve and sweep of the grass-green river, flowing between meadows and under alders and past rocky fastness and linking green valleys as a winding snake barred with emerald, what memories these suggest to every lad or lass, to every man or woman who has ever thrown a cast or trailed a line, or, for that matter, who has lain on their leaning banks, book in hand, or lost in dreams, or wandered the dewy ways at dusk. Does not the very mention of torrent and cataract and waterfall evoke happy memories? One can hear the tumultuous surge between heather-held banks, and see the rock-rooted bracken shake with the ceaseless spray: can see the wild leap and foaming collapse, so habitual, so orderly in disorder, that the ring-ousel flies heedlessly from her fragile eggs which a handful of this whirling water would crush and sweep away: can recall, as in dreams the mind rebuilds the phantoms of natural imagery, the long, white, wavering smoke down the sheer slope of some mountain-bastion, or the filmy yet motionless veils of delicate gauze hung high on the breasts of silent and remote hills.

What differences there are in these running waters. We hear much of "blue" rivers, of the silver flood of azure, and so forth. But

Running Waters

few rivers or brooks or burns are blue. Their azure colour is a mirage wrought by distance and the angle of vision, affected by the play of wind, by the quality of light, by the blueness of the sky. Every German poet has sung of the blue Danube, the blue Rhine. These rivers have no quality of blueness, save by reflection from above, at a distance, and at a certain angle of vision. Waters flowing from the Lake of Geneva and from the Lake of Lucerne are blue even on grey days and if looked at on the shadow-side of a bridge. We have many grey-blue and blue-white and azure-shadowed running waters, but we have more that are grass-green and far more that are dappled hazel and nut-brown and golden-brown and amber-shot black-brown. It is not easy to say which of these running waters one loves best: nor need one, nor should one try. It would be like thinking of a garden-close filled with wallflower and mignonette, carnations and sweet peas, dark violets and yellow pansies and blue love-in-a-mist, white tulips and lilies-of-the-valley and white roses, damask rose and the flusht morning-glory and the pink moss-rose and brier and eglantine, and saying which is best of these, which loveliest, which the most dear to the mind as well as to the eyes. But, still, we have doubtless

Running Waters

each some happy choice, some hidden predilection. That will depend on memories and associations. I read somewhere recently that a certain traveller could not anywhere find, could nowhere recall, any stream or river for him so poetical, so lovely in quiet beauty as the Yorkshire Ouse. My knowledge of that river is restricted to a brief intimacy at and near York, and my recollection of it is of a broad turbid stream between muddy banks. But that does not interfere with the giving full credit to that traveller's loyal affection. He would remember the Ouse among the sands of Egypt, or by the yellow flow of the Hooghly, or perhaps by the surge of some great river as the Mississippi; and it would flow through his mind in a serene pastoral beauty, bluer than any river which ever flowed in our grey North, and in a changeless light of May or June, with calling cuckoo and thridding swallow unmindful of seasons that come and go, and with green flag and tufted reed and trailing willow-branch as unfading as the memories to which they are for evermore wed. It would not be the Ouse that you or I look at from the muddy banks on a dull November day, or catch a glimpse of as the North Express whirls by. It would be the Ouse of boyhood and youth and the heart filled with a sweet trouble, perplext by a strange ache. It would be the Ouse at its loveliest, on a rare day, in an hour of the hours, flowing in midsummer-air fragrant with meadow-hay and wild-roses. It would be an Ouse more beautiful still: it would be subtly present in "the quiet waters" of the Psalmist, wherever the painter limned that delicate unrest, wherever the poet sang of the Stream's Secret. It would be, for him, the archetype of the flowing stream: *the* river.

And so, each will have his preference, if it be only one of temperament rather than of sentiment. The deep, broad, swirling river has its incalculable fascination. Its mysterious volume, so great a flood from perhaps so insignificant a source, from mayhap some shallow pool among stagnant marsh-lands with nothing of stir or motion but the hovering dragon-fly, the wheeling and wailing lapwing, and the slow, voiceless passage of wayfaring cloud: its devious way, like an interminable procession or the continuous winding column of an army seen from a great height: its arrivals and departures at quiet towns and noisy and defiling cities: its destiny, its ultimate blending with the devouring tide and overrunning wave . . . all this has become the commonplace of the poet and the romancist. Thames filled with every craft possible to be seen betwixt the Nore and Oxford; the Forth, winding in still loops under the walls of Stirling and grey Cambuskenneth; the Clyde, running past the hills of Dumbarton and Argyll, already salt with the sea-flood pouring in by the ocean-gates of Arran and Ailsa; the deep flood of Tay or Shannon; these, and others, will always have a host to praise and magnify. But many of us will dream rather of chalk-streams in Devon, of the rippling amber-yellow flood of Derwent in the Peakland valleys, of Tweed and Teviot, of slow streams among woods and bright rivers going like cold flame through wide straths and lowlands: of small narrow waters whose very names are wedded to beauty and to " old, unhappy, far-off things," Otterbourne, the Water of Urr, the Water of Quair, Allan Water. Above all will some of us think of those peat-stained bracken-dyed burns, that leap and dance and sing down the steep ways of rock and heather in the Scotland of our love.

For my own part I find myself in so great agreement with a friend, who expresses better than I can do the love and haunting spell of the brown hill-water (which is neither a

Running Waters

river nor exactly a stream nor yet a rivulet, but with something of each and more of what in the lowlands is a brook and in the highlands a burn, yet than the one is swifter and than the other is less debonair and impetuous) that I have been constrained to ask leave to let it appear here as a natural close of running waters at the end of this brief paper on a theme in whose very title lie old music and dream and subtly incalculable spell.

THE HILL-WATER

There is a little brook,
I love it well:
It hath so sweet a sound
That even in dreams my ears could tell
Its music anywhere.
Often I wander there,
And leave my book
Unread upon the ground,
Eager to quell
In the hush'd air
That dwells above its flowing forehead fair
All that about my heart hath wound
A trouble of care:
Or, it may be, idly to spell
Its runic music rare,
And with its singing soul to share
Its ancient lore profound:
For sweet it is to be the echoing shell
That lists and inly keeps that murmurous miracle.

Running Waters

About it all day long
In this June-tide
There is a myriad song.
From every side
There comes a breath, a hum, a voice:
The hill-wind fans it with a pleasant noise
As of sweet rustling things
That move on unseen wings,
And from the pinewood near
A floating whisper oftentimes I hear,
As when, o'er pastoral meadows wide,
Stealeth the drowsy music of a weir.
The green reeds bend above it;
The soft green grasses stoop and trail therein;
The minnows dart and spin;
The purple-gleaming swallows love it:
And, hush, its innermost depths within,
The vague prophetic murmur of the linn!

But not in summertide alone
I love to look
Upon this rippling water in my glen:
Most sweet, most dear my brook,
And most my own,
When the grey mists shroud every ben,
And in its quiet place
The stream doth bare her face
And lets me pore deep down into her eyes,
Her eyes of shadowy grey
Wherein from day to day
My soul is spellbound with a new surmise,
Or doth some subtler meaning trace
Reflected from unseen invisible skies.

Dear mountain-solitary, dear lonely brook,
Of hillside rains and dews the fragrant daughter,

Running Waters

Sweet, sweet thy music when I bend above thee,
When in thy fugitive face I look:
Yet not the less I love thee,
When, far away, and absent from thee long,
I yearn, my dark hill-water,
I yearn, I strain to hear thy song,
Brown, wandering water,
Dear murmuring water!

(W. S.)

THE SUMMER HERALDS

If the cuckoo, the swallow, and the night-jar be pre-eminently the birds of Summer (though, truly, the swift, the flycatcher, and the corn-crake have as good a title) the rearguard of Spring may be said to be the house-martin, the cushat, and the turtle. Even the delaying wheatear, or the still later butcher-bird may have come, and yet *Sweep-Sweep* may not have been heard about the eaves of old houses or under and over the ruined clay of last year's nests; the cushat's voice may not have become habitual in the greening woods; and the tireless wings of the turtle may not have been seen clipping the invisible pathways between us and the horizons of the south. But, when these come, we know that Spring has traversed the whole country, and is now standing ankle-deep in thrift and moondaisies in the last rocky places fronting the north sea. No one doubts that summer is round the corner when the flycatcher hawks the happy hunting-grounds of the apple-blossom, when the swift wheels over the spire

The Summer Heralds

of the village church, and when the wild-dove is come again. The first call of the cuckoo unloosened the secret gates. We are across the frontier in that first gloaming when we hear

> The clamour musical of culver wings
> Beating the soft air of the dewy dusk.

To these familiar and loved harbingers from the south should be added yet another welcome friend who comes to us in the rear-guard of the Spring, though, rather, we should say he becomes visible now, for the Bat has never crossed the seas. The house-martin has not had time to forget the sands of Africa before her wing has dusked the white pansies on the sunside of old redbrick English manors: but the bat has only to stretch his far stronger yet incalculably less enduring pinions and then loop through the dusk from ivied cave or tree-hollow or the sombre silences of old barns, ruined towers, or ancient belfries sheltered from rain and wind.

The Awakening of the Bat . . . yes, that too is a sign that Spring has gone by, singing on her northward way and weaving coronals of primrose and cowslip, or from her unfolded lap throwing clouds of blossom on this hawthorn or on this apple-orchard, or

The Summer Heralds

where the wind-a-quiver-pear leans over the pasture from the garden-edge, or where in green hollows the wild-cherry holds the nest of a speckled thrush. She will be gone soon. Before the cuckoo's sweet bells have jangled she will be treading the snows of yester-year. But no, she never leaves the circling road, Persephone, Earth's loveliest daughter. Onward forever she goes, young, immortal, singing the greening song of her ancient deathless magic far down below the horizons, beyond the lifting line of the ever upwelling world. And already Summer is awake. She hears the nightjar churring from the juniper to his mate on the hawthorn-bough, and in the dew among the green corn or from the seeding pastures the *crek-crāke! crek-crāke!* of the ambiguous landrail. This morning, when she woke, the cushats were calling from the forest-avenues, the bumblebee droned in the pale horns of the honeysuckle, and from a thicket newly covered with pink and white blossoms of the wild-rose a proud mavis saw her younglings at last take flight on confident wing.

A good symbol, that of the Awakening of the Bat. Darkness come out of the realm of sleep and dreams: the realm itself filled with the west wind and the dancing sunlight, sleep put away like a nomad's winter-tent and dreams become realities. Often I have wondered how it is that so little is commonly known of the bat-lore of our own and other races. Doubtless there is some book which deals with this lore. There may be some familiar one for aught I know, but I have never met with or heard of it.

Recently I tried in vain to get some such book dealing with the folklore and mythology of the bat. And yet in the traditional lore of all countries there are many allusions to this "blind bird of the dusk." The Greeks, the Romans, the Celts of Europe, the westering Gaels, had many legends and superstitions connected with it. To-day the Finn, the Magyar, the Basque and the island Gael keep some of the folklore that has ebbed away from other nations, or become confused, or remembered only by old folk in old out-of-the-way places. Somewhere I have notes of several bat-legends and fragments of bat-lore collected once for a friend, who after all went "to hunt the bat" before he could use them. That was the phrase which started the quest. He had read it, or heard it, I think, and wrote to me asking if I had ever heard the phrase "to hunt the bat" as synonymous with death. I have heard it once or twice in the last few years, and once in a story where the teller, speaking of an outlaw who was a great deer-hunter in the wilds of Inverness, was found dead "with the fork of an ash-root through his breast, pinned like a red fox he was, and he by that time hunting the bat in the black silence." It would be inapposite, here, to linger on this theme, but I am tempted to record one or two of these bat-lore fragments which I recall: and perhaps, from the scarcity of such traditional flotsam and jetsam, some readers and bat-lovers may be interested.

The bat, commonly called in Gaelic *an iallag*, or *dialtag*, though even in the one shire of Argyll at least six other common names might as likely be heard, is occasionally poetically called the *Bàdharan-dhu*, the dark wandering one. I remember being told that the reason of the name was as follows. In the early days of the world the bat was blue as the kingfisher and with a breast white as that of the swallow, and its eyes were so large and luminous that because of this and its whirling flight its ancient name was a name signifying "flash-fire"—though now become, with the Gaelic poet who told me this, *dealan-dhu badhalaiche choille*, " the little black wandering flame of the woods." But on the day of the Crucifixion the bat mocked at the

The Summer Heralds

agony of the Saviour, and while the redbreast was trying to pull out a thorn, now from Christ's hand, now from His foot, the bat whirled to and fro crying, "See how lovely I am! See how swift I am!" Christ turned His eyes and looked at it, and the blue and the white went out of the bat like the ebbing wave out of a pool, and it became blind and black and whirled away till it met the rising of night and was drowned in that darkness for evermore. And that is why the bat is seen in the dusk and at night, and wheels to and fro in such aimless wandering flight, with his thin almost inaudible voice crying, "See how blind I am! See how ugly I am!"

From the same source I had *dealan-dhu bais*, the little black flame (or flash) of death, and a still stranger note to the effect that bats are the offspring of lightning and smitten trees: the connection being more obvious to Gaelic ears, because *dealan-bàs* is one of the names of lightning.

The other name I heard as a child, and it long puzzled me. *Beuban-an-Athar-Uaibhreach:* literally, the malformed one of the Haughty Father. Now why should the bat be called *beuban*, a thing spoiled, wilfully malformed? "An t' Athair Uaibhreach" (of which *an*

The Summer Heralds

athar is the genitive) is one of the evasive names used by the Gael for Satan—for that proud and glorious angel, the Father of Evil, who fell from his high estate through inconquerable pride. Why, then, was the bat the malformed creature of Satan? It was years afterwards before I had the story told me, for my old nurse (from whom I heard the phrase) did not think the tale fitting for a child's ears. When Judas hanged himself on a tree, so the tale ran, and his soul went out lamenting on the wind, the Haughty Father flung that wretched spirit contemptuously back into the world. But first he twisted it and altered it four hundred and forty-four times, till it was neither human nor bird nor beast, but was likest a foul rat with leathern wings. "Stay there till the last day," he said, "in blindness and darkness, and be accursed for ever" . . . and that is why the bat (the *triollachan dhorchadas*, "the little waverer of the dark," or *triollachan fheasgair*, or little waverer of the dusk, as a more merciful legend has it) flies as he does, maimed, blind, accursed and feared, and shrieking in his phantom voice *Gu la' bais! Gu la' bais!* ("till the day of death" . . . *i.e.*, the Last Day).

In some parts of Argyll the bat is said to

The Summer Heralds

live for three generations of an eagle, six generations of a stag, and nine generations of a man. With less poetic exactitude I have been told that it lives thirteen years in flight and thirty-three years in all!—though equally authentic information avers that the average life of the bat is twenty-one years. A forester told me once that he did not think any bat lived longer than nine years, but he thought fifteen as likely as nine. On the other hand, he himself spoke, and as though for all he knew it might well be so, of an old tradition that a bat lives to a hundred years. This, I may add, I have heard again and again. The other day a fisherman from the island of Lismore gave the unexpected answer: " How old will the *tallag* be? Well, now, just exactly what the age of Judas was the hour he kissed Christ and betrayed Him, and not a day more and not a day less." Nothing explicit as to that, however, could be obtained. A gardener told me once a rhyme about how to get at the age of man, but I have forgotten it except that it was to the effect that a *losgunn* (a toad) was twice the age of an *easgunn* (an eel), and that a *diallag* (bat) was twice the age of a *losgunn*, and that *am fiadh* (the stag) was twice the age of a *diallag*, " and put ten to that and

The Summer Heralds

you'll have the allotted age of man" [*i.e.*, an eel is supposed to live about seven years to seven and a half years: a frog or toad to about fifteen: a bat to about thirty: a deer to about sixty]. I should add, however, that my informant was not sure if in the third instance it wasn't a *iolair* (eagle) instead of a deer.

One of the strangest English names for the bat (among over a score only less strange) is the Athern-bird—a Somerset term, I believe, whose meaning I do not know.

But now to return to the rear-guard of Spring of whom we spoke first. Yet the folk-lore of the house-martin is so familiar that it need not be alluded to. We all know that it is time to think of summer when the martin clings once more to her last year's clay-house under the eaves.

It is when the wild-doves are heard in the woods that one realises the Spring-Summer borderland is being crossed. When the cushat calls, all the clans of the bushes are at home, runs a Highland saying: meaning that every mavis and merle and finch is busy with hatching the young brood, or busier still feeding the callow nestlings. But when the voice of the turtle is heard in the land, then Summer has come over the sea on the south wind,

The Summer Heralds

and is weaving roses for her coronal and will be with us while we are yet unaware.

What a quantity of old lore one might collect about the dove, and as for the allusions in ancient and modern literature they must be legion—from the familiar Scriptural phrase about the turtle to Chaucer's "the wedded turtil with her hearté trewe," from Greek myth or Roman poem to Tennyson's "moan of doves in immemorial elms." Doubtless much of the dove-lore is so well known that it would be superfluous to repeat it hear. As the symbol of peace, of the Spirit, the dove herself is universally familiar. The turtle is also a symbol of mourning, and of old, as among the oak-groves of Dodona or before the fane of Hierapolis, was held sacred as the bird of prophecy, of the soul, and of the life after death. It is because of the loving faithfulness of the cushat that this bird was long ago dedicated to Venus; and it was because Venus presided over both birth and death that the dove became associated of old with scenes so opposite as marriage festivals and funeral rites. We are all familiar with the legend that the soul of a dying person may be seen departing like a flying dove, and so it was that even a tame pigeon came to be an unwelcome sight at the window where any

The Summer Heralds

one lay in serious illness. In a word, the peasant-invalid might take the bird to be a death-messenger, the bird of the grave. The most singular of these folk-superstitions, I think, is that in whose exercise a living pigeon used to be placed on the head of a dying man in order to attract the pain to the bird and so ease the sufferer. One wonders what became of the unfortunate pigeon.

The strangest of the northern legends is that Swedish one which makes the wild-dove the confidant of Baldur, the Scandinavian god of song and beautiful love, before he died "the white death" when the ancient world receded for ever at the advent of Christ. Still do they murmur in the woods of the immortal passion, the deathless love of the old gods, they who long ago passed away one knows not whither, with Baldur going before them harping, and singing a strange song. One Gaelic poetic name for the cushat is poetry itself; *Caoirean-na-coille*, "the murmur of the woods." The subtlest legend is that old-world Finnish identification of Aino the dove-maiden and Vaino, the male-Venus of the North, like Venus sea-born, like Venus the offspring of Zeus and Destiny, and as Aino or Vaino now the singer, now the presiding

The Summer Heralds

deity at marriage festival or during the lamentations for the dead.

How little we know of this Vaino of the *Kalevala*, or of that not less mysterious ancient Teutonic nature-god Wunsch, or of our Gaelic Angus Òg, son of heaven and earth; each of whom has the wild-dove for his own, his symbol and his mortal image. Each wove grass and plants and greenness of trees out of the earth and the rain, out of the sunshine and the wind; each spun flowers out of dew and moonlight and the rose and saffron of dawns and sunsets. Each, too, created strength in the hearts of men and power in their bodies, and wove beauty on the faces of women and children. Each became, thus, the god of happiness, of youth, of joy. And to each, finally, the doves were dedicated as their sacred birds, their mortal image among the illusions of the world. So here we pass back, pass away from the later tradition of mourning and death, to the old joyousness of Spring, of Spring who creates grass and plant and flower, the strength of men and the beauty of women and the gladness of children. Spring who turns when the apple-blossom fades and lets loose the doves of Summer.

THE SEA-SPELL

Old magical writers speak of the elemental affinity which is the veiled door in each of us. Find that door, and you will be on the secret road to the soul, they say in effect. Some are children of fire, and some of air, some are of earth, and some of water. They even resolve mortal strength and weakness, our virtue and our evil, into the movement of these elements. This virtue, it is of fire: this quality, it is of air; this frailty, it is of water. Howsoever this may be, some of us are assuredly of that ancient clan in whose blood, as an old legend has it, is the water of the sea. Many legends, many poems, many sayings tell of the Chloinn-na-Mhara, the children of the sea. I have heard them from fishermen, from inland-shepherds, from moorlanders in inland solitudes where the only visitors from the mysterious far-off deep are the wandering sea-mews or the cloud that has climbed out of the south. Some tell of the terror of the sea, some of its mysteriousness, some of the evil and of the evil things that

The Sea-Spell

belong to it and are in it, some of its beauty, some of its fascination (as the Greeks of old-time told of the sirens, who were the voices and fatal music and the strange and perilous loveliness of alien waters), some of the subtle and secret spell deep-buried in the hearts of certain men and women, the Chloinn-na-Mhara, a spell that will brood there, and give no peace, but will compel the spirit to the loneliness of the wind, and the outward life to the wayward turbulence of the wave. More than two thousand years ago the Great Pindar had these in mind when he wrote of that strange tribe among men "who scorn the things of home, and gaze on things that are afar off, and chase a cheating prey with hopes that shall never be fulfilled."

Elsewhere I have written much of this sea-spell, of the *Brònavara* (to Anglicise an island word), or Sorrow of the Sea, and do not wish to write here of that strange passion or sinister affinity: but of that other and happier Spell of the Sea which so many of us feel, with pleasure always, with delight often, at times with exultation, as though in our very heart were the sharp briny splash of the blue wave tossing its white crest, or of the green billow falling like a tower of jade in a seething flood. But, first, I recall that old legend

The Sea-Spell

to which I have alluded. Perhaps some folklorist may recognise it as gathered out of the drift common to many shores, may trace it even to those Asian inlands where so many of our most ancient tales mysteriously arose; but I have nowhere met with it in print, nor seen nor heard allusion to it, other than in a crude fashioning on the lips of simple Gaelic folk, nor even there for years upon years. There were once four cities (the Western Gael will generally call them Gorias and Falias, Finias and Murias), the greatest and most beautiful of the cities of those ancient tribes of beauty, the offspring of angels and the daughters of earth. The fair women were beautiful, but lived like flowers, and like flowers faded and were no more, for they were filled with happiness, as cups of ivory filled with sunlit dancing wine, but were soulless. Eve, that sorrowful loveliness, was not yet born. Adam was not yet lifted out of the dust of Eden. Finias was the gate of Eden to the South, Murias to the West: in the North, Falias was crowned by a great star: in the East, Gorias, the city of gems, flashed like sunrise. There the deathless clan of the sky loved the children of Lilith. On the day when Adam uttered the sacred name and became king of the world, a great sighing was

The Sea-Spell

heard in Gorias in the East and in Finias in the South, in Murias in the West and in Falias in the North: and when morn was come the women were no more awakened by the stirring of wings and the sunrise-flight of their angelic lovers. They came no more. And when Eve awoke by the side of Adam, and he looked on her, and saw the immortal mystery in the eyes of this mortal loveliness, lamentations and farewells and voices of twilight were heard in Murias by the margin of the sea, and in Gorias high-set among her peaks; in the secret gardens of Falias, and where the moonlight hung like a spear above the towers of Finias upon the great plain. The Children of Lilith were gone away upon the wind, as lifted dust, as dew, as shadow, as the unreturning leaf. Adam rose, and bade Eve go to the four solitudes, and bring back the four ancient secrets of the world. So Eve went to Gorias and found nothing there but a flame of fire. She lifted it and hid it in her heart. At noon she came to Finias and found nothing there but a spear of white light. She took it and hid it in her mind. At dusk she came to Falias and found nothing there but a star in the darkness. She hid the darkness, and the star within the darkness, in her womb. At moonrise she came to

The Sea-Spell

Murias, by the shores of the ocean. There she saw nothing but a wandering light. So she stooped and lifted a wave of the sea and hid it in her blood. And when Eve was come again to Adam, she gave him the flame she had found in Gorias and the spear of light she had found in Finias. "In Falias," she said, "I found that which I cannot give, but the darkness I have hidden shall be your darkness, and the star shall be your star." "Tell me what you found in Murias by the sea?" asked Adam. "Nothing," answered Eve. But Adam knew that she lied. "I saw a wandering light," she said. He sighed, and believed. But Eve kept the wave of the sea hidden in her blood. So has it been that a multitude of women have been homeless as the wave, and their heritage salt as the sea: and that some among their sons and daughters have been possessed by that vain cold fire, and that inappeasable trouble, and the restlessness of water. So it is that to the end of time some shall have the salt sea in the blood, and the troubled wave in the heart, and be homeless.

But thoughts like these, legends like these, are for the twilight hour, or for the silent people who live in isles and remote places. For most of us, for those of us who do not dwell by lonely shores and seldom behold the sea but in the quiet seasons, it is either a delight or an oppression. Some can no more love it, or can have any well-being or composure near it, than others can be well or content where vast moors reach from skyline to skyline, or amid the green solemnities of forests, or where stillness inhabits the hollows of hills. But for those who do love it, what a joy it is! *The Sea* . . . the very words have magic. It is like the sound of a horn in woods, like the sound of a bugle in the dusk, like the cry of wind leaping the long bastions of silence. To many of us there is no call like it, no other such clarion of gladness.

But when one speaks of the sea it is as though one should speak of summer or winter, of spring or autumn. It has many aspects. It is not here what it is yonder, yonder it is not what it is afar off: here, even, it is not in August what it is when the March winds, those still-blue courses, are unleashed; the grey-green calms of January differ from the purple-grey calms of September, and November, leaning in mist across the dusk of wavering horizons is other than azure-robed and circus-crowned May moving joyously across a glorious tossing wilderness of blue and white. The blue sea frothed with wind

The Sea-Spell

has ever been a salutation of joy. Æschylos sounded the note of rapture which has since echoed through poetry and romance: that "multitudinous laughter" struck a vibration which time has never dulled nor lessened. It has been an exultation above all in the literatures of the north. Scandinavian poetry is full of the salt brine; there is not a viking-saga that is not wet with the spray of surging seas. Through all the primitive tales and songs of the Gael one feels the intoxication of the blue wine of the running wave. In the Icelandic sagas it is like a clashing of shields. It calls through the Ossianic chants like a tide. Every Gaelic song of exile has the sound of it, as in the convolutions of a shell. The first Gaelic poet rejoiced at the call of the sea, and bowed before the chanting of a divine voice. In his madness, Cuchulain fought with the racing billows on the Irish Coast, striving with them as joy-intoxicated foes, laughing against their laughter; to the dark waves of Coruisk, in the Isle of Skye, he rushed with a drawn sword, calling to these wise warriors of the sea to advance in their proud hosts that he might slay them. Sigurd and Brynhild, Gunhild and Olaf, Torquil and Swaran and Haco, do they not sound like the names of waves? How good

The Sea-Spell

that old-world rejoicing in the great green wilderness of waters, in the foam-swept blue meads, in the cry of the wind and the chant of the billows and the sharp sting of flying scud? It is of to-day also. A multitude of us rejoice as those of old rejoiced, though we have changed in so much with all the incalculable change of the years. To-day as then the poets of the isles . . . the poet in the heart of each of us who loves the glory and beauty and in any degree feels the strong spell of the sea . . . answer to that clarion-music: as in this *Evoe!* by one of the latest among them:—

"*Oceanward, the sea-horses sweep magnificently, champing and whirling white foam about their green flanks, and tossing on high their manes of sunlit rainbow-gold, dazzling white and multitudinous, far as sight can reach.*

"*O champing horses of my soul, toss, toss on high your sunlit manes, your manes of rainbow-gold, dazzling white and multitudinous, for I too rejoice, rejoice!*"

And who of us will forget that great English poet of to-day, that supreme singer of—

"Sky, and shore, and cloud, and waste, and sea,"

who has written so often and so magically of the spell of the sea and of the elation of those who commit themselves to the sway and rhythm of its moving waters :—

" The grey sky gleams and the grey seas glimmer,
    Pale and sweet as a dream's delight,
As a dream's where darkness and light seem
    dimmer,
    Touched by dawn or subdued by night.
The dark wind, stern and sublime and sad,
Swings the rollers to westward, clad
With lustrous shadow that lures the swimmer,
    Lures and lulls him with dreams of light.

" Light, and sleep, and delight, and wonder,
    Change, and rest, and a charm of cloud,
Fill the world of the skies whereunder
    Heaves and quivers and pants aloud
All the world of the waters, hoary
Now, but clothed with its own live glory,
That mates the lightning and mocks the thunder
    With light more living and word more proud.

. . . . . .

"A dream, and more than a dream, and dimmer
    At once and brighter than dreams that flee,
The moment's joy of the seaward swimmer
    Abides, remembered as truth may be.
Not all the joy and not all the glory
Must fade as leaves when the woods wax hoary;
For there the downs and the sea-banks glimmer,
    And here to south of them swells the sea."

What swimmer too, who loves this poet, but will recall the marvellous sea-shine line in "Thalassius":

The Sea-Spell

"Dense water-walls and clear dusk waterways ..
The deep divine dark dayshine of the sea——"

It is this exquisite miracle of transparency which gives the last secret of beauty to water. All else that we look upon is opaque: the mountain in its sundown purple or noon-azure, the meadows and fields, the gathered greenness of woods, the loveliness of massed flowers, the myriad wonder of the universal grass, even the clouds that trail their shadows upon the hills, or soar so high into frozen deeps of azure that they pass shadowless like phantoms or the creatures of dreams—the beauty of all these is opaque. But the beauty of water is that it is transparent. Think if the grass, if the leaves of the tree, if the rose and the iris and the pale horns of the honeysuckle, if the great mountains built of grey steeps of granite and massed purple of shadow were thus luminous, thus transparent! Think if they, too, as the sea, could reflect the passage of saffron-sailed and rose-flusht argosies of cloud, or mirror as in the calms of ocean the multitudinous undulation of the blue sky! This divine translucency is but a part of the Sea-Spell, which holds us from childhood to old age in wonder and delight, but that part is its secret joy, its incommunicable charm.

SUMMER CLOUDS

For one who has lived so much among the hills and loves the mountain solitude it may seem strange to aver that the most uplifting and enduring charm in Nature is to be found in amplitude of space. Low and rolling lands give what no highlands allow. If in these the miraculous surprise of cloud is a perpetual new element of loveliness, it is loveliness itself that unfolds when an interminable land recedes from an illimitable horizon, and, belonging to each and yet remote from either, clouds hang like flowers, or drift like medusæ, or gather mysteriously as white bergs in the pale azure of arctic seas.

We are apt to be deceived by the formal grandeur of mountains, by the massed colours and contours of upbuilded heights, whether lying solitarily like vast sleeping saurians, or gathered in harmonious, if tumultuous, disarray. There is a beauty that is uniquely of the hills. The mountain lands have that which no lowland has. But in that company we shall not find what the illimitable

Summer Clouds

level lands will afford, what inhabits the wilderness, what is the revelation of the desert, what is the lovely magic of the horizons of the sea. By the sombre reaches of the Solway, in the fenlands of East Anglia, in the immensity of the great bog which cinctures Ireland, in the illimitable lowland from Flanders to the last brine-whitened Frisian meadows, I have seen a quality of aerial beauty that I have not in like loveliness elsewhere found. Who that in mid-ocean has long watched the revelation of distance and the phantasmagoria of cloud during serene days, or from island shores looked across limitless waters till the far blue line seemed lifted to the purple-shadowed bases of leaning palaces, can think of an excelling loveliness? Who that has seen the four-fold azure, in east and west, in north and south, over the desert, and watched the secret veils of a single pavilion of rose-flusht cumulus slowly be undone, till the vision is become a phantom, and the phantom is become a dream, and the dream is become a whiteness and stillness deep-sinking into fathomless blue, can forget that the impassive beauty of the wilderness is more searching and compelling than the continual miracle of wind-swept Alp and cloud-shadowed highland; that it has, in its majesty

Summer Clouds

of silence and repose, that which is perpetual on the brows of Andes and does not pass from Himalaya?

Perhaps in sheer beauty of pictorial isolation clouds are most lovely when viewed above sea horizons, from shores of islands, or promontories, or remote headlands. In the South this beauty is possibly more dreamlike, more poignantly lovely, than in the North. Certainly, I have nowhere known cloud beauty excelling that in the Mediterranean and Ionian seas, viewed from the Spanish coast, from the Balearic Isles, over against the mountain-bastions of Sardinia and Corsica, from the headlands of Sicily, where Ithaka and Zante are as great galleys in a magic ocean, where for weeks at midsummer the wine-dark waters are untroubled between the cliffs of Hellas and the sands of Alexandria. Perhaps. It is difficult to say of any region that there beauty is more wonderfully revealed than elsewhere. It comes, and is present, and is upgathered; as the wind, that has no home, that the shaken reed knows, that crumbles the crests of ancient hills; as the rainbow, which is the same aerial flame upon Helicon, upon Ida, on the green glen of Aghadoe, on the steeps of Hecla in the Hebrides, that gives majesty and wonder to the village green, and delivers mystery on the horizons of the frequented common. It is like light, whose incalculable arrivals are myriad, but which when most steadfast is most dreamlike, a phantom: as moonlight on the mysterious upturned face of great woods; or as when, on illimitable moors, the dew glistens on the tangled bent and pale flood of orchis where the lapwings nest; or in golden fire, as when at the solstice the sorrel in the meadows and the tansy in the wastes and the multitude of the dandelion are transmuted into a mirage of red and yellow flame; or in rippling flood of azure and silver, when the daysprings loosen; or in scarlet and purple and chrysoprase, when the South is as a clouded opal and the West is the silent conflagration of the world. There is not a hidden glen among the lost hills, there is not an unvisited shore, there is not a city swathed in smoke and drowned in many clamours, where light is not a continual miracle, where from dayset to dawn, from the rising of the blue to the gathering of shadow, the wind is not habitual as are the reinless, fierce, unswerving tides of the sea. Beauty, and Light, and Wind: they who are so common in our companionship and so continual in mystery, are as one in this—that none knows whence the one or the other is come, or where any has the last excellence or differs save in the vibration of ecstasy, or whither the one or the other is gone, when the moment, on whose wings it came or on whose brows it stood revealed, is no longer Eternity speaking the language of Time, but the silence of what is already timeless and no more.

It has been said, less wisely than disdainfully, that the chief element of beauty is destroyed when one knows the secret of semblance. Clouds, then, are forfeit in loveliness when one knows the causes of their transformation, their superb illusion? Not so. Has the rose lost in beauty, has she relinquished fragrance, for all that we have learned of her blind roots, the red ichor in her petals, the green pigment in her stem, her hunger that must be fed in coarse earth, her thirst that must be quenched in rain and dew, her desire that must mate with light? Is the rainbow the less a lovely mystery because we know that it is compact of the round, colourless raindrops such as fall upon us in any shower? Is the blue of an unclouded sky the less poignant for us if we know that the sunlight which inhabits it is there, not the yellow or red or suffused white which we discern, but itself an ineffable azure; that, there, the sun itself is not golden or amber or bronze, but violet-blue?

I remember it was complained once of something I wrote—in effect, that cloud was the visible breathing, the suspended breath of earth—that the simile was as inept as it was untrue. None who knows how cloud is formed will dispute the truth in similitude: as to disillusion, can that be "unpoetic" which is so strange and beautiful a thing? The breath of a little child born in the chill of dawn, the breath of old age fading into the soon untroubled surface of the mirror held against silent lips, the breath of the shepherd on the hills, of the seamen on dark nights under frost-blue stars, the breath of cows on the morning pastures, of the stag panting by the tarn, the breath of woods, of waters, of straths, of the plains, of the brows of hills, the breath of the grass, the breathing of the tremulous reed and the shaken leaf . . . are not these the continual vapour of life; and what is cloud but the continual breath of our most deep and ancient friend, the brown earth, our cradle, our home, and our haven?

If any reader wish to *feel* the invisible making of the cloud that shall afterward rise on white wings or stream like a banner from mountain-bastions, let him stand on the slopes

Summer Clouds

of a furrowed hill in this midsummer season. He will then feel the steady, upflowing tide of the warm air from the low-lying glens and valleys, a constant tepid draught, the breath of the earth. It will not be long before the current which shook yonder rose-flusht briar, which swayed these harebells as foam is blown, which lifted yonder rowan-branch and softly trampled this bracken underfoot, is gathered by scaur and sudden corrie to the sheer scarps of the mountain-summit, to be impelled thence, as a geyser is thrown from an imperious fount, high into the cold and windy solitude. There it may suddenly be transmuted to an incalculable host of invisible ice-needles, and become cirrus; to float like thistledown, or to be innumerably scattered in wisps and estrays, or long "grey-mares'-tails," or dispersed like foam among vast, turbulent shallows. Or it may keep to the lee-side of the mountain-summit, and stretch far like a serrated sword, or undulatingly extend like a wind-narrowed banner, covering as a flag the climbing armies of pine and boulder and the inscrutable array of shadow.

Cirrus . . . what a beauty there is in the familiar name: what beauty of association for all who love the pageant of cloud, and,

Summer Clouds

loving, know somewhat of the science of the meteorologist. It is not alone in this: memory and imagination are alike stirred by the names of the three other of the four main divisions of Cloud—the Cumulus, the Stratus, the Nimbus. From the grey and purple of earthward nimbus to the salmon-pink bastions of the towering cumuli, those unloosened mountains of the middle air, those shifting frontiers of the untravelled lands of heaven, and thence to the dazzling whiteness of the last frozen pinnacles of cirrus, all loveliness of colour may be found. Neither brush of painter nor word of poet can emulate those apparitions of gold and scarlet, of purple and emerald, of opal and saffron and rose. There every shade of dove-brown and willow-grey, every subterfuge of shadow and shine, can be seen.

The cloud-lover will know that these four great divisions are but terms of convenience. There are intervening children of beauty. Betwixt the earth-held, far-reaching nimbus and the climbing cumulus, whose forehead is so often bathed in the rarest fires of sunset, is the cumulo-nimbus. Between the cumulus and the stratus, whose habitual grey robe can be so swiftly made radiant in yellow and orange and burning reds, is the strato-

Summer Clouds

cumulus: a sombre clan in the upper wilderness, heavy with brooding rains, moving in dark folds, less persuaded of the great winds which may drive the as silent seeming stratus, some ten thousand feet higher it may be, at the lightning speed of the eagle. Between the stratus and cirrus there are the cirro-cumulus and the cirro-stratus. The former is in one form as commonly welcome as beautiful, the familiar "mackerel-sky," harbinger of fair weather—in another, it is the soft dappled sky that moonlight will turn into the most poignant loveliness, a wilderness of fleecy hillocks and delicate traceries. The latter is that drift-ice or broken-up snow-field enmassing which is so familiar. Both march from horizon to horizon in ordered majesty, though when they seem like idle vapours motionlessly suspended along the blue walls of heaven they are rustling their sheaves of frost-fire armour, are soaring to more than twenty thousand feet above the earth, and are surging onward with impetuous rush at the rate of from seventy to eighty miles an hour.

I have called them the children of beauty. But these children of cloud are many. In each division, in each subdivision, there is again complex division. In a Gaelic story or poem-saga they are called "the Homeless

Summer Clouds

Clan." It is a beautiful name. But they are not homeless whom the great winds of the upper world eternally shepherd, who have their mortal hour in beauty and strength and force, and, instead of the havens and graves and secret places of the creatures of earth, know a divine perpetual renewal.

THE CUCKOO'S SILENCE

There is silence now in the woods. That spirit of the south wind, that phantom voice of the green tides of May, has passed: that which was a wandering dream is become a haunting memory. Whence is the cuckoo come, whither does the cuckoo go? When our leaves grow russet and the fern clothes herself in bronze and pale gold, what land hears that thrilling call in ancient groves, or above old unvisited forests, or where arid declivities plunge into the gathering sands of the desert? Whither is gone Sinlinda, the summer bird, as the Esthonians call her: she who has been a voice in the far Orkneys (a daughter, it may be, of that cuckoo-queen who bore Modred to King Arthur, Modred the Pict who afterward wrought so great evil upon Arthur and his knights), or cried the sighing of vain love above the hills of the Gael, or in Sweden swung on the north wind as the *sorg-gök*, uttering "sorrow," or floated out of the east as the *trösle-gök*, calling "consolation"? When Finland loses her, and the

The Cuckoo's Silence

Baltic peasant no more counts with dread the broken cries, and she has passed from the Irish valleys, so that men and women are safe for another year from the wildness of wild love, whither is she gone? Like a dream her voice fades from Broceliande, is heard no more by Fontarabia, has no echo in the wood of Vallombrosa. In the last reaches of the Danube she no longer mocks love; above the Siberian steppe the exile no more hears her ironic *Go! Go!* from the dim Campagna she is lifted into silence, *sospir d'amore:* she is not heard across the waters of Corinth from that fallen temple where Zeus took her form upon him, nor is the shadow of her wings in that wild mountain-valley of Mykenai, where Agamemnon and Klytaimnestra sleep, where once the marble statue of divine Hera stood bearing on a sceptre her perilous image. Where, then, is she gone, she who from the dim Asian valleys to the Aztec wilderness, from one world to another, is the mysterious voice of wandering love; she who is, in one place, to be hailed with hymns of gladness, in another to be hearkened to with bowed head or averted eyes? For thus it is, even to-day, among the ancient remnant in Mexico and the Californian wilds, who hear with terror that foreboding flute-like voice calling out of the unseen world: thus it was in the Himalayan solitudes of old when the Sanskrit villagers hailed the cuckoo as a divine messenger, *Kakila*, the bird who knows all things, not only what has happened, but what shall happen.

She has troubled many minds, this wanderer. It could not be otherwise. What mysterious music, this, when through the grey lands of the north the south wind went laughing on a vast illimitable surge of green and foam of blossom? One morning, when the missel-thrush was silent and even the skylarks sank through the hazy stillness, a far cry would be heard, a sound from the unknown, a bell out of heaven. It would float bodiless through the blue air, or call softly like an imprisoned echo in the coverts of grey cloud. Then those who heard would know that Summer had ceased from wearing her robe of white and green and yellow, and with sun-browned hands was gathering roses for her May garland, her June coronal. The bird of love is come. The sighing heart, the beating pulse, know it. She is come, voice out of the sea, voice across waters, Aphroditê of sound. Long, long ago this voice, this dim-remembered myth, was transmuted into Orpheus in the south, into Lemminkainen by

The Cuckoo's Silence

the singers of the Kalevala, into Sigurd across the Scandinavian fjords, into Kukkolind along the Esthonian wastes into Cuchulaind among the Irish hills, into Coohoolin beside the foam of the Hebrides. My old nurse had a Gaelic song I have forgotten, all save its refrain, which was

> "*Gù-Gù, Gù-Gù,*
> *A cuislin a-ghràidh,*
> *Cuislin mo-chrìdhe!*"

> "*Cuckoo! Cuckoo!*
> *O pulse of love,*
> *Pulse of my heart!*"

In the first movement of the *oran* the singer called to the cuckoo to come, "Blue-bird of love." Why "blue-bird" I am unaware, though among the Finns and Esths "blue-bird" is a poetic analogue for the cuckoo. In the second lift of the *oran*, the singer cried, "It is come, it is come, bird of love, bird of joy." In the third fall the singer crooned, "It is gone, bird of sorrow, bird of foam, bird of the grey wind." And after each the swift and passionate or long, melancholy, and sorrowful refrain

> "*Gù-Gù! Gù-Gù!*
> *O cushleen a-ghrày*
> *Cushleen mo-chree!*"

The Cuckoo's Silence

"The returning one" the cuckoo is called in an old saga. It is the ancient mystery, Love, the son of Earth: the wildwood brother of him, that other Love, who puts aside the green branches of home to long for the shining stars, whose sighs unappeased by white breasts and dreams of one beautiful and far-off, made of the wandering rainbow, of the dew, of the fragrance of flowers. The one comes with the green wind and goes with the grey wind: the other puts on blindness as divine vision, and deafness as a sacred veil, and wooes Psyche.

All old primitive tales know the advent of this mysterious bird. Was not, as I have said, the divine Hera herself wooed thus by Zeus? In that ancient Heraion, in the heart of the Peloponnesos which Pausanias saw, he tells us of a statue of the goddess whose sceptre bore the image of this spring-born voice of eternal love and eternal illusion. The people loved it not, for in their eyes the story covered an evil thing: but the priests bowed before an ancient mystery, and the poets smiled, and the musicians paused and wondered and struck a new vibrant note. In every country there are oldtime tales of the cuckoo with the attributes of a god, or demigod, or at least of magic and illusion. When, in the great

The Cuckoo's Silence

Northern saga, Ilmarinen, the son of Wondersmith and the Air, goes north to woo the snow-bound princess . . . what but another lovely metaphor of Spring calling to the North to cover herself with the snow blossom of betrothal and the roses and honeysuckles of procreant love . . . he orders thus the outbringing of his sleigh:

> "Take the fleetest of my racers,
> Put the grey steed in the harness,
> Hitch him to my sledge of magic:
> Place six cuckoos on the break-board,
> Seven blue-birds on the crossbow,
> Thus to charm the northland maidens,
> Thus to make them look and listen
> As the cuckoos call and echo."

The wind, that grey steed, fleetest of racers, the calling of cuckoos, the northland maidens charmed to silence among awakening fields or amid the first green stirring of grass-blades and pointed leaf: is not Ilmarinen, son of Wondersmith and the Air, the veritable cuckoo-god?

If ever the cuckoo-myth find its historian one will learn how widespread and basic it is. We follow it from Orpheus himself to the myth of Saturn and Rhea, to that of Faunus and Fauna, to Siegfried in the north, to Cu-

The Cuckoo's Silence

chulain in the west—for the famous hero of the Gaels is, for all the bardic legends as to Setanta being Cu-chulain, the hound of Culain, as unmistakably a cuckoo-god as his Finnish or Esthonian namesake, Kukkolind. The base of all is the divine inspiration, the mysterious wandering Breath, the incalculable Word, "the heroic cuckoo," who awakens the green world, the world of blossom and leaf and the songs of birds and the sap in the trees and the mounting warmth in the blood, who, as the chroniclers say, "rouses the enchanted maid of spring from her long sleep." Of all these, whether it be Faunus, or Kullervo, or Kalevipoeg, or the Son of Mananan, or Cuchulain, the same thing may be said: they are bringers of Spring, champions of the sun, rhapsodes of the immemorial ecstasy, bacchids of the ancient intoxication.

One of the loveliest of these mythopœic dreams I heard first, at the break of June, years ago, at Strachur of Loch Fyne, in a season of cloudless blue by day and mellow amber by night, and when in the long-delaying dusk the voices of many cuckoos floated across the narrow loch from the shadowy woods of Claondiri. It was of Manan, the son of that ancient Manan the Gaelic Poseidon; and how he went to the north to woo

The Cuckoo's Silence

his beautiful sister, and strew her way with the petals of wild-rose, and fill her ears with the songs of birds, and the sighing of waters, and the longing of the wind of the west. But that I have told, and am more fully telling, elsewhere. Two summers ago, on the Sound of Morven, I was told a fragmentary legend of Conlay (Connleach), the son of Cuchulain, when a youth in Skye, and how he went to Ireland and, all unwitting, fought to the death with his father—as in the Greek tale of Oidipus, as in the Persian tale of Sohrab: and, unknowing relevancy or keeping to the ancestral word, the teller emphasised this old myth-tale of the cuckoo that knows not and is not known by its own offspring, by adding: "Aye, it was a meeting of cuckoos, that: father and son, the one not knowing the other any more than a cuckoo on the wind knows father or mother, brother or sister."

Of all the cuckoo-tales there is none lovelier than that told of our Gaelic hero in "The Wooing of Blathmaid." This sleeping queen or lost princess, whose name signifies "Blossom," lives on a remote island. With the Gaelic teller this island will be the Isle of Man, home of Mananan, that ancient god whose cold hands grope blindly along the shores of the world: with the Swede or Finn

The Cuckoo's Silence

or Esth it will be that other city set among cold forgotten waters, that other Mana. Cuchulain loves Blathmaid, and their wooing is so sweet that fragrance comes into flowers, and birds break into song. The voice of Cuchulain is the music of the world. Blathmaid hears it, awakes, moves to it in wondering joy. But a rival lord, Curoi the king, carries Blathmaid away. Cuchulain is left bound, and shorn of his long yellow hair. But he regains his strength and freedom, and follows Blathmaid. Her sign to him from the Dun where she is kept a prisoner is milk poured into the water that makes a gulf between the fortress and the leaning banks. In the end, Curoi is slain or driven away; Blathmaid hears the call of Cuchulain, and wanders into the beautiful green world with her lover. Here, every touch is symbolical. Cuchulain is the breath of returning life, Spring, symbolised in the Cuckoo, that "child of air" as the old northland poet calls his dream. Blathmaid is the awakening world: Blossom. Curoi is the wind of autumn, the fierce and silent magician Winter. The milk is but the emblem of melting streams, of the fluent sap.

But now, as I write, already midsummer is gone. The cuckoo is silent. The countryfolk still think it is become a hawk. The old

The Cuckoo's Silence

Cymric *Gwalchmei* (the cuckoo-son of Arthur and twin brother of Modred) is, Professor Rhys tells us, but an analogue of the Hawk of May. So, once more, we see the incalculable survival of tradition. Some say that the wandering clan has dispersed on the four winds. The sweet mysterious voice will be heard no more in the world till the wind of the south crosses the sea next far-off Spring, and the sound of the wings of swallows is come again. But "the bird of the sevens" is not yet gone. Seven weeks from the coming of the Voice to the hunger of the fledgeling seventeen weeks, and the fledgeling has left foster-parents and gone out upon the wind; seven and twenty weeks, and the bird fades away from the woodlands like mist.

It is gone: Midsummer, the songs of birds, the "wandering Voice." Already, with that old insatiate passion of the soul, we long for Blathmaid, so soon taken from us: long for that divine call to youth and love: long for Spring that shall come again, though it shall be but a sweet wandering voice, the call of the unknown, the promise of the unfulfilled. For we thirst for that invisible mystery whose voice floats above the veils of the world, and we would drink again of the old wonder and the old illusion.

THE COMING OF DUSK

At all seasons the coming of dusk has its spell upon the imagination. Even in cities it puts something of silence into the turmoil, something of mystery into the commonplace aspect of the familiar and the day-worn. The shadow of the great change that accompanies the passage of day is as furtive and mysterious, as swift and inevitable, amid the traffic of streets as in aisles of the forest, or in glens and on hills, on shores, or on the sea. It is everywhere the hour of suspense. Day has not receded into the confused past, already a shadow in eternity, and night has not yet come out of the unknown. Instinctively one feels as though crossing an invisible bridge over a gulf, perchance with troubled glances at the already dimming shore behind, or with dreaming eyes or watchful or expectant gaze on the veiled shore upon which we are almost come. In winter one can see dusk advancing like a mountain-shadow. In lonely places there is something ominous, menacing in the swift approach of the early winter-dusk, further

The Coming of Dusk

gloomed perhaps by the oncome of snow or rain or of a soughing wind moving out of low congregated cloud. In thronged streets it is not less swift, not less sombre; but the falling veils have hardly been secretly unloosened before they are punctuated by the white or yellow flare of the street-lamps. Hardly is breathing-space, there, between the stepping out of day and the stepping into night. The fear of darkness, which possesses towns like a great dread, has broken the spell with ten thousand lights: as the mind of man, which likewise dreads the naked darkness of thought and the white, remote, passionless stars of the spirit, hastens to hide its shadowy dusks and brooding nights with a myriad frail paper lanterns that a flying hand of rain will extinguish, or a breath of wind carry in a moment to the outer darkness.

But whatever hold upon the imagination the winter-dusk may have, however subtle a spell there may be in the gloamings of autumn, surely the coming of dusk has at no other time the enchantment of the long midsummer eves. It is then that one feels to the utmost the magic influences of the dimsea or dimsee, to use the beautiful old English west-country word. The further north one is the longer the suspense, the more magical the

The Coming of Dusk

slow gradual recession of the day-glow from vast luminous skies, the slow swimming into the earthward gloaming of incalculable shadow. What a difference between the lands of the south and the light-lingering countries of the north! The sudden night comes to the shores of Mediterranean while the rose of the west yet flames against the Cornish headlands; the Sicilian wave is dark while the long green billow, washing over Lyonesse, is still a wandering fire under cloudy banks of amethyst. And, in turn, shadow has come out of the sea upon Wales and fallen upon the upland watercourses from the norland fells while, in the Gaelic isles, purple and gold cloths are still piled deep upon the fiery threshold of the sunset: and when the last isles themselves are like velvet-dark barques afloat in a universe of opal and pale yellow and faint crimson, a radiant sun still blooms like a flower of fire among the white pinnacles of wandering berg and the everlasting walls of ice.

In June the coming of dusk is the audible movement of summer. The day is so full of myriad beauty, so full of sound and fragrance, that it is not till the hour of the dew that one may hear the breathing of the miraculous presence. The birds, who still sing early in

The Coming of Dusk

the month, and many even of those whose songs follow the feet of May, begin a new love-life at the coming of June, are silent; though sometimes, in the south, the nightingale will still suddenly put the pulse of song into the gloaming, though brieflier now; and elsewhere the night-loving thrush will awake, and call his long liquid notes above the wildgrowth of honeysuckle and brier. At the rising of the moon I have heard the cuckoos calling well after the date when they are supposed to be silent, and near midnight have known the blackcap fill a woodland hollow in Argyll with a music as solitary, as intoxicating, as that of a nightingale in a Surrey dell.

The thrush, the blackbird, the blackcap, the willow-warbler and other birds may often be heard singing in the dusk, or on moonlit nights, in a warm May: and doubtless it is for this reason that many people declare they have heard the nightingale even in regions where the bird never penetrates. Often, too, the nightingale's song is attributed to the blackcap, and even to the thrush or merle, simply because heard by day; for there seems to be a common idea that this bird will not sing save at dusk or in darkness or in the morning twilight. I doubt if the nightingale ever sings in actual darkness, and though the bird is most eager just before and at dawn, at moonlit or starlit dusk, or at full moon, it may be heard at any hour of the day. I have heard the song and watched the singer at full moon, and that not in deep woods but in a copse by the wayside. Strange that both name and legend survive in lands where the nightingale is now unseen. There is no question but that it was once plentiful, or at any rate often seen, in the Western Highlands; though now, it is said, not a bird of its tribe has crossed the Solway since the Union! It is still spoken of in Argyll and elsewhere, and not confusedly with any other woodlander. In no country has it a lovelier name than the Gaelic *Ros-an-Ceol*, the Rose of Music. I have heard it spoken of as the *smiol* or *smiolach*, the *eosag*, and the *spideag*, though this latter name, perhaps the commonest, is misleading, as it is applied to one or two other songsters.

In Iona, Colonsay, Tiree, and other isles, I have heard the robin alluded to as the *spideag*. I remember the drift, but cannot recall the text of a Gaelic poem where the nightingale (for neither in literary nor legendary language is any other bird indicated by "Ros-an-Ceol") is called the Sister of Sorrow, with an allusion to a singular legend, which in some variant or

The Coming of Dusk

another I believe is also found in the Austrian highlands, parts of Germany, and elsewhere, to the effect that if a nightingale come "with Song upon it" into the room of a sleeping person, that person will go mad, or that if the eyes of a nightingale found dead or slain be dissolved in any liquid, the drinker will become blind. I have heard, too, a tale (though the bird was there alluded to as the *smeor-achoidhche* or "night-thrush") where the nightingale, the owl, and the bat are called moon-children, the Moon-Clan; three birds, it is said, with three animals of the land and three of the water, three fish, three insects, three trees, three plants, three flowers, and three stones were thrown to the earth as a farewell gift the day the Moon died. Among the three birds the teller included the bat, and I daresay there are many who still regard the bat as a bird. The three animals of land and water were the weasel, the badger, and the fox, the seal, the otter, and the kelpie *(sic)*. The three fish were the fluke, the eel, and the moon-glistered herring. The three insects were the white moth, the grey gnat, and the cockchafer. The three trees were the ash, the thorn, and the elder. The three plants were the ivy, the moon-fern or bracken, and the mistletoe. The three flowers were the

The Coming of Dusk

meadowsweet, the white water-lily and the "lusavone" (? *Lus-Mhonaidh* . . .? Bog-cotton). The three stones were, I think, granite, basalt, and trap, though I am uncertain about the second and still more so about the third, which was called *clach-liath*, " the grey stone."

But though in the north the nightingale is no longer a haunter of the dusk, the other clans of the night are to be met with everywhere, "from the Rhinns of Islay to the Ord of Sutherland" as the Highland saying goes in place of the wider "from Land's End to John o' Groats." First and foremost is the owl. But of the owl and the nightjar and the midsummer night I wish to speak in a succeeding paper. The corncrake will next occur to mind.

The cry of the landrail is so like its popular name that one cannot mistake it. Some naturalists say the resemblance to the croaking of the frog may mislead the unwary, but there is an altogether different musical beat or emphasis in the call of the rail, a different quality of sound, a different energy; and it is difficult to understand how any ear familiar with nocturnal sounds could err in detecting the monotonously uniform *krex-krex* of the bullfrog from the large, air-swimming, harshly musical *crek-crāk*, with the singular suspense

The Coming of Dusk

so often to be noted after the first syllable. For all its harshness there are few sounds of the summer-dusk so welcome. It speaks of heat: of long shadow-weaving afternoons: of labour ceased, of love begun, of dreams within dreams. The very memory of it fills the mind as with silent garths of hay, with pastures ruddy with sorrel, lit by the last flusht glow or by the yellow gold of the moon, paling as it rises. The white moth is out; the dew is on the grass, the orchis, the ghostly clover; the flittermouse is here, is yonder, is here again; a late mallard flies like a whirring bolt overhead, or a homing cushat cleaves the air-waves as with rapid oars. As a phantom, a white owl drifts past and greys into the dusk, like flying foam into gathering mist. In the dew-moist air an innumerable rumour becomes a monotone: the breath of life suppressed, husht, or palpitant. A wilderness of wild-roses has been crushed, and their fragrance diffused among the dove-grey and hare-bell' blue and pansy-purple veils of twilight; or is it a wilderness of honeysuckle; or of meadowsweet; or of the dew-wet hay; or lime-blossom and brier, galingale and the tufted reed and the multitude of the fern? It is fragrance, ineffable, indescribable: odour

The Coming of Dusk

born under the pale fire of the moon, under the lance-thrusting whiteness of the Evening Star.

But before rain the persistent cry of the corncrake becomes loud, raucous, with a rasping intensity. The bird is commonly said to be a ventriloquist, but this I greatly doubt. I have watched the rail in many places, often within a few yards, more than once from the flat summit of a huge boulder set in the heart of a hillmeadow of grass and sorrel. Not once only have I heard "the King of the quails" unmistakably throw his voice a few score of yards away. Often a *crek-crāke* has resounded, and at some distance away, just as I have seen the stooping body of the *dream* (or *traon* or *treun-ri-treun*) slide through the grassy tangle almost at my feet: but the cry was not identical with that which a moment before I had heard, and surely it was not only distance but the difference of sex and the pulse of love which softened it to a musical call. Once, however, watching unseen from the boulder I have spoken of, I saw and heard a landrail utter its *crake* in three ways, first and for over a minute with its head to one side while it moved jerkingly this way and that, then for a few seconds (perhaps four or five times) with its head apparently thrown back, and then after a minute or two's silence and after a brief rapid run forward with out-thrust neck and lowered head, as though calling along the ground. In no instance was the call thrown as though from a distance, but unmistakably from where the bird moved or crouched. There had been no response to the first, a single echo-like *crek-crāke* followed the second, but to the third there came almost simultaneously calls from at least three separate regions.

Nor is the rail so invariably shy, so heedful of cover, as commonly averred. With silence and patience it may often be discerned before the seeding grass is too dense or the corn high. In a lonely place on the east shore of West Loch Tarbert in Cantire I have seen several corncrakes leave cover as fearlessly at those two other "sacred" or "blessed" birds, the lark and the red grouse, will leave the shelter of heather-clutch or grassy tussock: and one morning I was awaked at dawn by so near and insistent an iterance of the singular call that I rose and looked out, to discover three corncrakes awkwardly perched on a low rabbit-fence, while I counted four others running to and fro in the rough dew-glistered grass just beyond. There, by the way, a crofter spoke of the landrail as the

The Coming of Dusk

cearrsach, a name I have not elsewhere heard and am not sure of the meaning, unless it is "the lumpy" or "awkward one"; while an English factor knew it as the grass-drake or meadow-drake, and again as the night-crow —the latter obviously a survival from the Anglo-Saxon "nyghte-crake" or a name re-given from like association of ideas. The same shrewd farmer quite believed that a corncrake is governor and leader of each flock of quails, at any rate in the season of migration—an idea held by the Greeks of old and retained by the Greek and Sicilian quail-shooters of to-day, and obviously widespread, as the Germans call the landrail the quail-king (*Wachtelkönig*), the French "*le roi des cailles*," the Italians "*il re di quaglie*," and the Spaniards "*el rey de las cordinices*." However, if he had been a Gael he could have spoken of the quail only by hearsay most likely, for it is very rare in the Highlands, and for myself I have never seen one there. Its name (*garra-gart* or *garlan*) is not unique; and the common term *muir-eun* is solely biblical, "sea-bird" or "bird-from-oversea," because of the allusion in Numbers xii. 31.

But the dew is heavy on the grass: the corncrake calls: on a cloudy juniper the nightjar churrs: the fhionna or white moth

The Coming of Dusk

wavers above the tall spires of the foxglove. The midsummer eve is now a grey-violet dusk. At the rising of the moon a sigh comes from the earth. Down the moist velvety ledges of the dark a few far-apart and low-set stars pulsate as though about to fall, but continuously regather their tremulous white rays. The night of summer is come.

AT THE RISING OF THE MOON

"The dew is heavy on the grass: the corncrake calls: on a cloudy juniper the nightjar churrs: the fhionna or white moth wavers above the tall spires of the foxglove. The midsummer eve is now a grey-violet dusk. At the rising of the moon a sigh comes from the earth. Down the moist velvety ledges of the dark a few far-apart and low-set stars pulsate as though about to fall, but continuously regather their tremulous white rays. The night of summer is come."

With these words I ended my preceding essay, "The Coming of Dusk." There was not space there to speak of other, of so many of those nocturnal things which add so much to the mystery and spell of the short nights of summer: the arrowy throw of the bat, a shadowy javelin flung by a shadowy hand against a shadowy foe; the nightjar, the dusky clans of the owl, moonrise at sea or among pinewoods, the dance of the moths round certain trees, the faint woven cadence of the wheeling gnat-columns, the sudden scream of the heron or the wailing of seafowl, or the mournful noise of the moon-restless lapwing, wind in the grass, wind in the hollows of woods, wind among the high corries of the hills. These and a hundred other sounds and sights fill the summer-darkness: the hill-fox barking at the moonshine, the heather-cock in defiance of alarm, deer panting among the bracken, the splash of herring or mackerel on the moonlit breast of the bay, dogs baying a long way off and from farmstead to farmstead. One could not speak of all these things, or of the hundred more. In the meadows, in woods, on upland pastures, from beech-thicket to pine-forest, on the moors, on the hills, in the long valleys and the narrow glens, among the dunes and seabanks and along wave-loud or wave-whispering shores, everywhere the midsummer-night is filled with sound, with fragrance, with a myriad motion. It is an exquisite unrest: a prolonged suspense, to the dayworn as silence is, yet is not silence, though the illusion is wrought out of the multitudinous silences which incalculably intersperse the continuous chant of death, the ceaseless hymn of life.

Everywhere, but far north in particular, the summer night has a loveliness to which the least sensitive must in some degree yield,

At the Rising of the Moon

creates a spell which must trouble even a dulled imagination, as moonlight and the faintest rippling breath will trouble unquickened pools into a sudden beauty. It is a matter of temperament, of mood and circumstance rather, where one would find oneself, at the rising of the moon, in the prolonged twilights of summer. To be in a pinewood shelving to a calm sea breaking in continuous foam: or among mountain solitudes, where all is a velvety twilight deepening to a green darkness, till the sudden moon rests athwart one hill-shoulder like a bronze shield, and then slowly is lifted and dissolves into an amber glow along all the heights: or on great moors, where one can see for leagues upon leagues, and hear nothing but the restless crying of the curlew, the screech of a heron, the abrupt unknown cries and fugitive sounds and momentary stealthy rustlings of nocturnal solitudes. Or, again, on a white roadway passing through beech-woods: or on a gorse-set common, with the churring of a nightjar filling the dusk with the unknown surge and beat in one's own heart: or on the skirts of thatched hamlets, where a few lights linger, with perhaps the loud breathing and trampling of cattle: or in a cottage-garden, with mignonette and cabbage-roses and ghostly

At the Rising of the Moon

phlox, or dew-fragrant with musk and southernwood: or in an old manor-garden, with white array of lilies that seem to have drunk moonlight, and damask and tea-rose in odorous profusion, with the honey-loving moths circling from moss-rose to moss-rose, and the night-air delaying among tall thickets of sweet-pea. Or, it may be, on quiet sea-waters, along phantom-cliffs, or under mossed and brackened rocky wastes: or on a river, under sweeping boughs of alder and willow, the great ash, the shadowy beech. But each can dream for himself. Memory and the imagination will create dream-pictures without end.

Of all these midsummer-night creatures, alluded to here or in the preceding essay, there may be none more allied to poetic association than the nightjar, but surely there is none more interesting than the owl itself, that true bird of the darkness. That phantom-flight, that silent passage as from the unseen to the unseen, that singular cry, whether a boding scream or a long melancholy hoot or a prolonged too-whoo, how blent they are with one's associations of the warm husht nights of summer. But is not the nightjar also of the same tribe? Fern-owl is a common name; also jar-owl, heather-owl. I have

At the Rising of the Moon

heard it called the heather-bleat, though probably that name commonly indicates the snipe. How well I remember from childhood that puzzling riddle

"*The bat, the bee, the butterflee, the cuckoo and the gowk,
The heather-bleat, the mire-snipe; how many birds is that?*"

I was never "taken-in" by the first three, but as I had been told, or had somehow discovered, that the cuckoo was often companioned by the meadow-pipit I thought the latter must be the "gowk." So I guessed "four," taking the heather-bleat to be the nightjar: and it was long before I discovered that the answer was two, for only the cuckoo and the snipe were really named.

I wonder how many names the Owl has! Those alone which, like the archetypal name, derive from the old root-word *ul* (to howl or hoot or screech), must run to some thirty to forty at least, from the Anglo-Saxon "hule" and later "ullet" to the familiar "hoolet" or "hoolit" or "howlet," or again, the still current south English "ullud," "ullot," or "ullyet." We have many Gaelic names also, as (for the snowy or barn owl) "cailleach-bhan," the white auld wife, or "cailleach-oidhche," the night-witch; or (for the tawny owl) "bodach-oidhche," the night-bogle; or (for the screech-owl) the onomatopœic "corra-sgriachaig," or several terms meaning "long-eared" or "horned"; and three or four designations, either onomatopœic, as perhaps "ulacan" (though both in sound and meaning it is the same as the southland "hooligan"), or adaptations of the Teutonic root-word, as "Olcadan" or "ullaid." The name "yogle" may be heard along the Lothian, Yorkshire, and East Anglian coast-lands, and is doubtless a "lift" from the Danish "Katyugle" or "Katogle": indeed "catyogle," "catogle," and "catyool" (with the quaint by-throw "cherubim") occur in several parts of England. In Clydesdale I have often heard the horned owl called the "luggie" (long-ears). Some names with probably only local meaning I do not understand, as for example, the "Wite" (not the adjective, but possibly the old word for churchyard and even church); the "padge" or "pudge" of Leicestershire; the Jack-baker, billy-wix, and the eastland "will-a-wix." Is this the cry of the young owl awaiting food?) The "jilly," which I heard once at or near Windermere, is probably a corruption of the Gaelic "gheal" (white), as many north-Celtic names survive in that region. Our commonest

At the Rising of the Moon

name in the Highlands is "comhachag" (co-ach-ak) probably as onomatopœic a term as "cuach" or "cuthag" (coo-ak) for the cuckoo, or "fitheach" (*fee-ak*) for the raven. It is said that the longest poem on the Owl in any language is in Gaelic. The *Oran na Comhachaig* or Song of the Owl was composed by an aged Highland bard named Donald Finlay somewhere about three hundred years ago—about 1590 says one local account, though I do not know on what authority: *a rinn Domhnull Mac Fhionnlaidh nan Dan, sealgair 'us bard ainmeil Abrach, mu thiomchioll 1590* (done by Donald Finlay of the Songs, the celebrated Lochaber huntsman and poet, in or about 1590). I have again and again heard the second of its sixty-seven—in another version seventy—quatrains quoted in support of the theory that an owl lives at least a hundred years; some are credited with far greater age:

> "'S co-aoise mise do'n daraig,
> Bha na fhaillain ann sa choinnich,
> 'S ioma linn a chuir mi romham,
> 'S gur mi comhachag bhochd na sroine."

("I am old as the oak ... lit. 'the ancientness upon me is that of the oak' ... whose mossy roots spread wide: many a race have

At the Rising of the Moon

I seen come and go: and still I am the lonely owl of Srona.")

In every country the owl is a bird of mourning. It is also the bird of night pre-eminently (what a pity the old-English owl-light as a variant for twilight has become obsolete); the bird of moonlight or the Moon; the bird of Silence, of Ruin, of the Grave, of Death. In some places a dead owl is still transfixed to the outside of a door, to avert lightning. Perhaps it is for the same reason that a caged owl is held to be a dangerous co-inmate of a house during a thunderstorm. A thousand legends have woven this sombre raiment of associations, though the owl's only distinction from other birds of prey is that it can see in the dark and is nocturnal in habit. It loves solitary places, because there undisturbed, but is not all darkness solitary? In Syria the peasant calls the owl "the mother of ruins" which is poetically apt, as is the German, "the sorrowing mother," but our northern "night-witch" and the grim Breton "soul-harrier" (surely a survival of the Greek idea of the owl as a soul-guide) are unjust to an inoffensive bird whose concern is not with souls and graves and ruins but with rats and mice. A German naturalist has even, I remember, written to prove that the owl is pre-eminently a bird of love, of single-hearted devotion, "the dove of the night"; and there is a Danish poem about "the Silver-Spinner" weaving a thin invisible web in the dusk wherein to entangle and bring close the hearts of lovers. Old Donald Finlay of the Songs must have had some such idea in his mind when in his Song of the Owl he makes the bird say in effect, "I may be old and forlorn, but am not to be blamed for that: neither of rapine nor of lies have I ever been guilty: is there a grave anywhere that I have ever violated? and to the mate of my choice have I ever been faithless?"

This name of the Silver-Spinner, however, though often in Germany, Scandinavia, and our own country associated with the poetic legend alluded to, is really a romantic derivative from the ancient connection of the small owl with the Maiden Maid goddess who presided over spinning as one of her foremost womanly attributes. "The Woman's Bird," as the small owl is sometimes called, deserves the name, for in almost every language ancient and modern, except English and Finnish, its name is feminine. The sacred bird of Athens or the Lesbian Nyctimenê is still "the woman's bird" among the Australian aborigines: Sanskrit, Greek, Latin, Celtic, Icelandic,

At the Rising of the Moon

Vendish, German, French, Hungarian, all afford the same sex-indication. The great white owl, however, is the bird of heroes, wanderers, the night-foray, war, lightning, desolation, solitude, and death. It is said, I know not how demonstrated or traced, that the name Ulysses is but the variant of the Etruscan *Ulixé* or Sikulian *Oulixes*, words supposed to indicate the ululation of the owl's cry (in Italy I have heard the name of the sweet and plaintive little *aziola* or *aziolo* derived from the same source): and that it was given to the Homeric hero because he was the first to adventure sea-voyaging on moon-lit nights, because he too was a night-wanderer. But unless Ulixé or Oulixes be older than the Greek name, what of Odysseus? In like fashion some speculative philologists derive "Pallas" from the Turanian owl-name *Pöllö*.

I heard a singular fragment of owl-folklore once on the island of Arran. The narrator said the white owl had seven distinct hoots, but all I need recall here is that the seventh was when the "Reul Fheasgair" ceased to be the Evening Star and became the "Reul na Maidne," the Day-Star. Was this a memory of some myth associating the owl with the other world (or darkness or moontide or

At the Rising of the Moon

Night) disclosed every eve at the opening of the Gates of Dusk? . . . the time of sleep and dreams, of strange nocturnal life, of silence and mystery, between the soft white fire of the Vesper Star, the star of Labour as the Bretons call it, meaning that with its advent the long day's labour ceases, and its cold serenity when it has climbed the ramparts of the midsummer night, and, as Phosphoros, the Day-Star, Son of the Morning, flashes like a lance-point against the milky onflood of the dawn?

THE GARDENS OF THE SEA

(A MIDSUMMER NOON'S DREAM)

I recall a singular legend, where heard, where read, I do not remember, nor even am I sure of what race the offspring, of what land the denizen. It was to the effect that, in the ancient days of the world, flowers had voices, had song to them as the saying is: and that there were kingdoms among these populations of beauty, and that in the course of ages (would they be flower-æons, and so of a measure in time different from our longer or shorter periods?) satraps revolted against the dominion of the Rose, and tropical princes led new hosts, and scarlet forest-queens filled the jungle and the savannah with their chants of victory. And the end was a conflict so great that even the isles of the sea were shaken by it, and the pale green moss of polar rocks whispered of the great world-war of the peoples of Flowry. At last, after the shadow-flitting passage of an æon, the gods were roused from their calm, and, looking down

The Gardens of the Sea

into the shaken mirror of the world, beheld all their dreams and visions and desires no longer children of loveliness and breaths of song. In these æons while they had slept in peace the Empire of Flowry had come to a dissolution: race fought with race, tribe with tribe, clan with clan. Among all the nations there was a madness for supremacy, so that the weed in the grass and the flame-crowned spire of the aloe were at one in a fierce discontent and a blind lust of dominion. Thereupon the gods pondered among themselves. Kronos, who had been the last to wake and was already drowsy with old immemorial returning slumber, murmured: "A divine moment, O ye Brotherhood of Eternity, is a long time wherein to be disturbed by the mortal reflection of our dreams and the passions and emotions of our enchanted hearts."

And as all the calm-eyed Immortals agreed, Kronos sighed out the mandate of silence, and turning his face to Eternity was again among the august dreams of the Everlasting Ones.

In that long moment—for, there in the other world, it was but a brief leaning on their elbows of the drowsy gods while the fans of Immortal Sleep for a second stayed the vast waves of Peace—the divine messengers, or were they the listening powers and dominions

The Gardens of the Sea

of the earth, fulfilled destiny? From every flower-nation, from every people by far waters, from every tribe in dim woods and the wilderness, from every clan habiting the most far hills beyond the ever-receding pale blue horizons, song was taken as stars are pluckt away from the Night by the grey fingers of the Dawn. The Rose breathed no more a flusht magic of sound; the Lily no more exhaled a foamwhite cadence. Silence was come upon the wild chant of orchids in old, forgotten woods; stillness upon the tinkling cymbals of the little hands of the dim, myriad, incalculable host of blossom; a hush upon the songs of meadow-flowers; a spell upon the singing of honeysuckles in the white dews at the rising of the moon. Everywhere, from all the green tribes, from all the glowing nations of Flowry, from each and every of the wandering folk of the Reed, the Moss, and the Lichen, from all the Clans of the Grass, the added loveliness of song was taken. Silence fell upon one and all: a strange and awful stillness came upon the woods and valleys. It was then that the God of Youth, wandering through the husht world, took the last song of a single rose that in a secret place had not yet heard the common doom, and with his breath gave it a body, and a pulse

The Gardens of the Sea

to its heart, and fashioned for it a feather-covering made of down of the bog-cotton and the soft undersides of alder-leaf and olive. Then, from a single blade of grass that still whispered in a twilight hollow, he made a like marvel, to be a mate to the first, and sent out both into the green world, to carry song to the woods and the valleys, the hills and the wildernesses, the furthest shores, the furthest isles. Thus was the nightingale created, the first bird, the herald of all the small clans of the bushes that have kept wild-song in the world, and are our delight.

But in the hearts of certain of the green tribes a sullen anger endured. So the mysterious Hand which had taken song and cadence away punished these sullen ones. From some, fragrance also was taken. There were orchid-queens of forest-loveliness from whom all fragrance suddenly passed like smoke: there were white delicate phantoms among the grasses, from whom sweet odour was lifted as summer dew: there were nomads of the hillways and gypsies of the plain to whom were given the rankness of the waste, the smell of things evil, of corruption, of the grave. But to some, beautiful rebels of the peoples of the Reed, the Grass, and the Fern, the doom went out that henceforth their place

The Gardens of the Sea

should be in the waters ... the running waters of streams and rivers, the quiet waters of pools and lakes, the troubled waters of the seas along the coasts of the world, the ocean depths.

And that is how amid the salt bite of the homeless wave there grew the Gardens of the Sea. That is how it came about that the weed trailed in running waters, and the sea-moss swayed in brackish estuaries, and the wrack clung or swam in tangles of olive-brown and green and soft and dusky reds.

What a long preamble to the story of how the Seaweeds were once sweet-smelling blooms of the shores and valleys! Of how the flowers of meadow and woodland, of the sun-swept plain and the shadowy hill, had once song as well as sweet odours: how, of these, many lost not only fragrance but innocent beauty: and how out of a rose and a blade of grass and a breath of the wind the first birds were made, the souls of the green earth, winged, and voiced.

To-day I sit among deep, shelving rocks by the shore, in a desolate place where basaltic cliffs shut away the familiar world, and where, in front, the otherworld of the sea reaches beyond sight to follow the lifted wave against the grey skyline, or is it the grey lip of the

The Gardens of the Sea

fallen horizon? Looking down I can perceive the olive-brown and green seaweed swaying in the slow movement of the tide. Like drifted hair, the long thin filaments of the Mermaid's Locks (*Chorda Filum*) sinuously twist, intertwine, involve, and unfold. It is as though a seawoman rose and fell, idly swam or idly swung this way and that, asleep on the tide: nothing visible of her wave-grey body but only her long fatal hair, that so many a swimmer has had to cause dread, from whose embrace so many a swimmer has never risen. In the rock-set pools the flesh-hued fans of the dulse indolently stir. Wave-undulated over them are fronds of a lovely green weed, delicate, transparent: above these, two phantom fish, rock-cod or saithe, float motionless.

Idly watching, idly dreaming thus, I recall part of a forgotten poem about the woods of the sea, and the finned silent creatures that are its birds: and how there are stags and wolves in these depths, long hounds of the sea, mermen and merwomen and seal-folk. Others, too, for whom we have no name, we being wave-blind and so unable to discern these comers and goers of the shadow. Also, how old sea-divinities lie there asleep, and perilous phantoms come out of sunken ships and ancient weed-grown towns; and how there

The Gardens of the Sea

roams abroad, alike in the flowing wave and along the sheer green-darkening bodiless walls, an incalculable Terror that may be manifold, the cold implacable demons of the deep, or may be One, that grey timeworn Death whom men have called Poseidon and Mananan and by many names.

What a mysterious world this Tir-fo-Tuinn, this Land-Under-Wave. How little we know of it, for all that wise men have told us concerning the travelling tides, of currents as mysteriously steadfast in the comings and goings as the comets that from age to age loom briefly upon the stellar roads: how little, though they have put learned designations to a thousand weeds, and given names to ten thousand creatures to whom the whole world of man and all his hopes and dreams are less than a phantom, less than foam. The Gaelic poet who said that the man who goes to Tir-fo-Tuinn goes into another world, where the human soul is sand, and God is but the unloosened salt, tells us as much as the scientist who probes the ocean-mud and reveals dim crustacean life where one had believed to be only a lifeless dark. Above the weed-held palaces of Atlantis, over the soundless bells of Ys, above where Lyonesse is gathered in a foamless oblivion, the plummet may sink and

The Gardens of the Sea

lift a few broken shells, the drag-net may bring to the surface an unknown sea-snail or such a microscopic green Alga as that *Halosphæra viridis* which science has discovered in the great depths beyond the reach of sunlight: but who can tell, perchance how few who care to know, what Love was, long ago, when there were poets in Lyonesse: what worship was served by white-robed priests among the sunken fanes of Ys: what dreams withstayed and what passions beset the noble and the ignoble in drowned Atlantis, what empires rose and fell there, what gods were lauded and dethroned, and for how long Destiny was patient.

Even in the little pools that lie shoreward of the Gardens of the Sea what beauty there is, what obscure life, what fascinating "otherworld" association. This piece of kelp is at once *Fucus vesiculosus* and the long fingers of the Cailliach-Mhara, the Sea-Witch. This great smooth frond is . . . I do not know, or forget: but it is the kale of Manan, in seagroves of which that Shepherd pastures his droves of uncouth sea-swine. This green tracery has a Greek or Latin name, but in legend it is called the Mermaid's Lace. This little flame-like crest of undulating wrack has a designation longer than itself, but in tales of

The Gardens of the Sea

faerie we know it to be that of which the caps of the pool-elves are fashioned.

In the Isles seaweed has many local names, but is always mainly divided into Yellow Tails, Dark Tails, and Red Tails (*Feamainn bhuidhe, feamainn dubh,* and *feamainn dearg*). The first comprise all the yellowish, light-brown, and olive-brown seaware; the second all the dark-green, and also all green wrack; the third, the red. The common seaware or kelp or tang (*Fucus vesiculosus*) is generally called *propach*, or other variant signifying tangled: and the bladder-wrack, *feamainn bholgainn* or *builgeach*, "baggy-tails." I have at times collected many local names of these weeds, and not a few superstitions and legends. Naturally the most poetic of these are connected with the *Chorda filum* or Dead Man's Hair, which has a score of popular names, from "corpsy-ropes" to the occasional Gaelic *gillemu lunn*, which may be rendered "the wave's gillie" or "servant of the wave": with the drifted gulf-weed, whose sea-grapes are called *uibhean sìthein*, fairy eggs, and are eagerly sought for: and with the *duileasg*, or dulse. Even to this day, in remote parts, an ancient seaweed-rite survives in the propitiatory offerings (now but a pastime of island children) to the Hebridean sea-god Shony at

The Gardens of the Sea

Samhain (Hallowmass). The Shony, whose favours were won by a cup of ale thrown into the sea in the dark of the night, is none other than Poseidon, Neptune, Manan; for he is the Scandinavian sea-god *Sjoni*, viking-brought from Lochlin in the far-off days when the Summer-sailors raided and laid waste the Gaelic Isles.

It is singular how rarely seaweed has entered into the nomenclature and symbology of peoples, how seldom it is mentioned in ancient literature. Among our Gaelic clans there is only one (the M'Neil) which has seaware as a badge. Greek art has left us a few seaweed-filleted heads of Gorgons, and to sea-wrack the Latin poets have once or twice made but passing and contemptuous allusion. In the Bible ("whaur ye'll find everything frae a bat to a unicorn," as an old man said to me once) there is one mention of it only, in Jonah's words: "The depths closed me round about, the weeds were wrapped about my head."

THE MILKY WAY

With the first sustained breath or frost the beauty of the Galaxy becomes the chief glory of the nocturnal skies. But in midsummer even what amplitude of space, what infinite depths it reveals, and how mysterious that filmy stardrift blown like a streaming banner from behind the incalculable brows of an unresting Lord of Space, one of those Sons of the Invisible, as an oriental poet has it, whose ceaseless rush through eternity leaves but this thin and often scarce visible dust, "delicate as the tost veil of a dancing girl swaying against the wind." Perhaps no one of our poets, and poetry ancient and modern and of every country and race is full of allusions to the Galaxy, has more happily imaged it in a single line than Longfellow has done in

"Torrent of light and river of the air."

As a river, or as a winding serpent, or as a stellar road, it has imaginatively been conceived by almost every people, though many

The Milky Way

races have delighted in the bestowal of a specific name, as though it were not an aggregation of star-clusters and nebulæ, but a marvellous creature of the heavens, as, perhaps, we may conceive the Great Bear, or Orion, or moons-beset Jupiter, or Saturn among his mysterious rings. Thus in the Book of Job it is called the Crooked Serpent; the Hindûs of Northern India call it the Dove of Paradise (Swarga Duari), though they have or had a still finer name signifying the Court of God; and the Polynesians give it the strange but characteristic designation. "The Long, Blue Cloud-Eating Shark."

Last night I watched the immense tract for a long time. There was frost in the air, for I saw that singular pulsation which rightly or wrongly is commonly held to be an optical illusion, the aspect as of a pulse, or of an undulating motion of life such as one might dimly perceive in the still respiration of some sleeping saurian. There appeared to be countless small stars, and in the darker spaces the pale vaporous drift became like the trail of phosphorescence in the wake of a vessel: at times it seemed almost solid, a road paven with diamonds and the dust of precious stones, with flakes as of the fallen plumage of wings —truly *Arianrod*, the Silver Road, as the

The Milky Way

Celts of old called it. Of course it was no more than a fantasy of the dreaming imagination, but it seemed to me more than once that as a vast indefinite sigh came from the windless but nevertheless troubled sea there was a corresponding motion in that white mysterious Milky Way, so infinitely remote. It was as though the Great Snake—as so many bygone peoples called and as many submerged races still call the Galaxy—lay watching from its eternal lair that other Serpent of Ocean which girdles the rolling orb of our onward-rushing Earth : and breathed in slow mysterious response; and, mayhap, sighed also into the unscanned void a sigh infinitely more vast, a sigh that would reach remote planets and fade along the gulfs of incalculable shores.

As winter comes, the Milky Way takes on a new significance for pastoral and other lonely peoples, for shepherds and fisher-folk above all. Songs and poems and legends make it familiar to everyone. A hundred tales own it as a mysterious background, as Broceliande is the background of a hundred Breton ballads, or as Avalon is the background of a hundred romances of the Cymric and Gaelic Celt. The Hebridean islanders seldom look at it on still frosty nights without in the long idle hours recalling some old name

The Milky Way

or allusion, some ancient *rann* or *oran*, some *duan* or *iorram* of a later day, related to the mystery and startling appealing beauty of the Silver Road. It has many names on the lips of these simple men, who have little learning beyond the Bible and what life on the waters and life in the hearts of other simple men and women have taught them. Sometimes these names are beautiful, as "Dust of the World" (or universe, *an domhain*) or the "Kyle of the Angels" (the Strait or Sound): sometimes apt and natural, as "the Herring Way," and "the Wake": sometimes legendary, as "the Road of the Kings" (the old gods, from Fionn back to the Tuatha Dedannan) or as "the Pathway of the Secret People": sometimes sombre or grotesque, as "The Shroud" or as "the Bag of the Great Miller."

There is especial interest for us, of course, in the legendary associations of the Anglo-Saxon and Scandinavian and Celtic or Gaelic peoples. These, in common with the majority of western nations, image the Milky Way more as a "road" or "street" than as a serpent or than as a river—though the Norse have their *Midhgardhsormr*, connected in association with the *Weltum-Spanner* ("Stretcher-round-the-World") or Ocean-Stream.

I do not know when the Milky Way as a

The Milky Way

designation first came into common English use. Possibly there is no prior mention to that in Chaucer's *Hous of Fame*:

> "Se yonder, lo, the Galaxyë,
> Which men clepeth the Milky Wey"

—an allusion which certainly points to already familiar usage. It is now, I fancy, almost universal. Perhaps the old translator Eden was among the first to popularise it, with his rendering of the Latin *Via Lactis* and *Via Lactea* as "the Mylke way" and "Mylke whyte way." There has been no need to derive the term from the Italian *Via lattea* or the French *Voie lactée*, since Eden's use and Chaucer's preceded that of any French poet or romancist. Certainly the phrase became part of our literature after it passed golden from the mint of Milton (paraphrasing Ovid)—

> "Broad and ample road whose dust is gold,
> And pavement stars, as stars to thee appear
> Seen in the Galaxy, that milky way
> Which nightly as a circling zone thou seest
> Powdered with stars. . . ."

It is rarely now alluded to as the Galaxy, and probably never by unlettered people. In most parts of England for centuries, and it is said in many parts still, the common designation is

The Milky Way

"the Way of Saint James." This has a singular correspondence in the name popular among the French peasants, "the Road of Saint Jacques of Compostella." Originally a like designation was common in Spain, though for a thousand years the popular epithet runs *El Camino de Santiago*, after the Warrior-Saint of the Iberian peoples. I am told that "the Way of Saint James" is common in certain counties of England, but I have never heard it, nor do I wholly recall the reason of this particular nomenclature. In some form the road-idea continually recurs. How many readers of these notes will know that the familiar "Watling Street"—that ancient thoroughfare from Chester through the heart of London to Dover—was also applied to this Galaxy that perchance they may look at to-night from quiet country-side, or village, or distant towns, or by the turbulent seas of our unquiet coasts, or by still waters wherein the reflection lies and scintillates like a phantom phosphorescence. Watling Street does not sound a poetic equivalent for the Milky Way, but it has a finer and more ancient derivation than "the Way of Saint James." The word goes back to Hoveden's "Watlinga-Strete," itself but slightly anglicised from the Anglo-Saxon *Waetlinga Straet*, where the words mean the Path of the Wetlings, the giant sons of King Waetla, possibly identical with the giant sons of Turenn of ancient Gaelic legend, heroes who went out to achieve deeds impossible to men, and traversed earth and sea and heaven itself in their vast epical wanderings. Another curious old English name of the Galaxy, of great beauty in its significance, is "Walsyngham Way." Why the Galaxy should be so called might well puzzle us, were it not explained by the fact that up till near the middle of the sixteenth century one of the most common English names of the Virgin Mary was, "Our Lady of Walsyngham," from the fact that the Blessed Mother's chief shrine in the country was at Walsyngham Abbey in Norfolk. Further, as "the Way to Walsyngham" in common parlance signified the road to the earthly tabernacle of Mary, so "Walsyngham Way," as applied to the Galaxy, signified the celestial road to the virgin Mother in heaven. Much more barbaric is a name for the Milky Way still to be heard in Celtic Wales, *Caer Gwydyon*, the Castle or Fortress of Gwython. This Gwython or Gwydyon was a kind of Merlin Sylvestris. He was known as the Enchanter, the Wizard as we would say now, and was feared on this account, and because he was the son of Don,

The Milky Way

King of the Otherworld, Lord of the Secret People, the "fairies" of later tradition. Like Grania, the beautiful wife of Fionn, whose elopement with Dermid and their subsequent epical odyssey is the subject of one of the greatest and to this day most popular of Gaelic legendary romances, the wife of Gwython fled from his following vengeance from land to land, across seas, over mountains, "to the ends of the earth," and at last with her faery lover dared the vast untrodden ways of the remote skies. But long before they could reach Arcturus, or whatever the star or planet to which they fled, Gwython overtook them, led by the dust which these mortal if semi-divine fugitives made long and soundless dark blue roads of heaven. He slew them and their winged horses and their aërial hounds, and standing on the verge of space flung the heads and limbs and bodies into infinitude. Hence the meteors and falling stars which at the season of the autumnal equinox and at the approach of winter may still be seen whirling adown the bastions of high heaven. So terrible in tragedy, so titanic the deed, that to all eternity, or as long as our world endures, the phantom iteration of that mighty vengeance shall commemorate the inappeasable anger of Gwython the Enchanter. Is there

The Milky Way

not convincing evidence in the unpassing dust of that silent highway of the doomed lovers—the dust of the trampled star-way that no wind of space has blown to this side or to that, that no alchemy of sun or moon has burned up or like dew dissolved?

Besides "Watling Street," our Anglo-Saxon forbears had *Iringes Weg* or *Wec* and *Bil-Idun's Weg*; Iringe and Bil-Idun having been famous descendants of the Waetla already alluded to. They were warders of the Bridge of Asgard, the Scandinavian Heaven. In time this Asgard-Bridge came to be given as a name to the Milky Way . . . though the later poets applied the epithet also to the Rainbow. Readers of Grimm's *Teutonic Mythology* will remember that he cites many collateral instances. Thus the Vikings knew the Galaxy as *Wuotanes Straza*, or "Woden's Street"; the Dutch have in common use *Vronelden Straat*, "the women's Street"; and the German peasants commonly call it *Jakob's Weg*. The Westphalian term is singular and suggestive, "Weather Street." One wonders if there is any common idea that weather is in any way as closely associated with the Milky Way as are the vernal floods and that autumnal rains with the Pleiades. Probably the bestowal of the name is due to the fact that

The Milky Way

when the Galaxy is clear and bright and scintillant the weather is serene and dry. A more poetic designation is that of the Finns, who delight in the term *Linnunrata*, the Birds' Way, either from an old Finnish and Esthonian legend that once by a miracle all the songs of all the birds of the world were turned into a cloud of snow-white tiny wings, or from the more likely belief that it is the road of winged spirits on their passage from earth to heaven. This is, of course, a very ancient conception. The ancient Hindûs revealed it in the phrase "the Path of Ahriman": the ancient Norse as "the Path of the Ghosts" going to Valhalla: the ancient Gaels as the Hero-Way, leading from Earth to Flatheanas, the Abode of Eternal Youth. It is strange and suggestive that not only the North American aborigines called it "the Trail to Ponemah" (the Hereafter), but that people so rude as the Eskimo and the Bushmen of South Africa call it "the Ashen Path," the road of fire-ember signals, for the ghosts of the dead. Even the Patagonians speak of the Milky Way as the white pampas where their dead are immortal huntsmen rejoicing in the pursuit of countless ostriches.

But of all popular names I do not think any is more apt and pleasant than that common to the Swedish peasantry, who call the Galaxy

The Milky Way

Winter Gatan—i.e., "Winter Street." It is the Winter Street we must all travel some day, if the old poets say true, when the green grass grows on our quiet beds, when the loudest wind will not fret the silence in our tired minds, and when day and night are become old forgotten dreams. May we too find it the Pathway of Peace . . . not the least beautiful of the names of the Milky Way, not the least beautiful of the legends connected with that lovely wonder of our nocturnal skies.

SEPTEMBER

September: the very name has magic. In an old book, half in Latin half in English, about the months, which I came upon in a forgotten moth-eaten library years ago, and in part copied, and to my regret have not seen or heard of since, or anywhere been able to trace, I remember a singular passage about this month. Much had been said about the flowers of "these golden weekes that doe lye between the thunderous heates of summer and the windy gloomes of winter"; of those flowers and plants which bloom in gardens, and those, as the harebell and poppy and late-flowering gorse, which light the green garths of meadow and woodland; as the bryony, which trails among the broken copses and interweaves the ruddy masses of bramble; as the traveller's-joy, which hangs its frail wreaths of phantom-snow along the crests of every hedgerow of beech and hornbeam. Of the changing colours of the trees, too, the old writer had much to say: of the limes "that become wan and spotted as a doe," of the mountain-ash "that has its long fingers dyed redd and browne," of "the wyche-elme whose gold is let loose on the wind after nighte-frosts and cold dawnes." Nor did he forget that "greate beautie of mistes" which we all know; and he reached eloquence when he spoke of the apple-orchards and of the wall-fruits of "olde manor-gardenns"—"the peache that women and poetes doe make the queene of fruites," "the rich glowe and savour of the apricock," "the delicate jargonell that keepes the sweetes of France in olde warme English gardenns." Of wild-fruit, also, he had dainty words and phrases. Blackberries, "the darke-blue bilberry," the sloe "whose excellent purple bloode maketh so fine a comfort," "the dusky clustres of the hasel," "the green-smockt filberte," and so forth. Even upon mushrooms he had words of sun and wind and dew, so lightsome were they, ardent and joyous, with a swift movement— as though writ by one who remembered gathering "musherooms" in a sun-sweet dawn after a night of heavy dews, in company with another who laughed often in gladness and was dearest and fairest of all dear and fair things. "Howbeit," he added, after sorrowing that "many doe feare these goodly musherrooms as poysonis dampe weedes," "this dothe

September

in nowise abate the exceedynge excellence of Goddes providence that out of the grasse and dewe where nothing was, and where onlie the lytell worme turned in his sporte, comes as at the shakynge of bells these delicate meates."

Then, after some old-world lore about "the wayes of nature with beastes and byrdes" in this month, he goes further afield. "And this monthe," he says, "is the monthe of dreames, and when there is a darke (or secret) fyre in the heartes of poetes, and when the god of Love is fierce and tyrannick in imaginings and dreames, and they doe saye in deedes also, yett not after the midwaye of the monthe; butt whye I know not."

We hear so much of the poet-loved and poet-sung month of May, and the very name of June is sweet as its roses and white lilies and lavender, that it is become a romantic convention to associate them with "dreames" and the "tyrannick" season of "the god of Love." But I am convinced that the old Elizabethan or Jacobean naturalist was right. May and June are months of joy, but September is the month of "dreames" and "darke fyre." Ask those who love nature as the poet is supposed to love her, with something of ecstasy perhaps, certainly with underglow of

September

passion: ask those in whom the imagination is as a quickening and waning but never absent flame: ask this man who travels from month to month seeking what he shall never find, or this woman whose memories and dreams are sunny, howsoever few her hopes . . . and the chance will be that if asked to name the month of the heart's love, it will be September. I do not altogether know why this should be so, if so it is. There is that in June which has a time-defying magic: May has her sweet affinities with Spring in the human heart: in April are the flutes of Pan: March is stormy with the clarions of the winds: October can be wild with all wildness, or be the calm mirror of the passing of the loveliness of the green-world. There is not a month that has not its own signal beauty, so that many love best February, because through her surge of rains appear days of blue wonder, with the song of the missel-thrush tost like spray from bare boughs—or November, because in the grey silence one may hear the fall of the sere leaves, and see mist and wan blueness make a new magic among deserted woods—or January, when all the visible world lies in a white trance, strange and still and miraculous as death transfigured to a brief and terrible loveliness on the face of one sud-

September

denly quiet from the fever of youth and proud beauty. There is not a month when the gold of the sun and the silver of the moon are not woven, when the rose of sunset does not lie upon hills which reddened to the rose of dawn, when the rainbow is not let loose from the tangled nets of rain and wind, when the morning-star and the evening-star do not rise and set.

And yet, for some, there is no month that has the veiled magic of September.

"The month of peace," "the month of beauty," it is called in many Gaelic songs and tales; and often, "Summer-end." I remember an old *rann*, perhaps still said or sung before the peat-fires, that it was in this month God created Peace; again, an island-tale of Christ as a shepherd and the months as sheep strayed upon the hills of time. The Shepherd went out upon the hills, and gathered them one by one, and led them to the fold: but, before the fold was reached, a great wind of snow came down out of the corries, and on the left a wild flood arose, and on the narrow path there was room only, and that hardly, for the Shepherd. So He looked to see which one of the twelve He might perchance save, by lifting it in His strong arms and going with it alone to the fold. He looked long, for all

September

were the children of His Father. Then He lifted September, saying, "Even so, because thou art the month of fulfilment, and because thy secret name is Peace." But when He came out of the darkness to the fold, the Shepherd went back between the wild lips of flood and tempest, and brought to the fold June, saying, "Because thy secret name is Joy": and, in turn, one by one, He brought each to the fold, saying unto each, in this order, "May, because thy secret name is Love"; "April, because thou art made of tears and laughter"; "July, because thou art Beauty"; "August, thou quiet Mother"; "October, because thy name is Content"; "March, because thy name is Strife"; "February, because thy name is Hope"; "November, because thy name is Silence"; "January, because thou art Death"; and at the last, "December, whom I have left to the end, for neither tempest could whelm nor flood drown thee, for thy name is the Resurrection and the Life."

And when the tale was told, some one would say, "But how, then, was September chosen first?"

And the teller would say, "Because its secret name is Peace, and Peace is the secret name of Christ."

September

It is no wonder the poets have loved so well this month whose name has in it all the witchery of the North. There is the majesty of the hill-solitudes in it, when the moorlands are like a purple sea. It has the freshness of the dew-white bramble-copses, of the bracken become russet and pale gold, of the wandering frostfire along the highways of the leaf, that mysterious breath whose touch is silent flame. It is the month when the sweet, poignant second-song of the robin stirs the heart as a child's gladness among tears. "The singer of September," a Gaelic poet calls it, and many will recall the lovely lines of the old half-forgotten Elizabethan poet on the bird

"That hath the bugle eyes and ruddy breast
And is the yellow autumn's nightingale."

It is strange how much bird-lore and beast-lore lie with September. The moor-cock, the stag, the otter, the sea-wandering salmon, the corncrake, and the cuckoo and the swift, I know not how many others, have their tale told or their farewell sung to the sound and colour of September. The poets have loved it for the unreturning feet of Summer whose vanishing echoes are in its haunted aisles, and for the mysterious silences of the veiled arrivals

September

of Winter. It is the month of the year's fulfillings—

"Season of mists and mellow fruitfulness,
Close-bosom'd friend of the maturing sun."

And yet there are other Septembers than the Septembers of memory, than the Septembers of the imagination. For three years past the month has come with rains from the sea and cold winds out of the east and north. The robin's song has been poignantly sweet as of yore, but the dream-glow has been rare upon the hill and valley, and in the woods and on the moor-slopes the leaf has hung bannerets of dusky yellow, and the bracken burned dully without amber and flamelit bronze. This year, though, there has been some return of those September days which we believe in, while yet a long way off, as we believe in May, as we feel assured of June. This last June was truly a month of roses, and in May the east wind slept: but last year the roses trailed along flooded byways, and the east wind nipped bud and blossom through the bleak days of "the merry month," and a colourless and forlorn September must have chilled even that "darke fyre in the heartes of poetes" of which the old naturalist wrote.

September

There have been days of peace this year, and of the whole beauty of Summer-end. In the isles, among the hills, on forest lands and uplands, and by the long plains and valleys of the south, the September blue—which is part a flame of azure and part a haze of the dust of pearls—has lain over land and sea like a benediction. How purple the western moors, what depths of floating violet and pale translucencies of amethyst on the transfigured mountains. What loveliness of pale blue mist in the hollows of quiet valleys; what richness of reds and ambers where the scarlet-fruited ash hangs over the unruffled brown pool; what profuse gold and ungathered amber where the yellow gorse climbs the hillside and the armies of the bracken invade every windy solitude. How lovely those mornings when the dew is frost-white and the gossamer is myriad in intricate interlacings that seem woven of aërial diamond-dust. What peace in that vast serenity of blue where not the smallest cloud is seen, where only seaward the gannet may hang immeasurably high like a winged star, or, above inland pastures, the windhover poise in his miraculous suspense.

But, alas, only "days." It has not been the September of the heart's desire, of the poet's dream. The advance-guard of the equinox

September

has again and again come in force: the grey wind has wailed from height to height, and moaned among the woods. Even in the gardens the wall-fruits have hardly given the wonted rich warmth, though the apples have made a brave show. Yesterday there was a hush in the wind; a delicate frost lingered after a roseflusht dawn; and the inward light came out of the heather, the bracken and the gorse, out of the yellow limes and the amber planes and the changing oaks, and upon the hillside turned the great pine on the further crag into a column of pale gold and made the lichened boulders like the half-sunken gates of buried cities of topaz and jasper and chalcedony. But to-day vast masses of sombre cloud have been swung inland from the Atlantic, and the gale as the wild mournful sough that we look for in the dark months. It is in the firelight that one must recapture September. It lies hidden in that warm heart, amid the red and yellow flowers of flame; and in that other heart, which, also, has its "darke fyre," that heart in whose lands lit by neither sun nor moon are the secret glens where old dreams live again, and where the dreams of the hour are radiant in their new wonder and their new beauty.

THE CHILDREN OF WIND AND THE CLAN OF PEACE

I was abroad on the moors one day in the company of a shepherd, and we were talking of the lapwing that were plentiful there, and were that day wailing continuously in an uneasy wavering flight. I had seen them act thus, in this excess of alarm, in this prolonged restless excitement, when the hill-falcons were hovering overhead in the nesting season: and, again, just before the unloosening of wind and rain and the sudden fires of the thundercloud. But John Logan the shepherd told me that now it was neither coming lightnings nor drifting hawk nor eagle that made all this trouble among the "peewits." "The wind's goin' to mak' a sudden veer," he said—adding abruptly a little later, "an' by the same token we'll have rain upon us soon."

I looked at the cold blue of the sky, and at the drift of the few clouds trailing out of the east or south-east, and could see no sign of any change of wind or likelihood of rain.

"What makes you think that?" I asked.

"Weel," he answered literally, "I don't think it. It's the peewits an' the craws that ken swifter than oursel; it's they that tell, an' I think they're better at the business than thae folk wha haver awa' in the papers, an' are sometimes richt because they canna help it an' oftener wrang because it's maistly guess-work."

"Well, what do the peewits and the crows say?—though I haven't seen crow or rook or corbie for the last hour."

"Thae peewits an' a' the plovers are a' the same. If the win's gaun to leap out of the east intae the sooth-wast, or slide quickly from the north intae the wast, they'll gang on wheelin' an' wailin' like you for an hour or mair, an' that afore there's the least sign o' a change. An' as for the craws .., weel, if ye had been lookin' up a wee whilie ago ye'd 'a seen a baker's dozen go by, slantin' on the edge o' the win', like boats before a stiff breeze. Aye, an' see there! . . . there's a wheen mair comin' up overhead."

I glanced skyward, and saw some eight or ten rooks flying high and evidently making for the mountain-range about two miles away to our left.

"D'ye see that . . . thae falling birds?"

"Yes," I answered, noticing a singular occasional fall in the general steady flight, as though the suddenly wheeling bird had been shot: "and what o' that, John?"

"It's just this: when ye see craws flyin' steady like that an' then yince in a while drapping oot like yon, ye may tak' it as meanin' there's heavy rain no that great way aff: onyways, when ye see the like when thae black deils are fleein' straight for the hills, ye maun feel sure frae the double sign that ye'll hae a good chance o' being drookit afore twa-three hours."

One question led to another, and I heard much crow and corbie lore from John Logan, some of it already familiar to me and some new to me or vaguely half-known—as the legend that the corbies or ravens, and with them all the crow-kind, were originally white, but at the time of the Deluge were turned sooty-black because the head of the clan, when sent out by Noah from the Ark, did not return, but stayed to feed on the bodies of the drowned. "So the blackness of death was put on them, as my old mother has it in her own Gaelic."

"Your old mother, John?" I queried surprisedly: "I did not know you had any one at your croft."

"Aye, but I have that, though she's a poor

frail auld body an' never gangs further frae the hoose than the byre an' the hen-yaird. If ye want to hear more aboot thae birds an' the auld stories forenenst them, she'd mak' you welcome, an' we'd be glad an' prood to offer ye tea: an' I'll just tell ye this, that ye'll gie her muckle pleasure if ye'll hae a crack wi' her in the Gaelic, an' let her tell her auld tales in't. She's Hielan', ye ken: tho' my faither was oot o' Forfar, Glen Isla way. She's never got hold o' the English yet varra weel, an' to my sorrow I've never learnt the auld tongue, takin' after my faither in that, dour lowland body as he was. I ken enough to follow her sangs, an' a few words forbye, just enough to gie us a change as ye micht say."

I gladly accepted the shepherd's courteous offer; and so it was that an hour later we found ourselves at Scaui-vàn, as his croft was called, from its nearness to a great bleached crag that rose out of the heather like a light-ship in a lonely sea. By this time, his prognostications—or those rather of the wheeling and wailing lapwings, and the mountain-flying rooks—had come true. Across the wide desolate moors a grey wind soughed mournfully from the south-west, driving before it long slanting rains and sheets of drifting mist. I was glad to be out of the cold wet, and in the warm comfort of a room lit with a glowing peat-fire on which lay one or two spurtling logs of pine.

A dear old woman rose at my entrance. I could see she was of great age, because her face was like a white parchment seamed with a myriad of wrinkles, and her hands were so sere and thin that they were like wan leaves of October. But she was fairly active, and her eyes were clear—and even, if the expression may be used, with a certain quiet fire in their core—and her features were comely, with a light on them as of serene peace. The old-fashioned white mutch she wore enhanced this general impression, and I remember smiling to myself at the quaint conceit that old Mrs. Logan was like a bed-spirit of ancient slumber looking out from an opening of frilled white curtains.

It was pleasant to sit and watch her, as with deft hands she prepared the tea and laid on the table scones and butter and grey farrels of oatcake, while, outside, the wet wind moaned and every now and then a swirl of rain splashed against the narrow panes of the window, in whose inset stood three pots of geranium with scarlet flowers that caught the red flicker of the fire-flaucht and warmed the grey dusk gathering without.

The Children of Wind and the Clan of Peace

Later, we began to speak of the things of which her son John and I had talked on the moor: and then of much else in connection with the legendary lore of the birds and beasts of the hills and high moorlands.

As it was so much easier for her (and so far more vivid and idiomatic) she spoke in Gaelic, delighted to find one who could understand the ancient speech: for in that part of the country, though in the Highlands, no Gaelic is spoken, or only a few words or phrases connected with sport, sheep-driving, and the like. I had won her heart by saying to her soon after the tea—up to which time she had spoken in the slow and calculated but refined Highland-English of the north-west—*Tha mi cinnteach gu bheil sibh aois mhór* . . . "I am sure that you have the great age on you." She had feared that because I had "the English way" I would not know, or remember, or care to remember, the old tongue: and she took my hand and stroked it while she said with a quiet dignity of pleasure, *Is taitneach leam nach 'eil 'ur Gàidhlig air meirgeadh* . . . (in effect) "It is well pleased I am that your Gaelic has not become rusty."

It was after the tea-things had been set aside, and old Mrs. Logan had said reverently, *Iarramaid beannachadh* ("Let us ask a bless-

The Children of Wind and the Clan of Peace

ing "), that she told me, among other legendary things and fragments of old natural-history folklore, the following legend (or holy Christmas tale, as she called it) as to how the first crows were black and the first doves white.

I will tell it as simply but also with what beauty I can, because her own words, which I recall only as the fluctuating remembrance from a dream and so must translate from the terms of dream into the terms of prose, though simple were beautiful with ancient idiom.

Thus she began:—*Feumaidh sinn dol air ar n'-ais dlùth fichead ceud bliadhna*, which is to say, "We must go back near two thousand *(lit: twenty hundred)* years."

Yes, it is nigh upon twenty hundred years that we must go back. It was in the last month of the last year of the seven years' silence and peace. When would that be, you ask? Surely what other would it be than the seven holy years when Jesus the Christ was a little lad. Do you not remember the lore of the elders? . . . that in the first seven years of the life of the young Christ there was peace in the world, and that the souls of men were like souls in a dream, and that the hearts of women were at rest. In the second seven years it is said that the world was like an adder that sloughs its skin: for there was everywhere a troubled sense of new things to come. So wide and far and deep was this, that men in remote lands began moving across swamps and hills and deserts; that the wild beasts shifted their lairs and moaned and cried in new forests and upon untrodden plains; that the storks and swallows in their migration wearied their wings in high, cold, untravelled ways; that the narwhals and great creatures of the deep foamed through unknown seas; that the grasses of the world wandered and inhabited hills; that many waters murmured in the wilderness and that many waters mysteriously sank from pools and wellsprings. In the third seven years, men even on the last ocean-girdled shores were filled with further longing, and it is said that new stars were flung into the skies and ancient stars were whirled away, like dust and small stones beneath the wheels of a chariot. It was at the end of the third seven years that a Face looked out of Heaven, and that from the edges of the world men heard a confused and dreadful sound rising from the Abyss. Though the great and the small are the same, it is the great that withdraws from remembrance

The Children of Wind and the Clan of Peace

and the small that remains, and that may be why men have grown old with time, and have forgotten, and remember only the little things of the common life: as that in these years the Herring became the king of all fishes, because his swift gleaming clan carried the rumour of great tidings to the uttermost places of ocean; as that in these years the little fly became king over lions and panthers and eagles and over all birds and beasts, because it alone of all created things had remained tameless and fearless; as that in these years the wild-bees were called the Clan of Wisdom, because they carried the Word to every flower that grows and spread the rumour on all the winds of the world; as that in these years the Cuckoo was called the Herald of God, because in his voice are heard the bells of Resurrection.

But, as I was saying, it was in the last month of the last year of the seven years' silence and peace: the seventh year in the mortal life of Jesus the Christ. It was on the twenty-fifth day of that month, the day of His holy birth.

It was a still day. The little white flowers that were called Breaths of Hope and that we now call Stars of Bethlehem were so husht in quiet that the shadows of moths lay on them like the dark motionless violet in the hearts of pansies. In the long swards of tender grass the multitude of the daisies were white as milk faintly stained with flusht dews fallen from roses. On the meadows of white poppies were long shadows blue as the blue lagoons of the sky among drifting snow-white moors of cloud. Three white aspens on the pastures were in a still sleep: their tremulous leaves made no rustle, though there was a soundless wavering fall of little dusky shadows, as in the dark water of a pool where birches lean in the yellow hour of the frostfire. Upon the pastures were ewes and lambs sleeping, and yearling kids opened and closed their onyx eyes among the garths of white clover.

It was the Sabbath, and Jesus walked alone. When He came to a little rise in the grass He turned and looked back at the house where His parents dwelled. Joseph sat on a bench, with bent shoulders, and was dreaming with fixt gaze into the west, as seamen stare across the interminable wave at the pale green horizons that are like the grassy shores of home. Mary was standing, dressed in long white raiment, white as a lily, with her right hand shading her eyes as she looked to the east, dreaming her dream.

The young Christ sighed, but with the love

The Children of Wind and the Clan of Peace

of all love in His heart. "So shall it be till the day of days," He said aloud; "even so shall the hearts of men dwell among shadows and glories, in the West of passing things: even so shall that which is immortal turn to the East and watch for the coming of Joy through the Gates of Life."

At the sound of His voice He heard a sudden noise as of many birds, and turned and looked beyond the low upland where He stood. A pool of pure water lay in the hollow, fed by a ceaseless wellspring, and round it and over it circled birds whose breasts were grey as pearl and whose necks shone purple and grass-green and rose. The noise was of their wings, for though the birds were beautiful they were voiceless and dumb as flowers.

At that edge of the pool stood two figures, whom He knew to be of the angelic world because of their beauty, but who had on them the illusion of mortality so that the child did not know them. But He saw that one was beautiful as Night, and one beautiful as Morning.

He drew near.

"I have lived seven years," He said, "and I wish to send peace to the far ends of the world."

"Tell your secret to the birds," said one.

The Children of Wind and the Clan of Peace

"Tell your secret to the birds," said the other.

So Jesus called to the birds.

"Come," He cried; and they came.

Seven came flying from the left, from the side of the angel beautiful as Night. Seven came flying from the right, from the side of the angel beautiful as Morning.

To the first He said: "Look into my heart."

But they wheeled about him, and with new-found voices mocked, crying, "How could we see into your heart that is hidden"—and mocked and derided, crying, "What is Peace? Leave us alone! Leave us alone!"

So Christ said to them:

"I know you for the birds of Ahriman, who is not beautiful but is Evil. Henceforth ye shall be black as night, and be children of the winds."

To the seven other birds which circled about Him, voiceless, and brushing their wings against His arms, He cried:

"Look into my heart."

And they swerved and hung before Him in a maze of wings, and looked into His pure heart: and, as they looked, a soft murmurous sound came from them, drowsy-sweet, full of

The Children of Wind and the Clan of Peace

peace: and as they hung there like a breath in frost they became white as snow.

"Ye are the doves of the Spirit," said Christ, "and to you I will commit that which ye have seen. Henceforth shall your plumage be white and your voices be the voices of peace."

The young Christ turned, for He heard Mary calling to the sheep and goats, and knew that dayset was come and that in the valleys the gloaming was already rising like smoke from the urns of the twilight. When He looked back he saw by the pool neither the Son of Joy nor the Son of Sorrow, but seven white doves were in the cedar beyond the pool, cooing in low ecstasy of peace and awaiting through sleep and dreams the rose-red pathways of the dawn. Down the long grey reaches of the ebbing day He saw seven birds rising and falling on the wind, black as black water in caves, black as the darkness of night in the old pathless woods.

And that is how the first doves became white, and how the first crows became black and were called by a name that means the clan of darkness, the children of the wind.

STILL WATERS

Perhaps at no season of the year is the beauty of still waters at once so obvious and so ethereal as in Autumn. All the great painters of Nature have realised this crowning secret of their delicate loveliness. Corot exclaimed to a friend who was in raptures about one of his midsummer river scenes . . . "Yes, yes, but to paint the soul of October, *voilà mon idéal!*" Daubigny himself, that master of slow winding waters and still lagoons, declared that if he had to be only one month out of his studio it would have to be October, "for then you can surprise Nature when she is dreaming, then you may learn her most evanescent and most exquisite secrets." And our own Millais, when he was painting "Chill October" near Murthly, in Perthshire, wrote that nothing had ever caused him so much labour, if nothing had ever given him so much pleasure, in the painting, "for Nature now can be found in a trance, and you can see her as she is." A friend of the late Keeley Halswelle told me that this able artist (who was originally a

Still Waters

"figure" and "subject" painter) remarked to him that he had never realised the supreme charm of autumnal Nature among still waters till he found himself one day trying to translate to his canvas the placid loveliness of the wide, shallow reaches of the Avon around Christchurch. Doubtless many other painters, French and Dutch and English, have felt thus, and been glad to give their best to the interpretation of the supreme charm of still waters in autumn. What would Venice be without them . . . Amsterdam . . . Holland . . . Finland . . . Sweden? Imagine Scotland without this water-beauty, from Loch Ken to Loch Maree, from the Loch of the Yowes to the "thousand-waters" of Benbecula; or Ireland, where the white clouds climbing out of the south may mirror themselves in still waters all day till they sink beyond the Lough of Shadows in the Silent north.

The phrase is as liberal as "running water." That covers all inland waters in motion, from the greatest rivers to the brown burn of the hillside, from the melting of the snows in fierce spate to the swift invasion and troubled floods of the hurrying and confined tides. So "still waters" covers lakes and mountain-lochs, shallow meres, lagoons, the reaches of slow rivers, lochans, tarns, the dark, brown pools in peat-moors, or the green-blue pools in open woods and shadowy forests, the duckweed-margined ponds at the skirts of villages, the lilied ponds of old manor-garths and of quiet gardens, asleep beneath green canopies or given over to the golden carp and the dragon-fly beneath mossed fountains or beyond time-worn terraces. Often, too, and in February and October above all, the low-lying lands are flooded, and the bewildered little lives of the pastures crowd the hedgerows and copses. Sometimes for days, motionless, these mysterious lake-arrivals abide under the grey sky, sometimes a week or weeks pass before they recede. The crow flying home at dusk sees the pale cloud and the orange afterglow reflected in an inexplicable mirror where of late the grey-green grass and brown furrow stretched for leagues: the white owl, hawking the pastures after dusk, swoops so low on his silent wings that he veers upward from a ghostly flying image underneath, as a bat at sundown veers from the phantom of its purblind flight.

Delicate haze, cloud-dappled serenity, and moonlight are the three chief qualities of beauty in the charm of still waters. It is a matter of temperament, of the hour and occasion also no doubt, whether one prefer those

Still Waters

where another dream-world, that of human life, companions them in the ineffable suspense of the ideal moment, the moment where the superfluous recedes, where silence and stillness consummate the miraculous vision. Those moonlit lagoons of Venice, which become scintillating floods of silver or lakes of delicate gold, where the pole-moored *sandolò* thrusts a black wedge of shadow into the motionless drift, while an obscure figure at the prow idly thrums a mandolin or hums drowsily a *conzonnetto d'amore;* those twilit canals where old palaces lean and look upon their ancient beauty stilled and perfected in sleep; how unforgettable they are, how they thrill even in remembrance. In the cities of Holland, how at one are the old houses with the mirroring canals, in still afternoons when quiet light warms the red wall, and dwells on the brown and scarlet clematis in the cool violet and amber hollows of the motionless water wherein the red wall soundlessly slips and indefinitely recedes, hiding an undiscovered house of shadow with silent unseen folk dreaming out across invisible gardens. There are ancient towns like this in England also, as between Upsala and Elsinore to where old châteaux in Picardy guard the pollarded marais, or deserted Breton manors stand

Still Waters

ghostly at the forest-end of untraversed meres.

These have their charm. But have they for us the intimate and unchanging spell of the lakes and meres and other still waters of our own land? Nothing, one might think, could be more beautiful than to see in the Lake of Como the cypresses of Bellaggio and the sloping gardens of Cadenabbia meeting in a new underwater wonderland: or to see Mont Blanc, forty miles away, sleeping in snow-held silence in the blue depths of Lac Léman: or to see Pilatus and a new city of Lucerne mysteriously changed and yet familiarly upbuilded among the moving green lawns and azure avenues of the Lake of the Four Cantons. And yet leaning boulders of granite, yellow with lichen and grey with moss and deep-based among swards of heather and the green nomad bracken, will create a subtler magic in the brown depths of any Highland loch. There is a subtler spell in the solitary tarn, where the birch leans out of the fern and throws an intricate tracery of bough and branch into the unmoving wave, where the speckled trout and the speckled mavis meet as in the strange companionships of dreams. Enchantment lies amid the emerald glooms of pine and melancholy spruce,

Still Waters

when a dream-world forest underneath mirrors the last sunset-gold on bronze cones, and enfolds the one white wandering cloud miraculously stayed at last between two columnar green spires, flawless as sculptured jade.

Is this because, in the wilderness, we recover something of what we have lost? . . . because we newly find ourselves, as though surprised into an intimate relationship of which we have been unaware or have indifferently ignored? What a long way the ancestral memory has to go, seeking, like a pale sleuth-hound among obscure dusks and forgotten nocturnal silences, for the lost trails of the soul. It is not we only, you and I, who look into the still waters of the wilderness and lonely places, and are often dimly perplext, are often troubled we know not how or why: some forgotten reminiscence in us is aroused, some memory not our own but yet our heritage is perturbed, footsteps that have immemorially sunk in ancient dust move furtively along obscure corridors in our brain, the ancestral hunter or fisher awakes, the primitive hillman or woodlander communicates again with old forgotten intimacies and the secret oracular things of lost wisdoms. This is no fanciful challenge of speculation. In the order of psychology it is as logical as in the order

Still Waters

of biology is the tracing of our upright posture or the deft and illimitable use of our hands, from unrealisably remote periods wherein the pioneers of man reached slowly forward to inconceivable arrivals.

But whatever primitive wildness, whatever ancestral nearness we recover in communion with remote Nature, there is no question as to the fascination of beauty exercised by the still waters of which we speak, of their enduring spell. What lovelier thing in Nature on a serene and cloudless October day, than to come upon a small lake surrounded by tall elms of amber and burnished bronze, by beech and maple and sycamore, cloudy with superb fusion of orange and scarlet and every shade of red and brown, by limes and aspens tremulous with shaken pale gold? Beautiful in itself, in rare and dreamlike beauty, the woods become more beautiful in this silent marriage with placid waters, take on a beauty more rare, a loveliness more dreamlike. There is a haze which holds the fluent gold of the air. Silence is no longer quietude as in June; or a hushed stillness, as in the thunder-laded noons of July or August; but a soundless suspense wherein the spirit of the world, suddenly at rest, sleeps and dreams.

The same ineffable peace broods over all

Still Waters

still waters: on the meres of Hereford, on the fens of East Anglia, on lochs heavy with mountain-shadow, on the long grey Hebridean sheets where the call of the sea-wind or the sea-wave is ever near.

Truly there must be a hidden magic in them, as old tales tell. I recall one wherein the poets and dreamers of the world are called "the children of pools." The poet and dreamer who so called them must have meant by his metaphor those who look into the hearts of men and into the dim eyes of Life, troubled by the beauty and mystery of the world, insatiable in longing for the ineffable and the unattainable. So, long ago, even "ornamental waters" may have been symbols of the soul's hunger and thirst, emblems of the perpetual silence and mystery of his fugitive destiny!

Somewhere, I think it is in the *Kalevala*, occurs the beautiful metaphor of still waters "the mirrors of the world." Whoever the ancient singer was who made the phrase, he had in his heart love for still waters as well as the poet's mind. The secret of their beauty is in that image. It may be a secret within a secret, for the mirror may disclose a world invisible to us, may reflect what our own or an ancestral memory dimly recalls, may reveal

Still Waters

what the soul perceives and translates from its secret silences into symbol and the mysterious speech of the imagination.

Still Waters; it has the inward music that lies in certain words . . . amber, ivory, foam, silence, dreams: that lies often in some marriage of words . . . moonlight at sea, wind in dark woods, dewy pastures, old sorrowful things: that dwells in some names of things, as chrysoprase; or in some combination of natural terms and associations, as wind and wave; or in some names of women and dreams, Ruth, Alaciel, Imogen, Helen, Cleopatra; or in the words that serve in the courts of music . . . cadence, song, threnody, epithalamium, viol, flute, prelude, fugue. One can often evade the heavy airs of the hours of weariness by the spell of one of these wooers of dreams. *Foam*—and the hour is gathered up like mist, and we are amid "perilous seas in faëry lands forlorn": *Wind*—and the noises of the town are like the humming of wild bees in old woods, and one is under ancient boughs listening, or standing solitary in the dusk by a forlorn shore with a tempestuous sea filling the darkness with whispers and confused rumours and incommunicable things: *Ruth*—and sorrow and exile are become loveliness: *Helen*—and that immemorial desire is

Still Waters

become *our* desire, and that phantom beauty is become *our* dream and *our* passion. *Still Waters*—surely through that gate the mind may slip away from the tedious and unwelcome, and be alone among forests where the birch leans and dreams into an amber-brown pool, or by a mountain-lake where small white clouds lie like sleeping birds, or on moonlit lagoons where the reed and the reed's image are as one, and the long mirrors are unshaken by any wandering air, unvisited but by the passing soundless shadows of travelling winds.

THE PLEIAD-MONTH

From the Persian shepherd to the shepherd on the hills of Argyll—in a word, from the remote East to the remote West—November is known, in kindred phrase, as the Pleiad-Month.

What a world of legend, what a greater world of poetry and old romance, centres in this little group of stars. "The meeting-place in the skies of mythology and science," as they have been called by one of our chief astronomers. From time immemorial this remote starry cluster has been associated with festivals and solemnities, with auguries and destinies. On November 17, the day of the midnight culmination of the Pleiades, the great Festival of Isis was begun at Busiris: in ancient Persia, on that day, no petition was presented in vain to the King of Kings: and on the first of the month the midnight rites of our own ancestral Druids were connected with the rising of the Pleiades. To-day the South Sea Islanders of the Society and Tonga Isles divide the year by their seaward rising

The Pleiad-Month

and setting. The *Matarii i nia*, or season of the "Pleiades Above," begins when in the evening this stellar group appears on the horizon, and while they remain above it: the *Matarii i raro*, or season of the "Pleiades Below," begins when after sunset they are no longer visible, and endures till once again they appear above the horizon. The most spiritual and the most barbaric races are at one in considering them centres of the divine energy. The Hindûs imaged them as Flame, typical of Agni, God of Fire, the Creative Energy: the several Persian words, from the ancient *Perv* or the *Parur* of Hafiz or the *Parwin* of Omar Khayyam—derive from *Peru*, a word signifying "The Begetters"; and we know that the Greeks oriented to them or to their *lucida* not only the first great temple of Athenê on the Acropolis, but its successor four hundred years later, the Hecatompedon of 1150 B.C., and seven hundred years later the Parthenon on the same side. [The great shrine of Dionysos at Athens, the still earlier Asclepieion at Epidaurus, and the temple of Poseidon at Sunium, looked towards the Pleiades at their setting.] But far removed from these are the Malays and Pacific islanders, who more vaguely and crudely revere "the central fires," and even so primitive and remote a

The Pleiad-Month

people as the Abipones of the Paraguay River country worship them as their Great Spirit——*Groaperikie*, or Grandfather — and chant hymns of joy to this Pleiad-Allfather when, after the vernal Equinox, the mysterious cluster once more hangs visible in the northern sky.

It would be impossible, in a brief paper, to cover the ground of the nomenclature, of the literature, of scientific knowledge and speculation concerning the Pleiades. A long chapter in a book might be given to Alcyone alone—that bright particular star of which it has been calculated that, in comparison, our Sun would sink to a star below the tenth magnitude. Indeed, though the imagination strains after the astronomer's calm march with dazzled vision, our solar brilliancy is supposed to be surpassed by some sixty to seventy of the Pleiadic group, for all that our human eyes have from time immemorial seen therein only a small cluster of tiny stars, the "seven" of Biblical and poetic and legendary lore, from "the Seven Archangels" to the popular "Hen and her six chicks." Alcyone, that terrible torch of the ultimate heavens, is eighty-three times more refulgent than that magnificent star Sirius, which has been called the "Glory of the South": a thousand times larger than

The Pleiad-Month

our Sun. I do not know how Merope and Taygeta, Celeno and Atlas are, but Maia, that shaking loveliness of purest light, has been calculated to be four hundred times larger than the Sun, and Electra about four hundred and eighty times larger. When one thinks of this mysterious majesty, so vast that only the winged imagination can discern the illimitable idea, all words fail: at most one can but recall the solemn adjuration of the shepherd-prophet Amos, "*Seek Him that maketh Pleiades and Orion,*" or the rapt ecstasy of Isaiah, "*O day star, son of the morning.*"

A Gaelic poet has called them the Lords of Water, saying (though under different names, from the Gaelic mythology) that Alcyone controls the seas and the tides, that Electra is mistress of flood, that Taygeta and Merope and Atlas dispense rains and augment rivers and feed the well-springs, and that Maia's breath falls in dew. The detail is fanciful; the central thought is in accord with legend and old wisdom. I do not know how far back the connection of the Pleiades with water, particularly rains and the rising of rivers, has been traced. It runs through many ancient records. True, in one place, Hesiod speaks of "retreating from the burn-

The Pleiad-Month

ing heat of the Pleiades," and mention has already been made of the Hindu association of them with " Flame." But Hesiod's allusion is a seasonal trope, and natural to one living in a warm country where the coming of the autumnal rains coincides with days of sweltering closeness and heat. Moreover, Hesiod himself uses equally deftly other popular imagery as it occurs to him, speaking of the Pleiades, as Homer speaks, as Atlas-born; and again (with Pindar, Simonides and others) likening them to rock-pigeons flying from the Hunter Orion, doubtless from earliest mention of them in ancient legend as a flock of doves, or birds; and again as "the Seven Virgins" and "the Virgin stars"—thus at one with his contemporary, the Hebrew Herdsman-prophet Amos, who called them by a word rendered in the Authorised Version of the Bible as "the seven stars." As for the Hindu symbol, it must be remembered that fire was the supreme sacred and primitive element, and that every begetter of life in any form would naturally be thus associate. The Hindus called the Pleiad-Month (October-November) *Kartik*, and the reason of the great star-festival *Dibali*, the Feast of Lamps, was to show gratitude and joy, after the close of the wet season, for the coming of the Pleiad-days of dry warmth and beauty. The "sweet influences" of the Pleiades thus indicated will come more familiarly to many readers in Milton's

> "the grey
> Dawn and the Pleiades before him danc'd,
> Shedding sweet influence, . . ."

This ancient custom, the "Feast of Lamps," of the Western Hindus survives to-day in the "Feast of Lanterns" in Japan, though few Europeans seem to perceive any significance in that popular festival.

In general, however, we find the advent of the Pleiades concurrent, both in ancient and modern tradition, with springs and rains and floods: with the renewal of life. Thus the comment in the old *Breeches* Bible, opposite the mention of "the mystic seven" in that supreme line in Job: "which starres arise when the sunne is in Taurus, which is the spring time, and bring flowres." A Latin poet, indeed, used *Pliada* as a synonym of showers. Again and again we find them as the *Vergiliae*, Companions of the Spring. They are intimately connected too with traditions of the Deluge: and in this association, perhaps also with that of submerged Atlantis, it is suggestive to note that early in the sixteenth century Cortez heard in that remote, mysterious Aztec

The Pleiad-Month

otherworld to which he penetrated, a very ancient tradition of the destruction of the world in some past age at the time of their midnight culmination. A long way thence to Sappho, who marked the middle of the night by the setting of those wild-doves of the sky! Or, a century later, to Euripides, who calls them *Aelos*, our "Altair," the nocturnal time-keepers.

But to return to that mystery of seven. Although some scholars derive the word "Pleiades" or "Pliades," and in the singular "Plias," from the Greek word *plein*, "to sail," because (to quote an eminent living authority) "the heliacal rising of the group in May marked the opening of navigation to the Greeks, as its setting in the late autumn did the close"—and though others consider that the derivation is from *pleios*, the epic form of the Greek word for "full," or, in the plural, "many"—and so to the equivalent "a cluster," corresponding to the Biblical *Kimah* and the Arabic *Al Thurnyya*, the Cluster, the Many Little Ones—it is perhaps more likely that a less learned and ordinary classical reader may be nearer the mark in considering the most probable derivation to be from Pleione, the nymph of Greek mythology—"Pleione, the mother of the seven sisters," as she

The Pleiad-Month

was called of old. Such an one, too, may remember that certain Greek poets alluded to the Pleiades as the seven doves that carried ambrosia to the infant Zeus.[1] To this day, indeed, a common English designation for the group is "the Seven Sisters": and lovers of English poetry will hardly need to be reminded of kindred allusions, from Chaucer's "Atlantes doughtres seven" to Milton's "the seven Atlantic sisters" (reminiscent here, of course, of Virgil's "Eoæ Atlantides") or to Keats' "The Starry Seven, old Atlas' children." The mediæval Italians had "the seven doves" again *(sette palommiele)*, and to-day their compatriots speak of the "seven dovelets." It would be tiresome to go through the popular Pleiad-nomenclature of all the European races, and a few instances will equally indicate the prevalence, since the Anglo-Saxon *sifunsterri*. Miles Coverdale, in the first complete English Bible, comments on the passage in Job, "these

---

[1] On reading recently a work on mythological ornithology by Mr. D'Arcy Thompson I noticed that he traces the word Botrus, equivalent to a Bunch of Grapes (as the younger Theon likened the Pleiades) οἰνάς, a dove, so called from its purple-red breast like wine, οἶνος, and naturally referred to a bunch of grapes; or perhaps because the bird appeared in migration at the time of the Vintage. [And see his further evidence of Cilician coins.]

vii. starres, the clocke henne with her chickens"; and to-day in Dorset, Devon, and other English counties "the Hen and her Chickens" is a popular term, as it is in effect, with the Wallachians, and indeed, with or without the number seven, throughout Europe. The long continuity and vast range of this association with seven may be traced from the ancient Celtic "The Seven Hounds" to the still more ancient " seven beneficent sky-spirits of the Vedas and the Zend-Avesta " or to the again more ancient " Seven Sisters of Industry " of remote Chinese folklore. This feminine allusion in presumably the oldest mention of a popular designation for the Pleiades is the more singular from the kindred of the Roman writer Manilius—"The narrow Cloudy Train of female stars" . . . *i.e.*, no doubt, Pleione and her daughters.

Nor, again, is it possible to record the many picturesque or homely Pleiad-designations, ancient and modern, in literature and folklore. What range, indeed, to cover . . . since we should have to go back to two thousand years B.C. to recover that fine name, General of the Celestial Armies! It would be tempting to range through the poets of all lands. Think of such lovely words as those from the *Mu'allakât*, as translated by Sir William

The Pleiad-Month

Jones: "It was the hour when the Pleiades appeared in the firmament like the folds of a silken sash variously decked with gems": or that line in Graf's translation of Sadi's *Gulistân* . . . "as though the tops of the trees were encircled by the necklace of the Pleiades": or, of our own day, of a verse such as Roscoe Thayer's:

"slowly the Pleiades
Dropt like dew from bough to bough of the cinnamon trees,"

or lines such as that familiar but ever beautiful couplet in *Locksley Hall:*

"Many a night I saw the Pleiads, rising thro' the mellow shade,
Glitter like a swarm of fireflies tangled in a silver braid."

As for many of the names, what store of old thought and legend they enshrine. "Seamen's starres" our own King Jamie called them, after the popular use. The Finns call them "the Sieve," and the Provençals the "mosquito net," and the Italians "the Battledore." With the nomad Arabs they are "the Herd of Camels." Peoples so apart as the ancient Arabians, the Algerian Berbers of to-day, and the Dyaks of Borneo, have placed in them the seat of immortality. Races as widely severed as the Hebridean Gaels and certain Indian tribes have called them "the Dancers": to the Solomon Islanders they are "a group of girls," and (strange, among so primitive and savage a race) the Australian aborigines thought of them as "Young Girls playing to Young Men dancing." There is perhaps no stranger name than our Gaelic *Crannarain* (though *Grioglachan* or *Meanmnach* is more common), *i.e*, the baker's peel or shovel, from an old legend about a Baker and his wife and six daughters, itself again related to a singular Cuckoo myth.

But an end to this long excerpting from "starry notes"! In a later chapter, too, I propose to write of "Winter Stars," and the Great Bear, and Orion, and the Milky Way—and I must take warning in time to condense better and write "more soothly" as Chaucer has it. So, now, let me end with a quotation from Mr. D'Arcy Thompson's preface to his *Greek Birds*, to which I have alluded in a footnote. "As the White Doves came from Babylon or the Meleagrian Birds from the further Nile, so over the sea and the islands came Eastern legends and Eastern names. And our Aryan studies must not blind us to the presence in an Aryan tongue of these im-

The Pleiad-Month

migrants from Semitic and Egyptian speech, or from the nameless and forgotten language that was spoken by the gods."

Food for thought there, and in many of the other alluded-to clues of old forgotten faiths and peoples, for the Pleiad-Month!

What ages, what rise and fall of kingdoms and great empires, since the Arabian shepherd looked up from the illimitable desert and called this dim cluster, this incalculable congregation of majesty and splendour, *Al Najm*, "the Constellation"... "*the* Constellation": since the first wandering Bedouins halted in the moonlit Sahara to bow before *Al Wasat*, the Central One: since the poets of the Zend-Avesta hailed the overlordship of the Holy Seven! And still they rise, and set, changeless, mysterious. Still the old wonder, the old reverence lives . . . for not long ago I heard a tale told by a Gaelic story-teller who spoke of the Pleiades as the Seven Friends of Christ, and named them newly as Love, Purity, Courage, Tenderness, Faith, Joy, and Peace.

THE RAINY HYADES

"Where is the star Imbrifer? Let us adore it."

Years ago I remember coming upon this mysterious phrase in a poem or poetic drama by a French writer. The pagans, led by a priest, then went into the woods; and, in a hollow made of a hidden place swept by great boughs, worshipped a moist star. I forget whether the scourge of drought ended thereafter, and if winds lifted the stagnant branches, if rains poured through the leaves and mosses and reached the well-springs. I recall only the invocation, and some faint and broken memory of the twilight-procession of bitter hearts and wild voices, weary of vain lamentation and of unanswered prayers to sleeping or silent gods. But often I wondered as to Imbrifer, that dark lord with the sonorous name. Was he a Gaulish divinity, or, as his name signals, a strayed Latin? And was he, as our Manan of the West, a sea-deity, or a divinity of the clouds, clothed, like the shep-

The Rainy Hyades

herd Angus Sunlocks, in mist, so as the more secretly to drive before him down the hidden ways of heaven the myriad hosts of the rain? Or had he an angelic crest, with wings of unfalling water, as a visionary once portrayed for me a likeness of Midir, that ancient Gaelic god at whose coming came and still come the sudden dews, or whose presence, or the signs of whose passage, would be revealed and still are revealed by the white glisten on thickets and grasses, by the moist coolness on the lips of leaf and flower.

The name, too, or one very like it, I heard once in a complicated (and, alas, for the most part forgotten) tale of the Kindred of Manan, the Poseidon of the Gael: remembered because of the singular companionship of three or four other Latin-sounding names, which the old Schoolmaster-teller may have invented, or himself introduced, or mayhap had in the sequence of tradition from some forgotten monkish reciter of old. Aquarius and either Cetus or Delphinius (quaintly given as the Pollack, the porpoise) were of the astronomical company, I remember—and Neptheen or Nepthuinn (Neptune), notwithstanding his oneness with Manan's self.

But Imbrifer had faded from my mind, as though washed away by one of his waves of

The Rainy Hyades

rain or obliterated by one of his dense mists, till the other day. Then, as it happened, I came upon the name once more, in a Latin quotation in an old book. So, he was of the proud Roman clan after all! and, by the context, clearly a divinity of the autumnal rains, and of those also that at the vernal equinox are as a sound of innumerable little clapping hands.

Could he be an astronomical figure, a Zodiacal prince of dominion, I wondered. In vain I searched through all available pages connected with the Hyades, the Stars of Water: in vain, the chronicles of Aquarius, of Cetus and the Dolphin, of Hydra and Pisces and Argo, that proud Ship of March. But last night, sitting by the fire and hearing the first sleet of winter whistle through the dishevelled oaks and soughing firs, when I was idly reading and recalling broken clues in connection with the astrological "House of Saturn," suddenly, in pursuit of a cross-reference to some detail in connection with the constellation of Capricorn, I encountered Imbrifer once more. "Imbrifer, the Rain-Bringing One."

So, then, he is more than an obscure divinity of the woods and of remote ancestral clans! Greater even than Midir of the Dews,

The Rainy Hyades

one of the great Lords of Death: greater than the Greek Poseidon or the Gaelic Manan, heaven-throned among the older gods, though seen of mortals only on gigantic steeds of ocean, vast sea-green horses with feet of running waves and breasts of billows. For he is no other than one of the mightiest of the constellations, Capricorn itself! The name, in a word, is but one of several more or less obscure or forgotten analogues of this famous constellation, concerning which the first printed English astrological almanac (1386) has "whoso is born in Capcorn schal be ryche and wel lufyd"!

Imbrifer himself . . . or itself . . . is certainly not "wel lufyd" on many of these October and November days of floods and rains! *Imbrifer* . . . the very name is a kind of stately, Miltonic, autumnal compeer of our insignificant (and in Scotland, dreaded!) rain-saint of July, Swithin of dubious memory!

Truly a fit Constellation of late autumn, Capricornus.

"Thy Cold, for Thou o'er Winter Signs dost reign,
  Pullst back the Sun . . ."

as a bygone astronomical versifier has it.

The Rainy Hyades

Perhaps he had in mind Horace's "tyrannus Hesperiae Capricornus undae," who in turn may have recalled an earlier poet still, English'd thus:

> ". . . Then grevious blasts
> Break southward on the Sea, when coincide
> The *Goat* and *Sun:* and then a heaven-sent cold."

Many of us will remember with a thrill Milton's magnificent image

> ". . . Thence down amain
> As deep as Capricorn,"

and others will recall the often-quoted line of Dante in the *Paradiso* (relative of the Sun's entrance into Capricorn between January 18 and February 14).

"The horn of the Celestial Goat doth touch the Sun."

May and November are the two "fatal" months with the Celtic peoples: the first because of the influence of the Queen of Faerie (she has many names), and the second because of Midir, who sleeps in November, or, as another legend has it, "goes away" in that month. In that month too the Daughter

The Rainy Hyades

of Midir has departed on her long quest of her brother Aluinn Og (is this a legend or a confused traditionary remembrance, or a mythopoeic invention . . . I have come upon it once only), to find him asleep under the shaken fans of the Northern Lights, and to woo him with pale arctic fires, and auroras, and a faint music wrought out of the murmur of polar airs on a harp made of a seal's breastbone. It is but in another guise the old Greek legend of Persephone in the Kingdom of Aidoneus. Again, it is in November that the touch of Dalua, the Secret Fool or the Accursed of the Everlasting Ones, gives death. Once more, it is in November that Lîr holds his great banquet, a banquet that lasts three months, in Tir-fo-tuinn, the Country under the waves. In one way or another all these dreams are associated with the sea, with water and the Winter Solstice. By different ways of thought, of tradition, and of dreaming phantasy, the minds of this race or that people, of these scattered tribes or those broken clans, have reached the same strange goals of the imagination. The spell of Capricorn may be of the Waters of all time, since the Horned Goat of our Celtic forbears, the "Buccan Horn" of our Anglo-Saxon ancestors, the Latin "Imbrifer" or "Gelidus" or

The Rainy Hyades

"Sea-Goat" (in several variants), the Greek "Athalpees" or the commoner term signifying a Horned Goat, the ancient Egyptian Chnemu, God of the Waters, the perhaps as ancient Aztec Cipactli, imaged like the narwhal, the Chinese Mo Ki and the Assyrian Munaxa, both signifying Goat Fish—and so forth, East and West, in the dim past and the confused present,—are all directly or indirectly associated with the element of Water, with the Sea, or rains, storm and change and subtle regeneration. The Greek writers called the allied constellation of Aquarius Hydrochoüs, the Water-Pourer, in mythological connection (a Latin commentator avers) with Deucalion and the great Flood, that many believe to have been an ancestral memory of the Deluge which submerged Atlantis. The Anglo-Saxons gave it the same name, "se waetergyt." There is a breton legend in connection with Ys, that dim Celtic remembrance of vanished Lyonesse or drowned Atlantis, to the effect (for I know it only in modern guise) that on the fatal night when King Gradlon saw his beautiful city unloosened to the devouring waves by Dahut the Red, his Daughter, the Star of Water shook a fiery rain upon land and sea, and the floods of heaven fell, from the wake of the Great Galley (the Great Bear) to

The Rainy Hyades

the roots of the unseen tree that bears the silver Apples (the Pleiades), and as far as the hidden Well-springs (the Constellation of *Capricorn*) and The Mansion of the White King (the Constellation of Aquarius)—the White King being water personified.

Nearly all the ancient Greek and Asian analogues for the last named, Aquarias, relate to water. One of the few old-world exceptions was that Roman Zodiac on which the constellation figured as a peacock, symbol of Hêrê (Juno), because that in her month Gamelion (part January, part February) the sun enters this sign. The Greek Islanders of Ceos called it Aristaeus, in memory of a native Rain Bringer. Another name was Cecrops, because the Cicada or Field-cricket is nourished by the dews and has its eggs hatched by the vernal rains. It would be wearisome to collate superfluous instances. Enough, now, that the Arab, the Persian, the Syrian and the Israelite, were at one with the Hellene and the Anglo-Saxon in the designation of the Water-Pourer, or an equivalent such as the Arabian *Al Dalw*, the Well-Bucket: that in China of old its sign was recognised as a symbol of the Emperor Tchoun Hin, the Chinese Deucalion: and that still among the astrologers of Central Asia and Japan it has

The Rainy Hyades

for emblem the Rat, the far-Asiatic ideograph for water. Strange too that Star-Seers so remote as the Magi of the East and the Druids of the West should centrate their stellar science on this particular constellation. And, once more, not less strange that alike by the banks of the Euphrates where it was called the Star of Mighty Destiny, on the Arabian Sands where it was called the Fortune of all Fortune, and in the Druidic woods of the Gaul and the Gael where too it symbolised Fortune, a star of its group should be the Star of Fortune—the group alluded to by Dante in the *Purgatorio;*

> ". . . geomancers their Fortuna Major
> See in the Orient before the dawn . . ."

Again, is it tradition or coincidence that the Platonists of old held "the stairs of Capricorn" to be the stellar way by which the souls of men ascended to heaven, so that the constellation became known as the Gate of the Gods, and that to-day the astrologers and mystics of the West share the same belief? Even the Caer Arianrod of our Celtic forbears —the Silver Road, as generally given though obviously very loosely . . . and may not the name more likely, especially in connection

The Rainy Hyades

with a basic legend of the constellation of Corona Borealis, be the "Mansion of Ariand" (Ariadne)? . . . though commonly applied to the Milky Way or less often to the Northern Crown, is sometimes in its modern equivalent used to designate Capricorn. Naturally, to astrologers, this Constellation with that of Aquarius, is of greatest import, for at a certain time "the House of Saturn" is here to be discerned.

It is a drop from such sounding names as these to "the Skinker." Yet by this name our English forefathers probably knew in common speech the constellation of Aquarius. At any rate a Mr. Cock, "Philomathemat," in a rare book of some 200 years ago, *Meteorologiae*, speaks of Aquarius by this singular name, and as though it were the familiar and accepted designation: "Jupiter in the Skinker opposed by Saturn in the Lion did raise mighty Southwest Winds." Here again in this old English word, meaning a tapster, we have an analogue of the Water-Pourer, that universal Zodiacal sign of Aquarius.

But for all that Horace, and following him James Thomson in the *Seasons* ("Winter"), say of "Fierce Aquarius staining the inverted year," the constellation is more associated with the rain-tides of spring. It

The Rainy Hyades

is then, too, in mid-February to mid-March, that, following its passage through Capricorn, the Sun enters it—so that "benign" and not "fierce" becomes the apt epithet.

All these "watery constellations"—Aquarius, Capricorn, Cetus, the Dolphin, Hydra, Pisces—are set aside, in the mouths of poets and in the familiar lore of the many, for the Hyades, that lovely sestet of Taurus which in these winter-months are known to all of us, where they flash and dance south-east of the Silver Apples of childhood's sky—the clustered Pleiades. They have become the typical stars of the onset of winter—The Lords of Rain—"sad companions of the turning year" as an old Roman poet calls them, "the seaman noted Hyades" of Euripides, "the Boar-Throng" (feeders on the mast brought down in late October and November by the autumnal rains) of our Anglo-Saxon fathers, the "Storm-Star" of Pliny, the Moist Daughters of Spenser, so much more familiar to us in Tennyson's.

"Thro' scudding drifts the rainy Hyades
Vext the dim sea."

Of old the whole group was called Aldebaran, but now we recognise in that name only the

The Rainy Hyades

superb star whose pale-rose flame lights gloriously "the cold forehead of the wintry sky," to quote an undeservedly forgotten poet. And now, Aldebaran stands apart in Taurus, and the six storm-stars are torches set apart.

Well, the Season of the Rainy Hyades has come. The Water-Pourer, the Whale and swift Dolphin, Pisces ("Leaders of the Celestial Host" and "the Diadem of November"), Hydra the Water-Snake, every Rain-Star, from flashing Corona, Bride of the White Hawk, to the far southern torch of splendid Achernar in Eridanus the Celestial River, all have lent the subtle influences of the first of the Elements, Water. In the mystic's language, we are now in the season when the soul may least confusedly look into its life as in a shaken mirror, and when the spirit may "look before and after." For, they tell us, in the occult sense, we are the Children of Water.

To-night, looking at the Hyades, dimmed in a vaporous haze foretelling coming storm, as yet afar off, I find myself, I know not why, and in a despondency come I know not whence, thinking of and repeating words I read to-day in a translation of the *Bhagavad Gita*:—"I am in the hearts of all. Memory and Knowledge, and the loss of both, are all

The Rainy Hyades

from Me. There are two entities in this world, the Perishable and the Imperishable. All creatures are the Perishable and the unconcerned One is the Imperishable."

The unconcerned One!

WINTER STARS

I

To know in a new and acute way the spell of the nocturnal skies, it is not necessary to go into the exerlasting wonder and fascination of darkness with an astronomer, or with one whose knowledge of the stars can be expressed with scholarly exactitude. For the student it is needful to know, for example, that the Hyades are Alpha, Delta, Eta, etc., of *Tauri*, and lie 10° south-east of the Pleiades. But as one sits before the fireglow, with one's book in hand to suggest or one's memory to remind, it is in another way as delightful and as fascinating to repeat again to oneself how Tennyson in *Ulysses* speaks of this stellar cluster as

> " Thro' scudding drifts the rainy Hyades
> Vext the dim sea . . ."

or how Christopher Marlowe wrote of them

> " As when the seaman sees the Hyades
> Gather an army of Cimmerian clouds,
> Auster and Aquilon with winged steeds . . ."

to recall how Spenser alludes to them as "the Moist Daughters," or how our Anglo-Saxon ancestors called them "the Boar-Throng." One must know that Alpha of Boötes is the astronomical signature of the greater Arcturus, but how much it adds to the charm of this star's interest for us to learn that among its popular names are the Herdsman, the Bear-Watcher, the Driver of the Wain, and to know why these now familiar names were given and by whom. One may grasp the significance of the acquired knowledge that this vast constellation of Boötes stretches from the constellation of Draco to that of Virgo, and the numeration of its degrees in declination and ascension, and (if one may thus choose between the 85 and the 140 of astronomers) that it contains a hundred stars visible to the naked eye. But, for some of us at least, there is something as memorable, something as revealing, in a line such as that of the Persian poet Hafiz, as paraphrased by Emerson,

"Poises Arcturus aloft morning and evening his spear"—

or that superb utterance of Carlyle in *Sartor Resartus*,

"What thinks Boötes of them, as he leads his Hunting Dogs over the zenith in their leash of sidereal fire?"

Winter Stars

Not, I may add in parenthesis, that the seekers after astronomical knowledge should depend on the poets and romancers for even an untechnical accuracy. Literature, alas, is full of misstatements concerning the moon and stars. Few poets are accurate as Milton is magnificently accurate, his rare slips lying within the reach of a knowledge achieved since his day: or as Tennyson is accurate. Carlyle himself, quoted above in so beautiful a passage, has made more than one strange mistake for (as he once aspired to be) a student astronomer: not only, as in one instance, making the Great Bear for ever revolve round Boötes, but, in a famous passage in his *French Revolution*, speaking of Orion and the Pleiades glittering serenely over revolutionary Paris on the night of 9th August 1792, whereas, as some fact-loving astronomer soon pointed out, Orion did not on that occasion rise till daybreak. It has been said of the Moon, in fiction, that her crescents and risings and wanings are to most poets and novelists apparently an inexplicable mystery, an unattainable knowledge. Even a writer who was also a seaman and navigator, Captain Marryat, writes in one of his novels of a waning crescent moon seen in the early evening. The great Shakespeare himself wrote of the Pole Star as immutable, as the one unpassing, the one fixt and undeviating star—

> ". . . constant as the Northern Star,
> Of whose true fixed and lasting quality
> There is no fellow in the firmament."

This was, of course, ignorance of what has since been ascertained, and not uninstructedness or mere hearsay. Possibly, too, he had in mind rather that apparent unchanging aloofness from the drowning sea-horizon to which Homer alludes in the line beautifully translated "Arctos, sole star that never bathes in the ocean wave" . . . of which, no doubt, our great poet had read in the quaint delightful words of Chaucer (rendering Boetius)— "Ne the sterre y-cleped 'the Bere,' that enclyneth his ravisshinge courses abouten the soverein heighte of the worlde, ne the same sterre Ursa nis nevet-mo wasshen in the depe westrene see, no coveitith nat to deyen his flaumbe in the see of the occian, al-thogh he see other sterres y-plounged in the see."

That constellation "y-cleped the Bere," how profoundly it has impressed the imagination of all peoples. In every age, in every country, our kindred on lonely lands, on lonely seas, from caverns and camp-fires and great towers, have watched it "incline its ravishing

Winter Stars

courses" about the Mountain of the North, "coveting not" to drown its white fires in the polar seas. Here, however, it is strange to note the universality of the Ursine image with the Greeks and Romans and the nations of the South, and the universality with the Teutonic peoples of designations such as the Wain and the Plough. It was not till the Age of Learning set in among the Northern peoples that the classic term came into common use. Thus in a tenth-century Anglo-Saxon manual of astronomy the writer, in adopting the Greek Arctos (still used occasionally instead of the Bear), adds "which untaught men call Carleswæn," that is Charles's Wain, the Waggon. A puzzling problem is why a designation which primarily arose from an association of the early Greeks concerning Arkas, their imaginary racial ancestor, with Kallisto his mother, who had been changed into a great bear in the heavens, should also suggest itself to other peoples, to races so remote in all ways as the North American Indians. Yet before the white man had visited the tribes of North America, the red men called the constellation by names signifying a bear. The historian Bancroft has proved that alike among the Algonquins of the Atlantic and of the Mississippi, among the Eastern Narragansett nations and among the nations of the Illinois, the Bear was the accepted token.

Boötes, the Great Bear, the Little Dipper or Ursa Minor, these great constellations, with their splendid beacons Arcturus, the Triones or the Seven Hounds of the North, and the Pole Star—

> "By them, on the deep,
> The Achaians gathered where to sail their ships—

and in like fashion all the races of man since Time was have "gathered" the confusing ways of night on all lonely seas and in all lonely lands.

But best of all, to know this spell of the nocturnal skies, one should be in the company of fisher-folk or old seamen or shepherds, perchance unlettered but wise in traditional lore and leal to the wisdom of their fathers. How much more I value what I have heard from some shepherd on the wide dark moors, or from some islesman in a fishing-coble or drifting wherry, on moonless nights filled with a skyey "phosphorescence" as radiant as that a-dance and a-gleam in the long seethe of the wake of a ship, than what I have found concerning scientific star-names in books of astronomy. Nothing that I have since learned of "the Pointers" has impressed me so much

Winter Stars

as what I learned as a child of "the Hounds of Angus," nor, in later and fuller knowledge of Polaris, has the child's first knowledge of the mystery and wonder of "the Star of Wisdom," as pointed out and tale-told by an old Hebridean fisherman, or of "the House of Dreams," as sung to me in a forgotten ballad by a Gaelic woman of Argyll, been surpassed.

It was they—herdsmen and mariners, the wayfarer, the nomad, the desert-wanderer—who, of old, gave these names to which the nations have grown used. It was with the nomad that astronomy began. The Chaldæan shepherd, the Phœnician mariner, studied the stars and named them and the great constellations which group themselves from horizon to horizon in the nocturnal skies. They perceived strange symmetries, symbolic images, grotesque resemblances. The same instinct made the Arab of the Desert call the Pleiades the Herd of Camels, made the Akkadian call them the Wild Doves, made the Celtic hunter call them the Pack of Hounds, made the Teuton peasant call them the Hen and Chickens, made the Australian savage call them (in conjunction with the Bear) Young Girls playing to Young Men dancing: the same instinct, this, as made the ancient poet of the Zend-Avesta call them the Seven Beneficent Spirits, or made

Winter Stars

the modern poet of *Locksley Hall* liken them to a swarm of fireflies, or made the Gaelic poet of to-day image them as the Herring-Net. In a word, the instinct of poetry : which is as deep as hunger and thirst, as deep as love, as deep as fear, as deep as the desire of life. The instinct of the imagination to clothe the mysterious and the inexplicable in the raiment of the familiar or of recognisable and intimate symbol.

How infinitely it adds to the beauty of a star-name such as Aldebaran, or Alcyone, or Polaris, to know that to the swarthy nomads of the desert it imaged itself as one following in a skyey desert, a camel-driver tracking lost camels, a hound following a quarry, a warrior following a foe, a holy pilgrim tracking the difficult ways of God, so that no name seemed to them so apt as *Al Dabarān*, the Follower: to know that to the pastoral Akkadians or the early tillers and hunters of sea-set Greece, looking at the Pleiades in winter, Alcyone in its lovely group suggested the Nest of the Halcyon, the summer-bird who had flown to the remote depths of the sky to sit and brood there on a windless wave-unreached nest till once again "the Halcyon days" of calm settled on land and sea: or to know that to our own seafaring folk of old, the men who voyaged

Winter Stars

perilously in small and frail craft without compass and with little knowledge of the mysterious laws of the mysterious forces of earth and sea and heaven. Polaris was the one unchanging skyey beacon, the steadfast unswerving North Star; and so, lovingly called by our old Saxon forbears the *Scipsteorra*, the Ship-Star, and by the Elizabethan seafarers the Lodestar or Pilot-Star, and by the Hebridean fishermen the Home-Star, and by others the Star of the Sea—

"Constellations come, and climb the heavens, and go.
  Star of the Pole! and thou dost see them set.
    Alone in thy cold skies,
Thou keep'st thy old unmoving station yet,
Nor join'st the dances of that glittering train,
Nor dipp'st thy virgin orb in the blue western main.
    On thy unaltering blaze
The half-wrecked mariner, his compass lost,
    Fixes his steady gaze,
And steers, undoubting, to the friendly coast;
And they who stray in perilous wastes by night
Are glad when thou dost shine to guide their footsteps right."

The same spirit which animated Bryant when he wrote these verses in his beautiful "Hymn to the North Star," which made one of the Gaelic island-poets allude to it as the Star of

Winter Stars

Compassion, prevailed with these Chaldæan shepherds and Arabian nomads of old. They gave the familiar or beautiful names of love or intimate life, and in exchange the taciturn face of heaven lost its terrifying menace of silence, and the Night became a comrade, became the voice of the poets, of the sages, of the prophets and seers, the silver gateways of the Unknown.

The Hunter, The Herdsman, the Bear-Watcher, the Driver of the Wain—how much more we love Boötes, or, as Chaucer called the constellation, "ye sterres of Arctour," because of these simple names. The Herdsman, the Hunter, . . . the words strike the primitive music. The youth of the world is in them. In these few letters what infinite perspectives, what countless images. The Golden Age lies hid in their now impenetrable thickets. Through their branches we may look at the tireless hunter of to-day on the interminable pampas, at the bowed trailer in the dim savannahs of the Amazon, at the swarthy nomad on the wastes of Sahara guarding his camels like ships becalmed in a vast sea of sand, or may see the solitary mountain-shepherd in the hill-wildernesses of Spain or Italy, or the Northern herdsman toiling against wind and snow on our Gaelic hills.

Winter Stars

Here also is the romance of the stars, as well as that deeper and perturbing romance which is disclosed to us in the revelations of science. That sense of incalculable distances, of immeasurable periods, of unknown destinies and amazing arrivals, which haunts the imagination of the astronomer when he looks beyond the frontiers of ascertained knowledge, half-doubting perhaps whether even that be not a terrible illusory logic, is also here. One goes back, as in thought one recedes into the beautiful, impassioned wonderland of childhood. One seems to see mankind itself as a child, gone but a little way even yet, looking up trustfully or fearfully to the mysterious mother-eyes of a Face it cannot rightly discern, in its breath being Immortality, Eternity in its glance, and on its brows Infinitude.

WINTER STARS

II

Of all winter stars surely the most familiar is Polaris, the Pole Star or Lodestar: of all winter Constellations, the Plough, the Little Dipper (to give the common designations), Orion, and the lovely cluster of the Pleiades, are, with the Milky May, the most commonly observed stellar groups. One of our old Scottish poets, Gawain Douglas, writing towards the close of the fifteenth or early in the sixteenth century, thus quaintly brought them into conjunction—

"Arthurys hous, and Hyades betaikning rane,
Watlingtstrete, the Horne and the Charlewane,
The fiers Orion with his goldin glave."

Here possibly he has taken Arcturus for Polaris. Of old, the Lodestar and Arcturus (or, as often given in the North, "Arturus" or "Arthur" . . . a word itself signifying the

Winter Stars

Great or Wondrous Bear) were often confused. Sometimes, too, Arcturus stood for the whole constellation of Ursa Major— or, as we commonly call it, the Plough or the Wain, as, for example, in Scott's lines:

> "Arthur's slow wain his course doth roll,
> In utter darkness, round the Pole."

But it is obvious Gawain Douglas did not mean this to be understood, for in the second line he speaks of "Charlewane," i.e., Charles's Wain ... the Wain or Waggon being then, as it still is among country-folk, even more familiar a term than the Great Bear or than the Plough itself. Probably, then, he had in mind the Pole Star, the "House of Arthur" of the ancient British. His choice of the "rain-betokening Hyades" may be taken here as including the Pleiades, these "greater seven" in whom centres so much poetry and old legend. A previous paper has been devoted to the Milky Way, so that there is no need to explain why Watling Street should be analogous with the Galaxy. The "Horne" is the Little Dipper or Ursa Minor. Than "fierce Orion with his glistering sword" there is no constellation so universally familiar. If, then, to this category of the old Scottish poet, we add the star Aldebaran, and the constellation of Taurus or the Bull, we have more than enough Winter Lights to consider in one chapter.

Having already, however, dealt with "the watery constellations" we can be the more content now to ignore Alcyone, Maia, Taygeta, Electra, and the other Pleiadic stars of Taurus. This great constellation is one of the earliest in extant astronomical records: the earliest, it is believed. The stellar image of a Bull has occurred to many nations since the designations first arose among the ancient Cretans or Akkadians—if, indeed, in its origin it was not immeasurably more remote. East and West, in the deserts of the South and among the grey isles of the North, "the Bull" was recognised. To-day the Scottish peasant still calls it "the Steer," as his German kinsman does in *der Stier*, his French kinsman in *le Taureau*, his Spanish or Italian kinsman in *Toro*. When certain of the Greeks and Latins used *Keráon* and *Cornus* instead of *Tauros* and *Taurus*, they said merely the same thing—the Horned One. Virgil, as many will remember, utilises the image in the first "George":

Winter Stars

"When with his golden horns bright Taurus opes
The year . . ."

just as a poet of our own time, in a beautiful "Hymn to Taurus," writes:

". . . I mark, stern Taurus, through the twilight grey
The glinting of thy horn
And sullen front, uprising large and dim
Bent to the starry Hunter's sword at bay."

Among our own ancestors, the Druids made Taurus an object of worship, the Tauric Festival having been one of the grea events of the year, signalised when the sun first entered the imagined frontiers of this constellation. To-day, among the homesteads of our Scottish lowlands, the farm-folk tell of the Candlemas Bull who may be seen to rise in the gloaming on New Year's Eve and move slowly to the dark pastures which await his coming.

The particular stellar glory of this constellation is Aldebaran. This beautiful star has appealed to the imagination of all peoples. I do not know what were its earliest Celtic or Anglo-Saxon names. But as in Gaelic it is sometimes called "the Hound," this term may well be a survival from ancient days. If

Winter Stars

so, there is an interesting relation with the primitive Arabic name by which it is all but universally known. Aldebaran is *Al Dabarān*, the Follower: and, figuratively, a follower could hardly be better symbolised than by a hound. I recall a Gaelic poem on a legendary basis where the analogy is still further emphasised, for there Aldebaran is called "the Hound of the Pleiades," which is exactly what the Arabian astronomers implied in "the Follower." Another interesting resemblance is between "the red hound" of the Gaelic poet and legend and the *Rohini* of the Hindus, that word signifying "a red deer" . . . in each case the ruddy gleam of the star having suggested the name. Probably it was this characteristic which led Ptolemy to apply to the star the name "Lampadias" or the Torch-Bearer. In the narration of folk-tales I have more than once or twice heard Aldebaran alluded to as the star of good fortune, of "the golden luck." With us it is pre-eminently a winter-star, and may be seen at its finest from the latter part of January till the approach of the vernal equinox. Some idea of its luminosity may be gained from the fact that this is thrice the outglow of the Pole Star. How often I have stood on a winter's night, and watched awhile this small

Winter Stars

red "torch" burning steadfastly in the unchanging heavens, and thought of its vast journeys, of that eternal, appalling procession through the infinite deeps: how often I have felt the thrill of inexplicable mystery when, watching its silent fire in what appears an inexorable fixity, I recall what science tells us, that it is receding from our system at an all but an unparalleled velocity, a backward flight into the unknown at the rate of thirty miles a second.

It would be hopeless to attempt here even the briefest account of the primitive and diverse nomenclature, the mythology, the folk-lore of Orion . . . the Winter-Bringer, as this constellation is called in an old Scandinavian saga, identical thus with the marginal reading in the Geneva Bible relative to the reference to Orion in Job—"which starre bringeth in winter," an allusion to its evening appearance at the season of cold and storms. For these things are writ in the records of a hundred nations. They are alive in the poetry of all peoples. Centuries before our era, when Thebes was the greatest city of Greece, the poetess Corinna sang of this great Warrior, the Great Hunter, whose nightly course was so glorious above the dusky lands and waters of Hellas. Long after Pindar and the Greek poets, Catullus and Horace gave it a like preëminence in Latin literature. In our own poetry, many surely will recall from *Paradise Lost:*

". . . when with fierce winds Orion arm'd
  Hath vext the Red-sea coast, whose waves o'erthrew
Busiris and his Memphian chivalry . . ."

or Tennyson's beautiful line in *Locksley Hall:*

"Great Orion sloping slowly to the west . . ."

or, it may be, that epic of "Orion" upon which is based Richard Hengist Horne's claim to remembrance—or, once more, Matthew Arnold's fine allusion to Sirius and Orion in *Sohrab and Rustum:*

". . . the Northern Bear,
  Who from her frozen height with jealous eye
  Confronts the Dog and Hunter in the South."

Before Catullus or Pindar the Egyptians had identified Orion both with Horus and Osiris. Among the peoples of Israel the poets acclaimed the constellation as Nimrod, "the mighty Hunter" (or by another term signifying the Giant), "bound to the sky for rebellion against Jehovah." Among the Celtic races it has had kindred names, sometimes abstract, sometimes personal, as the Gaelic Fionn. A year or so ago I was told a sea-tale of the Middle Isles, in which was an allusion to this constellation as "the Bed of Diarmid." This is of especial interest, because of its connection with Fionn or Finn, the Nimrod, the great Hunter of the Gael. But in this story (a modern, not an ancient tale, though with more than one strange old survival) the major position is not held by Fionn, but by the Alban-Gaelic hero Diarmid, who is represented as succumbing under the spear thrust in his left side by the enraged Fionn, at last in grips with the daring chieftain who had robbed him of Grania. When questioned, my informant said he had heard a variant of this attribution, and that the constellation was an image of Diarmid with Grania hanging to his side in a swoon, because she and her lover have been overtaken by the wrath of Fionn . . . though from the description I was uncertain whether the latter indicated the star Sirius, or the rival constellation of the Great Bear. The Gaels of old called Orion *Caomai*, a name said to signify the Armed King: while the *Gall* (the Scandinavian races) applied the name *Orwandil*, but with what signification I do not know, though I have read somewhere

Winter Stars

that it stood for Hero, or for an heroic personage.

Of the chief stars in Orion there is not space here to speak. But of the splendid Rigel—as affluent in the mysterious science of the astrologer as in nocturnal light—pearly Anilam, of the Belt or Sword—ominous Bellatrix — ruddy-flamed Betelgeuze — of these alone one might write much . . . as one might write much of the Girdle or Staff itself, what Scott in *The Lay of the Last Minstrel* calls "Orion's studded belt." It has a score of popular names, from the Danish Frigge Rok (Freya's Distaff) to the seamen's "Yardarm," as, collectively, its three great stars have all manner of names in different countries, from the Magi, or the Three Kings or the Three Marys, to The Rake of the French Rhinelanders, or the Three Mowers of the Silesian peasant.

Those who have studied the mythology and folklore of the Pleiades will remember how universally the numeral seven is associated with their varying nomenclature. But there was, and still is among primitive peoples, not infrequent confusion in the use of "The Seven Stars" as a specific name. Although from China to Arabia, from India and Persia to the Latin countries of the South, the term

Winter Stars

almost invariably designates the Pleiades, in the folklore of many Western nations it is used for the seven planets, and in many Northern races it is often used for the seven brilliant stars of the Great Bear. Even the Biblical allusion to "The Seven Stars," as our own Anglo-Saxon ancestral *Sifunsterri*, does not necessarily indicate the Pleiades: many consider the seven great planets to be meant. There is a Shetland rune, common to all the north isles and to be heard in Iceland and Norway, known as the rune of sevens, and of which one of the invocatory lines is "And by da seven shiners." All kinds of interpretation have explained this, from the obvious "seven planets," or else the Pleiades, to the Seven Candlesticks of Revelation and I know not what besides. I have again and again asked fisher-folk or others from the Orkneys and Shetlands, and in all but one or two instances the answer has clearly indicated the Great Bear, occasionally Polaris and the Ursine Arcturus and their nearest brilliant "shiners." Again, *Crannarain*, one of the Gaelic names for the Pleiades, is, perhaps, as often applied to the Great Bear: the curious legend of the Baker's Shovel, implied in the Gaelic term, fitting equally.

Of the Great Bear, of the North Star, however, I have already spoken. Of Polaris itself, indeed, there is more than enough to draw upon. It is strange that "the Lamp of the North" should have so fascinated all the poets from the time of Homer till to-day, and yet that all have dwelled in the same illusion as to its absolute steadfastness. Nevertheless, Homer's

> "Arctos, sole star that never bathes in the ocean wave."

has both poetic truth and the truth of actuality.

It is a relief to put aside notes and pen and paper, and to go out and look up into the darkness and silence, to those "slow-moving palaces of wandering light" of which one has been writing. How overwhelmingly futile seems not only the poor written word, but even the mysterious pursuit of the far-fathoming thought of man. By the sweat of the brow, by the dauntless pride of the mind, we mortal creatures have learned some of the mysteries of the coming and going in infinitude of these incalculable worlds, of their vast procession from the unknown to the unknown. Then, some night, one stands solitary in the darkness, and feels less than the shadow of a leaf that has passed upon the

Winter Stars

wind, before these still, cold, inevitable, infinitely remote yet overwhelmingly near Children of Immortality.

BEYOND THE BLUE SEPTENTRIONS

TWO LEGENDS OF THE POLAR STARS

The star Septentrion is, for the peoples of the North and above all for the shepherd, the seaman and the wayfarer, the star of stars. A hundred legends embody its mystery, its steadfast incalculable service, its unswerving isolation over the Pole. Polaris, the North Star, the Pole Star, the Lodestar, the Seaman's Star, the Star of the Sea, the Gate of Heaven, Phœnice, Cynosure, how many names, in all languages, at all times. The Mongolian nomad called it the Imperial Ruler of Heaven: the Himalayan shepherd, Grahadāra, the Pivot of the Planets: the Arab knows it as the Torch of Prayer, burning for ever at the portal of the heavenly Mecca. It shines through all literature, since (and indeed long before) Euripides wrote his superb verse of how the two great Northern constellations which encircle Polaris, Ursa Major and Ursa Minor, the two "swift-wandering" Bears, "guard the Atlantean

Pole," till a poet of our own time wrote the less majestic but not less lovely line relating to these constellations which gives the title to this paper. In all ages, too, the dreaming mind of man has imagined here the Throne of the Gods, the Seat of the Mighty, the last Portal of the Unknown. It is the Flatheansas of our Gaelic ancestors, the ultimate goal of the heroic spirit: the Himinbiorg, or Hill of Heaven, of the Norsemen of old, and the abode of Heimdallr, the guardian of the bridge Bifröst (the Rainbow) which unites Asgard the Everlasting with that brief whirling phantom, the Earth. It is Albordy, "the dazzling mountain on which was held the Assembly of the Gods" of the ancient Teutonic peoples: the mysterious Mount Mēru, the seat of the gods, of the Aryan dreamers of old, and the Hindû sages of later time: "the holy mountain of God" alluded to in Ezekiel —so, at least, it has been surmised.

"The blue Septentrions" . . . Boötes with Arcturus, the Great Bear, the Lesser Bear, the Pointers or the Northern Hounds, the North Star . . . what legend, what poetry, what romance, what wonder belongs to these stars and constellations which guard the marches of the Arctic North. To the mass of what is already extant, what need to add further matter? And yet there is ever new justification in that continual need of the soul to hear over and over again, and in ever-varying ways, even the most fragmentary runes or sagas of this unfathomably mysterious stellar universe which encloses us with Silence and Beauty and Wonder, the three Veils of God —as the Hebridean islesman, the Irish Gael of the dreaming west, and the Arab of the Desert alike have it.

I have elsewhere spoken of the legendary association of Arthur (the Celtic-British King and the earlier mythical Arthur, semi-divine, and at last remote and celestial) with Arcturus, that lovely Lamp of the North, the glory of Boötes. But now, I may add what there I had to omit.

In all European lands, and above all in the country of the West, there is none without its legend of King Arthur. The Bretons claim him as theirs, and the places of his passage and exploit are familiar, though only the echo, only the phantom of a great fame ever reached Arvôr. In the Channel and Scilly Isles the story runs that there is Lyonesse, and that Arthur sleeps in a cavern of the seas. The Cornish folk and their kindred of Somerset and Devon believe there is not a rood of ground between Camelot and

Beyond the Blue Septentrions

Tintagel where the great King has not dwelt or passed. Wales calls him her son, and his chivalry her children, and the Cymric poets of a thousand mabinogion have sung his heroic fame. Clydesdale, that more ancient home of the Cymri, has dim memories older than what Taliesin sang: Arthur's Seat hangs above Edinburgh, a city so old that a thousand years ago its earlier name was forgotten; and from the Sidlaw to the Ochil, from blue Demyat to grey Schiehallion, old names and broken tradition preserve the obscure trails of a memory fallen into oblivion, but not so fallen that the names of Arthur and Queen Guinevere and wild-eyed Merlin of the Woods have ceased to stir the minds of the few who still care for the things that moved our fathers from generation to generation. The snows of the Grampians have not stayed the wandering tale: and there are still a few old people who recall at times, in the winter story-telling before farm-kitchen fires, how the fierce Modred, King of the North, made Queen Gwannolê his own, and how later, in a savage revenge, Arthur condemned her to be torn asunder by wild horses. Lancelot passes from the tale before it crosses the Border, and as it goes north (or is it not that as it comes south?) Merlin is no more a courtier but a wild soothsayer of the woods, Queen Wanders or Gwannolê or Guinevere is tameless as a hawk, and Arthur himself, though a hero and great among his kind, is of the lineage of fire and sword.

Where is Joyeuse Gard? Some say it is in the isle Avillion off the Breton shores: some that it is in Avalon, under the sacred hill of Glastonbury: some that it is wet with the foam of Cornish Seas: others aver that it lies in fathomless silence under the sundown wandering wave and plunging tide. Another legend tells that it leaned once upon the sea from some lost haven under Berwick Law, perhaps where North Berwick now is, or where Dirleton looks across to Fidra, or where the seamews on ruined Tantallon scream to the Bass.

Arthur himself has a sleeping-place (for nowhere is he dead, but sleeps, awaiting a trumpet-call) in "a lost land" in Provence, in Spain, under the waters of the Rhine. To-day one may hear from Calabrian shepherd, or Sicilian fisherman, that the Great King sleeps in a deep hollow underneath the Straits of Messina. And strangest of all (if not a new myth of the dreaming imagination, for I have not been able to trace the legend beyond a modern Slavonic ballad) among the Carpathian Highlands, is a nameless ancient tomb lost in a pine-forest, where at mid-winter a bear has been seen to rise, walking erect like a man, crowned with a crown of iron and gold holding a single shining stone magnificent as the Pole Star, and crying in a deep voice, "*I am Arthur of the West, who shall yet be king of the World.*"

Strange indeed, for here among the débris of the lost history of Arthur—that vast shadowy kingly figure whose only kingdom may have been the soul of primitive races, and whose sword may have been none other than the imagination that is for ever on its beautiful and perilous quest—here among that débris of legend scattered backward from the realms of the north across Europe is one, remote as it is, which brings us back to the early astronomical myth that identifies the great Celtic champion with the chief constellation of the north.

But as I have heard this fragment of our old lost mythology related in a way I have not seen in any book, I will give it here altered but slightly if at all from one of the countless legends told to me in my childhood.

At sunset the young son of the great King Pendragon came over the brow of a hill that stepped forward from a dark company of mountains and leaned over the shoreless sea which fills the west and drowns the north. All day he had been wandering alone, his mind heavy with wonder over many things. He had heard strange tales of late, tales about his heroic father and the royal clan, and how they were not as other men, but half divine. They were not gods, he knew, for they could be slain in battle or could die with the crowding upon them of many years: but they were more terrible in battle than were the greatest of men, and they had vision and knowledge beyond the vision and knowledge of the druids, and were lordly beyond all men in mien and the beauty of courtesy, and lived beyond the common span of years, and had secret communion with the noble and invisible company. He had heard, too, of his destiny: that he, too, was to be a great king, as much greater than Pendragon, than Pendragon was above all the kings of the world. What was Destiny, he wondered. Then, again, he turned over and over in his mind all the names he could think of that he might choose for his own: for the time was come for him to put away the name of his childhood and to take on that by which he should be known among men.

Beyond the Blue Septentrions

He came over the brow of the hill, and out of the way of the mountain-wind, and, being tired, lay down among the heather and stared across the grey wilderness of the sea. The sun set, and the invisible throwers of the nets trailed darkness across the waves and up the wild shores and over the faces of the cliffs. Stars climbed out of shadowy abysses, and the great chariots of the constellations rode from the west to the east and from the north to the south. His eyes closed, but when he opened them again to see if a star quivering on the verge of the horizon had in that brief moment sprung like a deer above the drowning wave or had sunk like a white seabird passing out of sight, he saw a great and kingly figure standing beside him. So great in stature, so splendid in kingly beauty was the mysterious one who had so silently joined him, that he thought this must be one of the gods.

"Do you know me, my son?" said the kingly stranger.

The boy looked at him in awe and wonder, but unrecognisingly.

"Do you not know me, my son?" he heard again . . . "for I am your father Pendragon. But my home is yonder, and there I go before long, and that is why I have come to you as a vision in a dream . . . " and, as he spoke he pointed to the constellation of the *Arth*, or Bear, which nightly prowls through the vast abysses of the polar sky.

When the boy turned his gaze from the great constellation which hung in the dark wilderness overhead, he saw that he was alone again. While he yet wondered in great awe at what he had seen and heard, he felt himself float like a mist and become like a cloud, and, as a cloud, rise beyond the brows of the hills, and ascend the invisible stairways of the sky.

When for minutes that were as hours he had moved thus mysteriously into the pathless and unvisited realms of the air, he saw that he had left the highest clouds like dust on a valley-road after one has climbed to the summit of a mountain; nor could he see the earth save as a blind and obscure thing that moved between the twilights of night and dawn.

It seemed to him thereafter that a swoon came over him, in which he passed beyond the far-off blazing fires of strange stars. At last, suddenly, he stood on the verge of Arth, or Arth Uthyr, the Great Bear. There he saw, with the vision of immortal not of mortal eyes, a company of most noble and

Beyond the Blue Septentrions

majestic figures seated at what he thought a circular abyss but which had the semblance of a vast table. Each of these seven great knights or lordly kings had a star upon his forehead, and these were the stars of the mighty constellation of the Bear which the boy had seen night after night from his home among the mountains by the sea.

It was with a burning throb at his heart that he recognised in the King of all these kings no other than himself.

While he looked, in amazement so great that he could hear the pulse of his heart, as in the silence of a wood one hears the tapping of a woodpecker, he saw this mighty phantom-self rise till he stood towering over all there, and heard a voice as though an ocean rose and fell through the eternal silences.

"Comrades in God," it said, "the time is come when that which is great shall become small."

And when the voice was ended, the mighty figure faded into the blue darkness, and only a great star shone where the uplifted dragon-helm had brushed the roof of heaven. One by one the white lords of the sky followed in his mysterious way, till once more were to be seen only the stars of the Bear.

Beyond the Blue Septentrions

The boy-king dreamed that he fell as a falling meteor, and then that he floated over land and sea as a cloud, and then that he sank as mist upon the hills of his own land.

A noise of wind stirred in his ears, and he felt the chill dew creep over his hands like the stealthy cold lip of the tide. He rose stumblingly, and stood, staring around him. He was on the same spot, under the brow of the hill that looked over the dim shoreless seas, now obscure with the dusk. He glanced upward and saw the stars of the Great Bear in their slow majestic march round the Pole. Then he remembered.

He went slowly down the hillside, his mind heavy with thought. When he was come to the place of the King his father, lo, Pendragon and all his fierce chivalry came out to meet him, for the archdruid had foretold that the great King to be had received his mystic initiation among the holy silence of the hills.

"I am no more Snowbird the child," the boy said, looking at them fearlessly, and as though already King. "Henceforth I am Arth-Urthyr,[1] for my place is in the great Bear which we see yonder in the north."

[1] Pronounced *Arth-Uir*, or *Arth-Ur*. In ancient British *Arth* means Bear, and *Uthyr* great, wondrous.

So all there acclaimed him as Arthur, the wondrous one of the stars, the Great Bear.

"I am old," said Pendragon, "and soon you shall be King, Arthur, my son. So ask now a great boon of me and it shall be granted to you."

Then Arthur remembered his dream.

"Father and King," he said, "when I am King after you I shall make a new order of knights, who shall be strong and pure as the Immortal Ones, and be tender as women, and simple as little children. But first I ask of you seven flawless virgin knights to be of my chosen company. To-morrow let the wood-wrights make for me a round daïs or table such as that where we eat our roasted meats and drink from the ale-horns, but round and of a size whereat I and my chosen knights may sit at ease."

The King listened, and all there.

"So be it," said the King.

Then Arthur chose the seven flawless virgin knights, and called them to him.

"Ye are now Children of the Great Bear," he said, "and comrades and liegemen to me, Arthur, who shall be King of the West. And ye shall be known as the Knights of the Round Table. But no man shall make a mock of that name and live: and in the end that name shall be so great in the mouths and minds of men that they shall consider no glory of the world to be so great as to be the youngest and frailest of that knighthood."

And that is how Arthur, the son of Pendragon, who three years later became King of the West, read the Rune of the Stars that are called the Great Bear and took their name upon him, and from the strongest and purest and noblest of the land made Knighthood, such as the world had not seen, such as the world since has not known.

. . . .

Very different, a cruder legend of the Pole star, the drift of which I heard some months ago from a fisherman of Ross, "foregathered with" in the Sound of Morvern.

One day, Finn, before he was born the King of the West, a thousand years earlier than that and maybe thousands more on the top of that thousand, went hunting a great bear beyond the highest mountains in Ross and Sutherland. It came to the Ord, and then, seeing there was no more land, it went into the sea with an awesome plunge, like Iceland in the story before it swan away from Scotland, so that the fish were knocked out of the nets and the fishing cobles were thrown on the shores like buckies, and the tides ran like hares till they leaped into the sea again at the rocks of Wick and over Cromarty Cliffs. Ay, it is said a green wave ran right through the great Kirk at Inverness; and that away across the lands of Mackenzie and Chisholm, of Fraser and Gordon, a storm of foam blew like snow against the towers and steeples of Aberdeen. At least all this might well have been, if in those old ancient days there had been any Aberdeen or Inverness to see it, or if there were cobles and nets then, as, for all you or I or the wind know, there may have been. Well, the Bear swam away due north, and Finn after it and his great hounds Luath and Dorch. It took then a month to come up with it, and then it was among mountains of solid ice with the sea between hard as granite. Then it came to the place where there's an everlasting Rainbow. The Bear climbed this, to jump to the other side of the Pole, but Luath ran up one side and Dorch the other and Finn hurled his great shining spears, one after the other: so that down the bear came with a rush, and so great was the noise and stramash that the icebergs melted, and out flew thousands of solanders and grey swans and scarts and God knows what all, every kind of bird that is with a web to its foot. The hounds fell into the water, and the Bear lay on a floe like a wounded seal, but Finn never moved an inch but put spear after spear into the Bear. "Well, you're dead now," he said; "and if you're not, you ought to be," he added, seeing that the Bear was up again and ready to be off.

"This can't go on," said God Allfather, so He swung a noose and sagged up the Bear into the black Arctic sky. But the hounds hung on to its tail, and so were carried up too. And as for Finn, he took the hero-leap, and with one jump was on the Pole, and with the next was in the Northman's Torch *(Arcturus)*, and with the third was on the Hill of Heaven itself. And that's where he went back to on the day he died after his three hundred years of mortal life. He has never moved since, and he won't move again, till Judgment Day. And by the same token, you can see the Great Bear prowling round the Pole still, and Finn the Watchman never letting him go by, night or day, day or night, and far away down are the two Hounds that herd the Great Bear and his mate. And when these come too near, Finn hurls his spears, and that's when we see the Northern Lights. And behind the streamers and the auroras and the rainbows and the walls of ice Finn looks into the Garden of Eden—Paradise as they say, just the Flatheanas of the old tales, the old songs. And who would be doubting it?

WHITE WEATHER

A MOUNTAIN REVERIE

To be far north of the Highland Line and among the mountains, when winter has not only whitened the hill-moors but dusted the green roofs of every strath and corrie, may not have for many people the charm of the southward flight. But to the hill-born it is a call as potent as any that can put the bitter-sweet ache into longing hearts. There is peace there: and silence is there: and, withal, a beauty that is not like any other beauty. The air and wind are auxiliary; every cloud or mist-drift lends itself to the ineffable conspiracy; the polar breath itself is a weaver of continual loveliness often more exquisitely delicate than the harebell, often incalculable or immeasurable, or beautiful with strangeness as moonlight on great waters, or the solitary torch of Jupiter burning his cold flame in the heart of a mountain-tarn. There is no soundlessness like it. And yet the silence is relative; is, in a word, but an imagination

White Weather

laid upon an illusion. If there is no wind on the moor, there may be a wandering air among the lower heights. If so, many hollows of rocks, caverns lost in bracken, caves of hill-fox and badger, sudden ledges haunted by the daw and the hoodie and filled with holes as though the broken flutes of the dead forgotten giants of old tales, will make a low but audible music; a lifting and falling sighing, with singular turnings upon itself of an obscure chant or refrain, that just as one thinks is slipping into this side knowledge and is almost on the edge of memory, slides like rain along that edge and vanishes, vague as an unremembered fragrance. Or, if the suspense be so wide that not a breath moves lower than where the corries climb towards the very brows of the mountains, one will surely hear, far up among the time-hollowed scarps and weather-sculptured scaurs, that singular sound which can sink to a whimpering, as of unknown creatures or lost inhuman clans strayed and bewildered; or can be as though unseen nomads were travelling the mountainway with songs and strange flutes and thin wailing fifes; or can rise to a confused tumult as of embattled hosts, or to a crying and a lamentation more desperate than the cries of men and a lamenting as of that mysterious and dreaded clan, the Grey Children of the Wild. The wind, in truth, is almost always to be heard, near or far. Sometimes the eye may learn, where the ear fails: as when one is in a glen or strath or on a shore or moor, and, looking up, may see smoke rising from the serrated crests or the curving sky-lines, like the surf of vast billows—to realise soon, that this volcanic apparition means no more than that vast volumes of driven snow are being lifted by the north wind and whirled against and over the extreme mountain-bastions. *Trath chaidleas 's a ghleann an t-àile*, "when the air sleeps in the glens," goes a Gaelic saying, "you may hear the wind blowing in the high corries *mar chaithream chlàr*," like the symphony of harps.

Then, too, it is rare that the snowy wilderness is without voice of mountain torrent, for even when frost holds the hill-world in a grip so terrible that the smaller birds cannot fly in the freezing air, there are rushing burns of so fierce a spate that the hands-of-ice are whirled aside like foam, and the brown wave leaps and dashes from rock to rock, from granite ledge to peaty hollow, from brief turbulent channels to chasms and crevasses whence ceaselessly ascends the damp smell of churned surge, above which as ceaselessly rises a phantom spray. Again, there is that strange, continual earth-movement, the alarm of all unfamiliar wayfarers. Who suddenly unloosened that rush of rock and earth yonder? What enemy moved that boulder that leapt and hurtled and crashed downward and beyond, but a score yards away? Of what elfin-artillery are those rattling stones the witness? What hand, in the silence, thrust itself through the snow and crumbled that old serrated ledge, where, a week ago, the red deer stood sniffing the wind, where, yesterday perhaps, the white ptarmigan searched the heather?

Moreover we are in the domain of the eagle, the raven, and the corbie. They are seldom long silent there. And that sudden call on the wind? . . . what but the Merry Folk, *Clann Aighean Siubhlach*, the Wandering Deer-Clan, passing like drifting shadows over white heather-pastures lost to view? It is long since the love-belling of the stags made musical the mountain-side: was not "the Silence of the Deer" the first sign of winter come again? But that cry was the cry of hunger—a *guth acaimeach*, a sobbing voice, as once I heard a prosaic roadmender unprosaically and with kindly sympathy allude to

White Weather

the winter-bleat of the snow-famished deer. And that other bleating: of sheep left upon the hills, and overtaken by the White Weather. How goes the sound, the translated echo of their mournful iteration, that is now a long ululation of lament and now a rising and falling bleating as of confused words? The same roadmender I speak of said—after himself lamenting in sympathy *tha 'm fuachd a muigh's a staigh an diugh* . . . "the cold is outside and inside to-day"—that it went like this: *Tha sinn cèarr, tha sinn cèarr, tha sinn cèarr 's gun fhios againn!* . . . "We are astray we are astray, we are astray and have lost our bearings!"

Up here everything may have a snow-change "into something rich and rare." It was in a hill-solitude, in white weather such as this, that, for example, I heard from an old shepherd names for the eagle, the corbie, and the ptarmigan that I had not elsewhere heard, nor have seen in print, though for long now I have been collecting all whenever and wherever chance permits the Gaelic and Lowland names of birds and animals. The corbie he called *An t-Eun Acarachd*, the Merciless, literally, "the bird without compassion," no doubt with thought of its love for young lambs or its savage lust for the eyes

White Weather

of stricken or dying sheep. The ptarmigan he called *An t-Eun (Adhar or Aidhre)*, the bird of the snow or frost—though this is but a variant, of course, of the more familiar *Sneacag* or *Eun-an-Sneachel*. When he spoke of the eagle simply as *An t-Eun Mòr*, the great bird, that seemed less noteworthy, but when he added, *Abù! An t-Eun Mòr Abù*, I was puzzled. I thought he meant *aboo* to simulate the *Iolair's* cry, though it sounded much more like the muffled hoot of the great owl than the eagle's screech. He said he remembered that was the eagle's name in an old tale he had often heard his mother tell when he was a child. I never thought of it as *Abù*, however, till one day I came upon this word in a Gaelic dictionary and found it entered as being an ancient war-cry of the Gael. Truly, a fit survival, for a wild slogan that has ages ago died away from the Gaelic hills to live still among these desolate mountains, around those wind-tortured scarps and scaurs, in the scream of the golden eagle. The old man had a special bird-name for most of the birds he spoke of or about which I asked him. Doubtless he was as good a naturalist and with as good a right to make names as any ornithologist who would know what the old man could not know, and would

White Weather

be familiar with common and other names that would be unfamiliar there among the far hills, or, at least, to the old mountaineer, for whom the hill-birds were the best of company. For the curlew, for instance, though he knew the common Scots name, Whaup, he had the good name *An t-Eun Chaismeachd*, "the bird of alarm"—how good a name (though perhaps equally applicable to the grey plover, the green whistler, or the lapwing) must be obvious to all who have walked the moorland or travelled the hillside. And where an islesman or a man of the mainland coasts would, for swiftness, use a comparison such as *cho luath ri sgadan*, "as swift as a herring," he would say, *cho luath ris na feadag*, "as swift as the plover."

White Weather, he said, was always first "called" by the linnet, the "heather lintie" so loved of Scots song-writers, to which he gave several names ("out of a good ten that will be known to any one whatever"), one a curious blend of Scots-Gaelic, *Shilfa-monaidh* (*i.e.*, the moor-chaffinch), another a pretty name, *Breacan-Beithe*, "little speckled one of the birch." But even he, for all his hill-wisdom, could not tell me why it is that when the lapwing come again after the great winter-end storm about mid-March, welcome pioneers of the Spring that is stealing slowly up through the glens and straths of the south, they always, if they nest on the slope of a hillside, choose the east side for their unsheltered homes and where to lay their eggs. Do they so love the bleak wind of the east? Hardly any bird takes so little trouble with the nest: often it is but the frost-hardened delve of a cow's hoof, a tangle of bent, or the hollow of a misplaced stone. I have heard that this is truer of the mainland than of the isles, but I have not found it so. Last March or April I remember that on the long, low-hilled and mainly "upland" island where I then was, not a single lapwing's nest but was on the east slope of grassy brae or sloping moor or pasture. But though he could not say a word on so strange, almost so inexplicable a habit, he could be positive as to the age of the eagle, and especially as to one aged *iolair* that he often saw on Maol-Aitonnach, the great hill that was half the world and more to him: namely, that the king-bird lived to be three hundred years. And he computed it thus; that an eagle lives three times less than an oak, and three times more than a deer. There is a familiar proverb that "*Tri aois feidh aois firein; tri aois firein aois craoibh dharaich*," "thrice the age of a deer,

White Weather

the age of an eagle" ("ferain," "fireun," and "fiolair" are variants of "iolair," whose more ancient name is "antar" *(an t-ar)*, one of the oldest names in the Gaelic language); "thrice the age of an eagle, the age of an oak." The stag lives a hundred years, or so it is universally believed: therefore the eagle lives three hundred, and the oak's age is at least nine hundred years. I recall, in connection with the eagle, a singular saying which I heard many years ago and have not since heard or anywhere encountered, to the effect that between dusk and dawn a bat's flight will be the equivalent of a thousand miles, that between dawn and dusk a swallow will cover a thousand miles, and that a thousand miles is the measure of an eagle's flight between sunrise and sunset.

Well, I must leave Maol-Ationnach, and the snow-held hills. Everywhere, now, the White Weather may have spread. Far south, listeners may hear the *honk-honk* of the travelling solander, that most musical and thrilling of all nocturnal sounds or of winter-dawns: or, like phantom-voices from the world of dreams, the *kuilliyak-ee, kuilliyak-o* of the wild swans, the *Clann righ fo gheasan*, the Enchanted sons of Kings, who, as they wheel through the snowy twilight under the dawn-

White Weather

star may remember the dim lands of the north, and a great mountain that rises among white and silent hills and looks down upon a black tarn I know of, so dark in the grip of black-frost, and so strangely spared of the snow, that not a white wing rests there, or floats overhead, but is mirrored as an enchanted sail in an enchanted sea.

ROSA MYSTICA

(AND ROSES OF AUTUMN)

> . . . *Rosa Sempiterna*
> *Che si dilata, rigrada, e ridole*
> *Odor di lode al Sol.* . . .

Sitting here, is an old garden by the sea, it is difficult for me to realise that the swallow has gone on her long flight to the South, that last night I heard countless teal flying overhead, and before dawn this morning the mysterious *honk-honk* of the wild-geese. A white calm prevails. A sea of faint blue and beaten silver, still molten, still luminous as with yet unsubdued flame, lies motionless beneath an immeasurable dome of a blue as faint, drowned in a universal delicate haze of silver-grey and pearl. But already a change to pale apple-green and mauve is imminent. A single tern flashes a lonely wing along a grey-green line that may be where sky and sea meet, or may be the illusion of the tide refluent from green depths. On the weedy rocks I cannot see even a sleeping seamew: on the havened

Rosa Mystica

stretch of yellow-white sand a dotterel runs to and fro in sudden aimless starts, but as suddenly is still, is all but unseen with her breast against a rock covered with the blue-bloom of mussels, and now is like a shadow licked up by twilight.

Along the husht garden-ways beside me and behind me are roses, crimson and yellow, sulphur-white and pale carnation, the blood-red damask, and a trailing-rose, brought from France, that looks as though it were live flame miraculously stilled. It is the hour of the rose. Summer has gone, but the phantom-summer is here still. A yellow butterfly hangs upon a great drooping Marechal Niel: two white butterflies faintly flutter above a corner-group of honey-sweet roses of Provence. A late hermit-bee, a few lingering wasps, and the sweet, reiterated, insistent, late-autumn song of the redbreast. That is all. It is the hour of the rose.

> " *C'est l'heure de la rose*
> *L'heure d'ambre et flamme,*
> *Quand dans mon âme*
> *Je sens une Blanche Rose*
> *Éclose.*"

To-night the sea-wind will go moaning from the west into the dark north: before dawn a steely frost will come over the far crests of the hills. To-morrow the garden will be desolate: a garden of phantom dreams. They have waited long, spell-bound! but the enchantment is fallen; in a few hours all shall be a remembrance. What has so marvellously bloomed thus late, so long escaped devastating wind and far-drifting rains and the blight of the sea, will pass in a night. Already, a long way off, I hear a singular, faint, humming sound, like stifled bees. So . . . the foam of storm is on the skerries of the seaward isles. Already from the north, a faint but gathering chill comes on the slanting wings of twilight. I rise with a sigh, thinking of an old forgotten refrain in an old forgotten poem:

> *"Ged tha thu 'n diugh 'a d'aibheis fhuar,*
> *Bha thu nair 'a d'aros righ—"*

> *"(Though thou art to-day a cold ruin*
> *Thou wert once the dwelling of a king.)"*

In the long history of the Rose, from the time when the Babylonians carried sceptres ornamented now with this flower now with the apple or lotus, to the coming of the Damask Rose into England in the time of Henry VII.: from the straying into English gardens, out of the Orient, of that lovely yellow cabbage-

Rosa Mystica

rose which first came into notice shortly after Shakespeare's death, or from Shakespeare's own "Provencal rose," which is no other than the loved and common cabbage-rose of our gardens: from the combes of Devon to the straths of Sutherland, to that little clustering rose which flowered in Surrey meads in the days of Chaucer and has now wandered so far north that the Icelander can gather it in his brief hyperborean summer: from Keats's musk-rose—

"The coming musk-rose, full of dewy wine,
The murmurous haunt of flies on summer eves—"

to that Green Rose which for more than half a century has puzzled the rose-lover and been a theme of many speculations . . . a thousand wise and beautiful things have been said of this most loved of flowers and not a few errors been perpetuated.

What has become of the Blue Roses to which in 1800 a French writer, Guillemeau, alludes as growing wild near Turin? They are no less phantoms than some of the rose-allusions which the poet has made sacrosanct, that to the rhetorician have become an accepted convention. Again, we are told and retold that the cult of the rose is a modern and not an ancient sentiment. Even, it is said, the allusions of the Latin poets are not those of lovers and enthusiasts. It is the Rose of Catullus, we are reminded, that blooms in the old Italic literature, the flower of festival, of Venus and Bacchus, alluded to more for its associations and its decorative value than for love borne to it or enthusiasm lit by it as by a fragrant flame.

All this may be so, and yet I am not persuaded that the people of ancient days did not love this flower of flowers as truly as, if perhaps differently than, we do. It is true that the ancients do not appear to have regarded nature, either in the abstract or in the particular, in the way characteristic of peoples of modern times and above all of our own time. But literary allusiveness does not reveal the extent or the measure of the love of objects and places. It is almost inconceivable, for example, that so beauty-loving a people as the Greeks did not delight in the rose. The fact that only a mere handful of roses may be culled from all the poetry of Hellas, here a spray from Sappho, a wine-flusht cluster from Anacreon, a dew-wet bloom from Theocritus, a few wild-roses from the Anthology, an epithet from Homer, an image from Simonides or Pindar, a metaphor in some golden mouth,

Rosa Mystica

this paucity—so singular compared with the Rose of Poetry in our English speech, from Chaucer's "Rose of Rhone" to W. B. Yeats's "Rose on the Rood of Time," loved and sung through a thousand years. Such paucity does not necessarily mean that only a few poets casually alluded to this supreme flower, and that it was unnoticed or unloved of the many. Doubtless rose-chaplets were woven for lovers, and children made coronals, and at mourning ceremonies and marriage festivals these flowers were strewn. The very fact that Sappho called the rose the queen of flowers showed that it was distinguished from and admired among even the violets, pre-eminently the flowers of Athens. That she likened a yonng maiden to a rose is as indicative as when an Arab poet likens his love to a delicate green palm, or as when a northern poet speaks of her as a pine-tree swaying in the wind or a wave dancing on the sea.

Then, again, the Rose would not have been consecrated to Venus, as an emblem of beauty: to Eros, as an emblem of love: to Aurora, as an emblem of Youth: and to Harpocrates, as an emblem of silence, if this symbolic usage were not such as would seem fit and natural. That roses, too, were in general demand is evident alone from their far-

Rosa Mystica

famed culture and the great trade in them at Paestum, the Lucanian town colonised by the Greek Sybarites five hundred years B.C. All mediæval and later literature is full of the beauty and fragrance of the rose; but were it not so, one could infer that the flower was held in high esteem from the fact that it has for ages been the wont of the Popes to have a golden rose exquisitely finished, and, when consecrated, to present it to some Catholic monarch as a token of special regard. Thus it seems to me that were there not a single allusion to the rose by any great poet from Homer to Sappho, from Anacreon to Theocritus, we might yet discern the love of the ancient Greeks for this flower from, let us say, a single surviving phrase such as the anonymous lovely epitaphial prayer-poem in the Anthology:—" May many flowers grow on this newly-built tomb; not the dried-up Bramble, or the red flower loved by goats; but Violets and Marjoram, and the Narcissus growing in water; and around thee may all Roses grow."

In Persia and the East, from Hindustân to Palestine, from remotest Asia to Abyssinia and Barbary, the Rose has ever been loved and honoured. Sâdi of the Rose-garden and many another has sung of it with ecstasy.

Rosa Mystica

The Hindû god Indra, even Buddha himself, suffered for robbing a paradisaical garden of a rose. How suggestive it is, that the Eve of the Aztec garden of Eden sinned, not for plucking an apple but a rose: it was a fatal rose, too, that the Eve of primitive Mexican legend gathered to her undoing and that of all her descendants.

What innumerable legends centre round this flower. In every country and in either hemisphere, north of the Equator, the poet and the myth-maker and the legend-weaver have occupied their imaginations to enhance its beauty, to deepen its significance.

Long ago Bion told how the rose sprang from the blood of the wounded Adonis, the supreme type of beauty, and of the tears of Venus. An older Hellenic legend declares that the rose was originally white, till Eros, dancing among the gods, upset a goblet of nectar upon Venus's flower, which thereupon became red. Christian legend, on the other hand, would have it that the red rose sprang from the brands which had been lighted at Bethlehem to burn to death a Christian virgin-martyr. Remote from Syria as from Greece, the Scandinavian legend arose that this flower was white till Baldur, the god of Youth and Love, bled at the coming of Christ—akin to

Rosa Mystica

which is a Gaelic legend, that the flower was white till a drop of Christ's blood fell from the Cross . . . a variant of which is that the robin, who plucked at the thorns in Christ's forehead till they stained its breast red, leaned exhausted against a wild white-rose on Calvary, which ever after was red as blood. I do not know the origin of the legend save that it is Teutonic in its present colour and shape, of how the Crown of Thorns was woven of the Briar-Rose, and how the drops that fell from the thorns became blood-hued blooms, Teutonic also, I think, is the legend that Judas made a ladder of the rose-briar with which to reach the closed doors of heaven; hence why it is that the name Judas-Stairs is given to the Briar in some parts of Germany to this day, and why the scarlet hips are called *Judasbeeren*.

Most beautiful of surviving rose-customs is that akin to what is still done in some remote parts of Europe, the placing of an apple into the hand of a dead child, so that the little one may have something to play with in Paradise. I know of a dead Irish girl into whose right hand was placed a white rose, and of a drowned fisherman in whose hand was placed a red rose, symbols of spiritual rebirth and of deathless youth. Against this must be set the strange and widespread aversion to throwing a rose into a grave, or even letting one fall or be lowered there. ("It is throwing red life away" it was explained to me once,—with the grim addition, "and Death will at once be hungry for more of the rose-thrower.")

Again, I recall an old legend of the last rose of summer, long anterior to the familiar song so named: a legend of how at Samhain (Hallowmass) when of old was held the festival of summer ended and of winter begun, a young Druid brought a rose to the sunward Stones and, after consecration and invocation, threw it into the sea.

To-day, sitting in my old garden amid many roses, and looking westward across a waveless, a moveless sea, now of faint apple-green and fainter mauve lost in a vast luminous space of milky, violet-shadowed translucency, I dream again that old dream, and wonder what its portent then, what its ancient significance, of what the symbol now, the eternal and unchanging symbol. For nothing is more strange than the life of natural symbols. We may discern in them a new illusion, a new meaning: the thought we slip into them may be shaped to a new desire and coloured with some new fantasy of dreams or of the unspoken and nameless longing in the heart: but the symbol

Rosa Mystica

has seen a multitude of desires come and go like shadows, has been troubled with many longings and baffled wings of the veiled passions of the soul, and has known dreams, many dreams, dreams as the uncounted sand, the myriad wave, the illimitable host of cloud, rain that none hath numbered. The symbol of the Lily has been the chalice of the world's tears; the symbol of the Rose, the passion of uplifted hearts and of hearts on fire; in the symbol of the Cross has dwelled, like fragrance in a flower, the human Soul. The salt, mutable, and yet unchanging sea has been the phantom in which empires have seen Time like a shadow, the mirage by which kings have wept and nations been amorous in a great pride. The Wind, that no man has seen, on whose rushing mane no hand has been laid, and in whose mouth has been set no bridle since the world swung out of chaos on chariots of flame, . . . has not that solitary and dread creature of the deeps been fashioned in our minds to an image of the Everlasting, and in our hearts been shaped to the semblance of a Spirit?

A rose, laid on a stone-altar in the sunfire, and thrown into the sea, with strange hymns, with supplication . . . what a symbol this of the desires that do not die with nations, the

Rosa Mystica

longings that outlive peoples, the grass of prayer that Time has trampled upon and left and forever leaves green and virginal!

To give that, that lovely fragrant flame of the old material earth, to the altars of the bowed spirit: to clothe it in the fire of heaven: to commit it to the unassuaged thirst of the everlasting graves of the sea . . . . Surely, here, an image of that Rosa Mundi which has been set upon the forehead of the world since time was, that Rose of Beauty, that Rose of Time, that Rose of the World which the passion of the soul has created as a prayer to the Inscrutable: the Rose of the Soul, of you, of me, of all that have been, of all that are, of all unborn, that we lay upon our places of prayer, and offer to the Secret Fires, and commit to desolation, and sorrow, and the salt and avid hunger of Death? What came of that mystical wedding, of the world we know and the world we do not know, by that rose of the spirit, committed thus in so great a hope, so great a faith? The Druid is not here to tell. Faith after Faith has withered like a leaf. But still we stand by ancestral altars, still offer the Rose of our Desire to the veiled Mystery, still commit this our symbol to the fathomless, the everlasting, the unanswering Deep.

THE STAR OF REST

A FRAGMENT

Rest—what an OCEANIC word! I have been thinking of the unfathomable, unpenetrable word with mingled longing, and wonder, and even awe.

What depths are in it, what infinite spaces, what vast compassionate sky, what tenderness of oblivion, what husht awakenings, what quiet sinkings and fadings into peace.

Waking early, I took the word as one might take a carrier-dove and loosed it into the cloudy suspense of the stilled mind—and it rose again and again in symbolic cloud-thought, now as an infinite green forest murmurous with a hidden wind, now in some other guise and once as Ecstasy herself, listening . . . .

AN ALMANAC

*Our Elder Brother is a Spirit of Joy: therefore,
in this new year, Rejoice!*

In January the Spirit dreams,
And in February weaves a Rainbow,
And in March smiles through Rains,
And in April is clad in White and Green,
And in May is the Youth of the World,
And in June is a Glory,
And in July is in two Worlds,
And in August is a Colour,
And in September dreams of Beauty,
And in October Sighs,
And in November Wearieth,
And in December Sleeps.

"I am Beauty itself amid Beautiful things"
(Bhagavad Gita).

BIBLIOGRAPHICAL NOTE

By Mrs William Sharp

THE contents of this volume represent the earlier and the later writings of William Sharp as "Fiona Macleod," separated by an interval of ten years. "The Tragic Landscapes" from *The Sin-Eater* were written in 1893. "The Silence of Amor," written in 1895, formed a section of the 1st Edition of *From the Hills of Dream* (1896); and was published—with Foreword and additions, some of which are retained in the present edition—in book form in America in 1902 by Mr. T. Mosher (Portland, Maine). One or two of these prose rhythms were incorporated in later work —in the Introduction to *The Sin-Eater*, and in "Iona," for example.

The Nature-Essays gathered together in the posthumous volume *Where the Forest Murmurs* (Newnes 1906) were written during the years 1903-5 for *Country Life*, at the request of Mr. P. Anderson Graham (to whom the volume was dedicated) with the exception of "At the Turn of the Tide" which appeared in *The Fortnightly* in 1906, and of the fragment "Rest" found on the author's writing table, after his death at Castello di Maniace, Sicily.

The titular nature-paper "Where the Forest Murmurs" forms a part of the second volume of selected tales published in the Tauchnitz collection in 1905

Bibliographical Note

under the title of *The Sunset of Old Tales*. The first volume, *Wind and Wave*, appeared in 1902; and has been admirably translated into German by Herr Winnibald Mey under the titles of *Wind und Woge* and published by Herrn Eugen Diederichs (Jena and Leipzig). Several of the tales have been translated into French by Monsieur Henri Davray and have appeared in *Le Mercure de France*, and will eventually be issued in book form; they have also been translated into Swedish and into Italian. The Tauchnitz volume of *The Sunset of Old Tales* (1905) contains an "After Dedication" which may very appropriately be reprinted as conclusion to the present volume of Nature-Essays:

"Had I known in time I would have added to the Dedicatory Page the following tribute, which now I must be content to add here; yet not wholly regretfully so, for, with its recognition of a new and beautiful justice, as well as a rare and beautiful generosity, it forms, because of the great deed, which it records, a fitting close to this book and *Wind and Wave*. In both, perhaps, is heard too much, too often, the refrain of Gaelic sorrow, the refrain of an ancient people of the hills and glens and grey wandering arms of the sea, in the days of farewell, or, at best, of a dubious, a menacing transmutation. Decade by decade, year by year, Scotland has been more and more entangled in the mesh of the crudest and most selfish landlordism. From the Hebrid Isles and the mountains of Sutherland to the last heather walls of Cheviot, the blight of a fraudulent closing of the hills and the glens, the woods and the waters, has shut away their own land from the Scottish people. Surely one may hope at last for the coming of the great Restitution, of a nobler

Bibliographical Note

ideal ownership, when one has lived to witness so great and so significant a public deed as that of Mr. Cameron Corbett.

DEDICATED ALSO
TO
CAMERON CORBETT, M.P.

whose free gift to the people, for all time, of a vast tract of Mountain-lands and Loch-shores, in Eastern Argyll, is not only the noblest contemporary gift bestowed on Scotland, but an augury of the possible redemption of that all but 'preserved-away' country from the grip of selfish landowners and from the injustice of fraudulent and often iniquitous game-laws."

CPSIA information can be obtained
at www.ICGtesting.com
Printed in the USA
LVOW13s2229090218
566055LV00008B/173/P